Werther's Goethe and the Game of Literary Creativity

Werther's Goethe and the Game of Literary Creativity

DEIRDRE VINCENT

UNIVERSITY OF TORONTO PRESS
Toronto Buffalo London

© University of Toronto Press Incorporated 1992
Toronto Buffalo London
Printed in Canada
Reprinted in 2018
ISBN 0-8020-5018-2
ISBN 978-1-4875-8499-3 (paper)

Printed on acid-free paper

Canadian Cataloguing in Publication Data

Vincent, Deirdre Winifred Joy, 1943–
  Werther's Goethe and the game of literary creativity

  Includes bibliographical references.
  ISBN 0-8020-5018-2

  1. Goethe, Johann Wolfgang von, 1749–1832. Werther.
  2. Goethe, Johann Wolfgang von, 1749–1832 –
  Criticism and interpretation. I. Title.

  PT1980.V55 1992   833'.6   C92-093950-3

This book has been published with the help of a grant from the Canadian Federation for the Humanities, using funds provided by the Social Sciences and Humanities Research Council of Canada. Publication has also been assisted by a generous grant from the University of Toronto Women's Association.

Man muß schreiben, wie man lebt, erst um sein selbst willen, und dann existiert man auch für verwandte Wesen.

Italienische Reise, 5.10.1787

Contents

INTRODUCTION 3

1 **Werther, Goethe, and Charlotte von Stein** 15
   Life, Love, and Writing 1775–89 22

2 **Writing and Rewriting 1776–90** 71
   Literary Game-playing 72
   Werther 1776–86 88
   Other Works Revised 1786–9 92

3 **The Changes in Werther** 121
   Albert 123
   Lotte 133
   Werther 151
   The Editor's Report 186

4 *Werther*: **The Case for a Rereading** 213
   The Final *Werther* in the Light of the Final *Tasso* 213
   Goethe on Writing and Being Read 231
   A Closer Look at Our Critical Responses to *Werther* 239
   Werther: A Summary of the Need for Review 249

APPENDIX 259

BIBLIOGRAPHY 261

Werther's Goethe and the Game of Literary Creativity

Introduction

Two very powerful yet seemingly contradictory urges lie at the root of Goethe's literary creativity, obliging us, his readers, to engage in a provocative game of informed guesswork. From very early on the poet felt the urge to record and give shape to all the significant events, emotions, and reflections of his life, and having done so, to present the results to a reading or listening public. This we know from the repeated stress he himself laid on the autobiographical, even confessional, nature of his writings,[1] and from his richly documented eagerness for details of response to his work.[2] However, eager though he was to write and for his works to meet with informed approval, he also felt impelled to write in such a way as to conceal a great deal from his reader or critic. The more significant the work was for him in personal terms, the more marked was his paradoxical urge towards self-revelation and self-concealment at one and the same time.

In reviewing his past life in pensive mood in 1779, when he was just thirty years old, he made the following reference to his love

---

1 For example, *Dichtung und Wahrheit*, Bk. 2, ch. 7, in *Goethes Werke: Hamburger Ausgabe*, ed. E. Trunz, 1978, [HA] 9:283; also to Sara von Grotthus, in 1801 (*Goethe über seine Dichtungen*, ed. Hans Gerhard Gräf, 1901–14, here 2,2:no.1037); to Rochlitz, 27 July 1807 (ibid. 2,3:no.2226); Johann Peter Eckermann, *Gespräche mit Goethe in den letzten Jahren seines Lebens*, 1982, 631f.; conversation with Soret, February 1832 (*Goethes Gespräche*, based on the original ed. of Flodoard Freiherr von Biedermann, enlarged and ed. by Wolfgang Herwig, 1965–87, here 3,2:839; subsequent references to this work appear as Biedermann/Herwig with the page number).

2 Throughout the nine volumes of Gräf one finds Goethe repeatedly eliciting interpretative comments on his works, e.g.: (on *Faust*) 2,2:no.1065, 1090a, 1094, 1143, 1199, 1219, 1420, etc.; (on *Götz*) 2,3:no.2125, 2134, 2199, 2216, 2286, etc.; (on *Iphigenie*) ibid.:no.2465, 2510, 2516, 2517, 2527, 2529, 2559, etc.

of secrets and hidden relationships: 'Zu Hause aufgeräumt, meine Papiere durchgesehen und alle alte [sic]³ Schalen verbrannt ... Stiller Rückblick aufs Leben ... wie ich besonders in Geheimnissen, dunkeln, imaginativen Verhältnissen eine Wollust empfunden habe.'⁴ Some thirty years later he referred to this same delight in secrets in rather more explicit terms, explaining how it had always been a conscious principle behind his writing. Refuting the then current critical opinion that the lines of his 'Dedication' to *Faust* clearly reflected the troubled situation of 1808, he said:

> Daß die Stanzen der Zueignung meines Faust vorläufig gut gewirkt, ist mir sehr angenehm zu hören; doch muß ich zur Steuer der Wahrheit und zu Ehren meines, wenn ich nicht irre, ziemlich verkannten Inneren, versichern, daß diese Strophen ... ihre Entstehung keineswegs den Tribulationen der Zeit verdanken ... So viel habe ich überhaupt bei meinem Lebensgange bemerken können, daß das Publikum nicht immer weiß wie es mit den Gedichten, sehr selten aber, wie es mit dem Dichter dran ist. Ja ich leugne nicht, daß, weil ich dieses sehr früh gewahr wurde, es mir von jeher Spaß gemacht hat, Versteckens zu spielen.⁵

Playing hide and seek with his readers and critics either in the role of writer or self-interpreter was something that Goethe did throughout his life, and although he has provided us with a great many interpretative comments on what he wrote, many of these comments are more misleading than helpful, many formulated in terms of the image of himself and his works that he sought to foster in later years – the image of a talented and sensitive representative of his age and of mankind in general. He undoubtedly was such a representative, but his retrospective discovery of himself in these terms as he reviewed his earlier writings led at times to a distortion, sometimes wilful, sometimes unconscious, of what had led him to write as he did and the original purpose of that writing. But then for him the primary task of

---

3 Here, as elsewhere throughout this study, quoted material has been presented in its original form, which accounts for the seemingly faulty spelling at times and for certain inconsistencies of form or style.
4 *Goethe Tagebücher der sechs ersten Weimarischen Jahre*, ed. Heinrich Düntzer, 1889, 165
5 To K.F. von Reinhard, 22 June 1808, in *Goethes Briefe*, ed. Karl Robert Mandelkow, 1965, 3:79; subsequent references to this edition appear as HA *Briefe*, followed by the volume and page numbers.

Introduction 5

the author was simply to write, and not to provide pointers or clues that would facilitate an explanation of his texts. As he said rather angrily to Luden in 1806: 'Der Dichter soll nicht sein eigener Erklärer sein ... Es ist die Sache des Lesers, des Ästhetikers, des Kritikers, zu untersuchen, was er mit seiner Schöpfung gewollt hat.'[6] This was a logical standpoint, of course, given Goethe's wish both to reveal himself through what he wrote and simultaneously to hide behind it. As we read in a letter to Jacobi as early as 1774: 'Sieh Lieber, was doch alles schreibens anfang und Ende ist die Reproduktion der Welt um mich, durch die innere Welt die alles packt, verbindet, neuschafft, knetet und in eigner, Form, Manier, wieder hinstellt, das bleibt ewig Geheimniss Gott sey Danck, das ich auch nicht offenbaaren will den Gaffern u. Schwäzzern.'[7]

Tied in with Goethe's love of secrecy were very specific notions about how he wished to be read and very clear ideas about the nature of literary works. In his poem 'Gedichte sind gemalte Fensterscheiben,' for example, he declares that the reader must be willing to step into the very heart of the work of literature, to enter it with an appreciative and observant eye that alone enables him to penetrate the meaning and beauty of the poem (HA 1:326).[8] But the true reader, as Goethe calls him, is also able to sense the state of mind of the poet behind the work. 'Der Zustand des Schreibenden,' he wrote to Rochlitz in 1822, 'teilt sich dem wahren Leser sogleich völlig mit.'[9] Note: the *true* reader. In the course of his life Goethe came to form a clear image in his mind of the type of person for whom he wrote as one who shared his goals and preoccupations and for whom his works were therefore readily accessible.[10] Fundamental to the poet's image of the ideal reader was a belief that the act of reading, when properly carried out, was in itself a creative act, a productive encounter for the reader between minds on the same wavelength.[11] Without the right kind of

---

6 Gräf 2,2:no. 1065; see also F.W. Riemer on Goethe's love of riddles and secrets and his refusal to help others interpret his works (*Mittheilungen über Goethe*, 1841, 1:239–52, here 246).
7 HA *Briefe* 1:166
8 Cf. Goethe's motto to the *Noten und Abhandlungen, West-Östlicher Divan*, HA 2:126.
9 22 April 1822; HA *Briefe* 4:35
10 See Eckermann 253 (11 October 1828); also note 20, chapter 4.
11 Cf. Goethe's letter to Schiller (19 November 1796), responding to Körner's critical

readers, whom Goethe termed 'kindred spirits' ('verwandte Wesen'), the act of writing would be purely egotistical.[12] Thus it was in the 'true reader' that the poet placed his hopes for all that he wrote. Although one may disagree with particular elements of Heinz Schlaffer's critical appraisal of Goethe's novels, one must concede that the distinction he makes between an exoteric and an esoteric level of meaning in the works has an undoubted validity, a validity implicitly endorsed over and over again by Goethe himself.[13] And so the question must be asked: how well do we of the literary-critical fraternity read Goethe's works?

A recent book by Albrecht Schöne would seem to suggest that we tend not to do it very well.[14] Schöne deals with only three fairly short texts (*Die Harzreise im Winter*, *Alexis und Dora*, and part of the original 'Walpurgisnacht' from *Faust*), attempting to show how accepted views originating either with the author or with an influential critic have led us away from rather than towards a real understanding of each of these works. The errors in interpretation which Schöne points out all seem to spring essentially from a failure to honour the text by close and scrupulous reading. But such reading is by no means an easy task, as even Goethe himself knew. As an octogenarian he commented to Eckermann in 1830: 'Die guten Leutchen wissen nicht, was es einem für Zeit und Mühe gekostet, um lesen zu lernen. Ich habe achtzig Jahre dazu gebraucht und kann noch nicht sagen, daß ich am Ziel wäre.'[15]

The current state of *Werther*-scholarship tends to bear out Goethe's awareness that reading is no easy matter. How one reads depends of course to some extent on one's perception of what one is reading – a very formal letter from an intimate friend might be perceived as ironic or humorous, for example, while the mere text of the letter might give no cause for such an interpretation. And here we have a central prob-

---

insights into *Wilhelm Meisters Lehrjahre* (HA *Briefe* 2:245); also his letter to Rochlitz, 13 June 1819 (ibid. 3:456).
12 See the *Italienische Reise*, 5 October 1787 (HA 11:413).
13 Heinz Schlaffer, 'Exoterik und Esoterik in Goethes Romanen,' 1978. The exoteric-esoteric distinction stems originally from Goethe – see HA 14:67; also the letter to Franz Passow, 20 October 1811 (HA *Briefe* 3:168).
14 Albrecht Schöne, *Götterzeichen, Liebeszauber, Satanskult: Neue Einblicke in alte Goethetexte*, 1982
15 Eckermann 611 (25 January 1830)

lem in our reading of *Werther*, a problem that has existed ever since the publication of the second version in 1787: despite even deliberate attempts to approach the novel as a work of literature without regard for the biography of its author, the fact is, more often than not the reader-critic's awareness of Goethe's life continues to play a major role in how this second version is interpreted. Now whereas there may be a ready justification for exploring links between the life experiences and the works of an avowedly autobiographical writer such as Goethe, in fact the biographical background to *Werther* seems to have been inadequately explored and poorly applied for a surprisingly long time. The result is that the text of the second edition of the novel seems not to have been subjected to any penetrating scrutiny to this day. It has been assumed for the past two hundred years or so that a chain of events that took place in Goethe's life in Wetzlar in 1772 and in Frankfurt in 1774 provided the background to both versions of *Die Leiden des jungen Werther(s)*. Indeed, this assumption has gained such a hold in critical scholarship on *Werther* that one now feels a certain self-consciousness in going over old ground by referring to these events, as Rudolf Käser's reference to them in a recent treatment of *Werther* as 'jedem Schüler global bekannt' clearly demonstrates.[16] But however well-known the links between Goethe's own experiences and his original version of the novel may be, the conviction that these same experiences lay behind the alterations made in Version Two seems to me improbable and in need of re-examination for reasons that will become clear in due course.

A brief word or two should perhaps be said first about the overall direction taken by critics who have chosen to deal with this novel, which is currently enjoying a sharp resurgence of scholarly interest. The first wave of scholarship tended to concentrate on the autobiographical nature of the work, on details of Goethe's relationship with Charlotte Buff and J.C. Kestner in Wetzlar from June to September 1772, on Jerusalem's suicide and Kestner's detailed account of it in a letter to Goethe a short time later, and on Goethe's second 'Werther'-experience with Maximiliane LaRoche just prior to his putting pen to paper in 1774. For some time now, however, the biographical approach

---

16 Rudolf Käser, *Die Schwierigkeit, ich zu sagen: Rhetorik der Selbstdarstellung in Texten des 'Sturm und Drang,'* 1987, 133

has been downplayed, even derided, on the grounds that the work must stand or fall on its own merits, regardless of actual events and experiences behind the writing. It is not difficult to see why this should be so, given the somewhat primitive, positivistic attitude of many nineteenth-century *Werther*-scholars. Goethe himself was enraged by contemporary reactions to the work and resented the constant desire of those around him to pin him down, and his novel with him, to an admission of the absolute identity of what he had written with what he had experienced. Yet although our more modern scholars may seem at first glance to be on the right path in turning away from biographical knowledge in order to interpret the work itself, if one looks more closely at what is actually being produced, one finds that a great deal falls into the category of involuntary sleight of hand. The fact is, the autobiographical content of *Werther* has been so deeply internalized by critical readers that it has become a hidden starting-point for our everything-other-than-biographical approach to the novel. Let me just offer a few examples of the unquestioned assumptions that currently lie at the heart of *Werther*-scholarship:

1 Goethe, it is widely believed, wrote the whole Werther-trauma out of his system in 1774 and went on to gain increasing distance from it inwardly, in part because of the new duties to which he had to attend in Weimar, in part because of the soothing and ennobling influence exerted on him by Charlotte von Stein.
2 Equally widespread is the conviction that the young Goethe, having arrived in Weimar as a somewhat wild and unruly rebel against most of the rules and limitations imposed on the individual by society, swiftly came to endorse and actively support the value system of the aristocracy, to whose ranks he was only too eager to belong.
3 With particular reference to *Werther*, it is believed that Goethe, obliged to co-operate in the reissuing of his collected works by Göschen because of the proliferation of inferior, pirated editions in the late 1770s and early 1780s, set about reworking his *Werther* with a more mature and thus necessarily more critical eye. In doing so, one of his chief aims, it is believed, was to show greater fairness to his friend, Johann Christian Kestner, who had come off rather badly as the prototype of the Albert figure in the original version.

Each of these assumptions has had and continues to have serious implications for *Werther*-scholarship in its attempts to come to grips with the differences between the first version of the novel, published in 1774, and the second, published thirteen years later in 1787. For example, Dieter Welz in his book *Der Weimarer Werther*, which appeared in 1973 and which has since become a valued work for scholars, makes the case that the more polished, less breathless, less passionate style of the revised *Werther* is incontrovertible evidence of Goethe's mature acceptance of the norms of court society in Weimar.[17] Erich Trunz, also espousing the theory of calm maturity, tells us that the second version was written during a period of emotional serenity in Karlsbad shortly before Goethe left for Italy,[18] while Peter Müller and others concentrate on the implicit social message of the novel first pointed to by Heine, taking for granted that such an interpretation is supported by the change which is supposed to have taken place in Goethe during his first period in Weimar.[19] This alleged change is represented as a development away from 'd[ie] hypochondrisch[e] Unbehaglichkeit der Wertherposition' to the achievement of 'das gesunde und ruhige Bewußtsein eines bedeutenden Leistungsvermögens.'[20] I cite only one critic as the representative of many. For quite some time now scholars have been convinced that the more substantial changes Goethe saw fit to introduce when rewriting the novel represent the establishment of an aesthetic and critical distance between the author and his central character – a rejection of the original Werther, in other words.[21] Now while this seems to fit in with what we think we know of Goethe's development and therefore to offer a plausible reading of the changes he made, it in fact represents an untenable oversimplification that ignores the reality of the life he

17 Dieter Welz, *Der Weimarer Werther: Studien zur Sinnstruktur der zweiten Fassung des Werther-Romans*, 1973
18 HA 6:559. The notion that Goethe had achieved a greater maturity and serenity is shared by Hans Reiss – cf. 'Die Leiden des jungen Werthers,' 1969, 18ff.
19 See Peter Müller, 'Die Aufhebung des Wertherproblems,' in *Zeitkritik und Utopie in Goethes 'Werther,'* 1983, 205–20. Cf. Welz 13; also Konrad Burdach, *Die Wissenschaft von deutscher Sprache*, 1934, 68.
20 Müller 209f.
21 Such an interpretation is offered or implied, for example, by Hans Reiss (18f.); Welz, passim; Eric Blackall, 'The Fictive Editor,' in *Goethe and the Novel*, 1976, 44–55, here 53: 'We must be able to see [Werther's anguish] as something askew ...'

lived and how he wrote during his first phase in Weimar. And from oversimplifications misreadings often result, such as that by Welz, for example, who in summarizing the second version of the novel proclaims with a flourish: 'Das Wertherschicksal [wird] nicht länger als Anklage gegen die große Ordnung der Dinge, sondern als Tragikomödie einer gescheiterten Existenz dargestellt.'[22]

We modern *Werther*-critics all share a host of beliefs about the path which Goethe's development took, based on a knowledge of his life. We know that his raw subject matter was the life he lived and the thoughts he had on the subject of life in general. This he himself readily admitted, not once but many times, among them with reference to *Die Wahlverwandtschaften*, a work with evident thematic links to his first novel.[23] Here, it seems to me, lies the trouble with *Werther*-criticism in general, for we bring to our reading of the text each time a set of presuppositions that result in an unconsciously mediated response to the work. We know, or at least we think we know, that there are major links between Goethe and his Werther, between Lotte and Charlotte Buff, between Albert and Kestner, her fiancé. For two centuries now the awareness of these links has dominated the reading of the second version of the novel, sometimes overtly, sometimes not, but always in play at some level. We readers are convinced that we are in command of the facts that make up the real-life background to *Werther*, and we have been convinced of this for a very long time indeed. The widespread nature of these convictions is very clearly demonstrated by Thomas Mann's novel, *Lotte in Weimar*, for example, for in identifying Werther with Goethe and Lotte with Charlotte Buff (albeit forty years on), Mann was simply drawing on a double equation first made by the readers of the original novel in 1774, an equation which, right down through the years of critical perusal of *Die Leiden des jungen Werther*, has never been questioned. Unfortunately, we all know the Wetzlar story behind Goethe's novel so well that we have never stopped to ask ourselves whether it truly underlies the second version as it did the first. What if a very different part of Goethe's personal life had an important role to play in the rebirth of Werther? 'Wiedergeburt' – the term is not mine, but Goethe's.[24]

22 Welz 35
23 Eckermann 267 (February 1829)
24 See *Goethes Briefe an Charlotte von Stein*, ed. Julius Petersen, 1923, P1592 (14 July

This question needs to be asked and possible answers to it explored because the contrastive scholarly interpretations of *Werther* up to now, even where they have explicitly eschewed the biographical approach, have all too often been based on the supposed facts of Goethe's life underlying Version One. Changes he made in the rewriting are generally regarded as changes introduced by a man for whom the torment of unrequited love is a thing of the past, and interpreted accordingly. I do not mean to suggest any duplicity on the part of scholars, but simply to point out how difficult it has become to read *Werther* without bringing certain old, preconceived ideas to bear on the text. That Goethe at times wilfully, at times unconsciously, led his contemporaries, and through them posterity, astray has certainly not helped matters either. His love of secrets and self-concealment as a principle of writing, together with our background assumptions affecting how we read both versions of the novel, have given rise to a number of theories and assertions that need to be reviewed.

Michael Bernays claimed over a century ago that the two versions were quite separate and distinct from each other,[25] and Gottfried Fittbogen made a similar observation some forty years later,[26] but by and large this distinction has been ignored. Scholars and critics either feel free to write on the original version of the novel as if it were not different in any significant sense from the revised version,[27] or they declare it better for no readily discernible reason,[28] or they omit to deal with significant changes made in the rewriting.[29] An exception is Robert Riemann, who saw in the second version an intensification of the first, and not only in the introduction of the farmboy story, but

---

1786). Future references in my text appear as P followed by the number of the relevant letter. References in my notes appear as P followed by the letter number with the date of writing in parentheses. Where reference is made to Petersen's notes, the volume and part numbers are given, then the page number.

25 *Der junge Goethe*, with an introduction by Michael Bernays, 1875, 1:lxxviif.
26 Gottfried Fittbogen, 'Die Charaktere in beiden Fassungen von Werthers Leiden,' 1910, 557
27 For example, Roger Paulin, ' "Wir werden uns wieder sehn!": On a Theme in *Werther*,' 1980; Klaus Müller-Salget, 'Zur Struktur von Goethes "Werther," ' 1981
28 For example, Thomas Saine, 'Passion and Aggression: The Meaning of Werther's Last Letter,' 1980; Müller-Salget 542; Hans Gose, Goethes '*Werther*,' 1921, 2
29 Emil Staiger, for example, omits all mention of the added story of the young farmhand and seems to see little reason to explore the other changes made in Version Two (*Goethe*, 1952–9, 1:147–73, 526–46).

elsewhere as well; in his view the most passionate passages of all in either version are those that were added in the rewriting.[30] And if one looks closely, it seems that the text lends more support to this claim than to many others. But why should his be such an unrepresentative view? It seems to me possible that the discrepancy here may have to do both with an undeveloped awareness of how Goethe wrote and with the negative attitude that has developed in scholarly criticism towards the use of biography as an aid in evaluating the changes that any writer undergoes and that are reflected in his works. And yet to turn one's back categorically on biographical exploration in approaching a writer such as Goethe seems unwise – which is not to say that any one of his works can be adequately read or interpreted in terms of even the most detailed, most accurate biographical chart imaginable.

What I propose to attempt in the following pages is an examination of the many ways in which Goethe used his literary talent; I shall also consider the various functions that writing appears to have had in his life chiefly between 1776 and 1786, a much more productive period in literary terms than has generally been claimed. I shall explore something of his relationship with his own material once written, whether fragmentary or complete, and attempt to establish a feasible explanation for why he so often rewrote existing works sometimes with substantial, sometimes insubstantial, alteration. By means of a detailed examination of the changes he made to the original *Werther* for its republication in 1787 in the light of how he related to and wrote his other material around that time, I hope to raise for consideration the possibility that our reading of the second version to date may in fact reflect more of us as critics than it does of Goethe as author or of the work itself as text. Paradoxical though it may perhaps seem, one of my chief aims is to highlight the need for a more attentive scrutiny of the text of Version Two without regard for any notions of biography – paradoxical, since I myself feel obliged to present in some considerable detail a particular part of the author's biography and to consider the changes made to the work in the light of that period. I feel obliged to do so, not in order merely to substitute one possible biographical reading of the text for another, but in order to highlight the plausibility of such a new reading, and by so doing to open up our minds to

---

30 Robert Riemann, *Goethes Romantechnik*, 1902, 208

possibilities other than those already represented by the prevailing scholarly views on the rewritten novel. A sound aesthetic evaluation of the later version seems long overdue. My task here is to help to lay the groundwork for such an evaluation.

While several major works were begun or worked on during Goethe's first decade in Weimar, the only significant literary task he brought to completion before leaving for Italy was the rewriting of *Werther*. *Egmont, Iphigenie,* and *Tasso* all remained incomplete and were taken with him, each in large measure an embodiment of some phase of his past life and experience from which he could not bring himself to part until he had re-created them to his own satisfaction, a satisfaction part literary, part personal, as we shall see. Of immense importance for the poet's literary output between 1776 and 1789 was his relationship with Charlotte von Stein, and I mean to show that in this relationship lie important clues that help us to understand more clearly how he wrote, challenging us to think again about a great many of the changes he chose to make to *Werther*, changes of interest and significance in terms of his development both as a man and as a writer.

1
Werther, Goethe, and Charlotte von Stein

Had Goethe not left us with such a wealth of specific information on just about every important period and relationship in his life, his total silence on Charlotte von Stein and the first ten years in Weimar would not seem so remarkable. Aware of the gap, and wishing to fill it at least in part in subsequent years, he wrote the *Tag- und Jahreshefte*, a careful, if less than absorbing, account of his life as administrator, scientific researcher, and public personality, but the veil of silence over the more highly personal aspects of his first decade in Weimar was never lifted. *Dichtung und Wahrheit* deals in some detail with events in his life up to early 1775; Weimar and Charlotte lie beyond. It seems that for some reason he could never bring himself to provide a full record of the period 1775–86 in the way he did for the years before and after – as if he could never quite gain the inner distance from Charlotte that he gained from other great loves such as Friederike Brion and Lili Schönemann.

Denied sufficient information by Goethe himself about this particular relationship, we have developed a distorted picture of it, with unfortunate consequences for our understanding and evaluation of a great deal of the poet's literary output in the early Weimar years. We ought not to blame ourselves entirely for this, however, as we were *meant* to develop an inaccurate view both of the relationship and of the works that were so central to it. Neither Goethe nor Frau von Stein wished the truth of their life together to become known to anyone – indeed, they worked very hard to ensure that it remained a deep secret known only to themselves. The situation in which they were placed dictated a certain degree of subterfuge right from the start, of course. Charlotte von Stein was a married woman of the court and one for whom the good opinion of others was of paramount importance, so it was necessary for them to take care to observe all the visible proprieties of social behaviour when others were around. At first Goethe strongly objected to the exaggerated demands imposed on him by Frau von Stein's concern for appearances, but he came to consent to them quite early on and in so doing seems unwittingly to have fostered her natural inclination to control the relationship. Her need to dominate arose only partly from the situation in which she found herself as a married lady of the court; in larger part it seems to have sprung from a deep-seated emotional insecurity, and in the end the two together made rupture a virtual inevitability.

The reality of life at the Weimar court, as perceived by Charlotte von Stein, both attracted and repelled Goethe, involving him in a constant round of deceit which at times he enjoyed, at others abhorred. The difference in his response depended on the extent to which the game fostered or hindered his own hopes and wishes in regard to his beloved. Although everyone in court circles was well aware of the deep friendship that existed between Frau von Stein and the poet, almost no one knew anything of the truth of their relationship,[1] and they went to great lengths to ensure that no one should find out, chiefly because of her fear of censure, even in the most trivial of matters.

Perhaps the best single example of the lengths to which they went is the extraordinary tale of their use of 'du' and 'Sie.' Here we can glimpse something of the tension, anxiety, and underlying excitement that were part of the ongoing subterfuge they employed in their dealings with one another in public and even in the company of close friends for over a decade. Just two months after his arrival in Weimar in November 1775 Goethe had already begun to balk at the artificial constraints being placed by Frau von Stein on their written intimacy, and he continued for six long years to plead with her to write the more natural 'du' form of address in her notes and letters to him. Not until November 1781 did his pleas bear fruit, however, and even then

---

1 The one notable exception was Goethe's friend, Karl Ludwig von Knebel, and even he was not fully aware of the truth; cf. Goethe's letter to Frau von Stein, P489 (29 October 1780). See footnote 24, chapter 1.

not altogether consistently.[2] Clearly, Frau von Stein's fear was that a note or letter might go astray and reveal to others that she and Goethe were on familiar terms, for not even those closest to them knew that they habitually addressed each other in private with the more intimate 'du' form, even though it was common knowledge that they spent a great deal of time together.[3] Goethe fell in with her wish that this be kept secret, and even the Herders, whom he counted among his best friends at the time, were unaware right up to 1787 of the familiar tone he and Frau von Stein used to each other until a mix-up occurred in his correspondence from Italy and a letter for her was sent by mistake in an envelope addressed to the Herders. Herder forwarded this letter to her at once, and from her attempt to cover up the truth of the previous eleven years in a hastily penned note of thanks as soon as she realized what had happened,[4] we can fairly conclude that throughout the whole decade before Goethe went to Italy, she and he addressed each other as 'Sie' when in the company of other people, despite the early intimacy of their private relationship. Thus every meeting at which others were also present during those years must have meant the enactment of a false little drama by both of them. It is not difficult to imagine how constraints like these, in spite of all love of concealment, should have come to pall in the end on a man whose belief in the worthiness of court values was always less than absolute. There can be no doubt, however, that the game of secrecy and subterfuge appealed to Goethe for some considerable time, once he had overcome his initial opposition to it. One only needs to look at what and how he wrote at this time and to read his letters to Charlotte up to 1786 to see how willingly he engaged in it. The fact is, an extraordinary degree of interplay between secret disclosure and open conceal-

---

2 See P763 (12 December 1781). Goethe's first written use of 'du' to Frau von Stein was in a very early letter (26 January 1766 [P6]). His ongoing objection even to her sporadic use of the formal mode of address in her letters to him re-emerged as late as August 1784 – see P1287.
3 Cf. Wilhelm Bode, *Charlotte von Stein*, 1919, 257: 'Vor Niemand machten die Beiden ein Geheimnis aus ihrer nahen Freundschaft. Nur das "Du" brauchten sie immer heimlich; wenn Fritzchen den Sekretär Goethes spielte, ward seine Mutter mit dem steiferen "Sie" angeredet.' For more evidence of widespread awareness in Weimar of their special relationship see Heinrich Düntzer, *Charlotte von Stein: Goethes Freundin*, 1874, 1:222; the title of this work is shortened to *CvSt* below.
4 See Petersen 1,2:545 (Charlotte von Stein [CvSt] to Herder, 31 August 1787).

ment permeated the relationship between Goethe and Frau von Stein in Weimar society from beginning to end, enabling them to engage in game-playing in matters both large and small, both literary and non-literary.

Since Goethe's death scholars and critics have continued to accept as truth the carefully constructed drama that he and Charlotte consciously played out on their own little stage in Weimar. A great many of our misconceptions both about the poet and about Frau von Stein appear to have originated with Heinrich Düntzer, who in 1874 published a two-volume work entitled *Charlotte von Stein: Goethes Freundin*.[5] Düntzer's dedication on the first page of his book ('Meiner guten Mutter geweiht') offers an unsettling intimation of the biased view he may have of his subject, and as one reads on, comparing what he has to say with those letters and diaries of Goethe's on which he draws, one realizes that he is indeed incapable of objective evaluation. Unaware of his own bias, Düntzer presents the whole relationship in terms that are highly favourable to Frau von Stein – so favourable, indeed, that they represent a distortion of the truth. The fact is, she was far from being that model of serenity or that paragon of virtue which he depicts for us, even though the view of her that he presents remains in essence the standard view even today. While Düntzer may emphasize rather more than many others the impact of Frau von Stein on Goethe's writing process during the Weimar years, an unfortunate sense of awe and reverence hovers over almost every line that he writes about her, and this has coloured our ideas on the role she played in Goethe's life and writings from 1776–86. Convinced that she sought at all times to calm and soothe the poet, to tame his passion, and to foster the nobler aspects of his being, Düntzer omits or misinterprets such evidence as there is to suggest that Frau von Stein encouraged anything other than a platonic relationship between Goethe and herself. He omits, for example, the most important part of the most important letter in the whole relationship – the very part that Charlotte von Stein herself underlined – but he carefully cites what comes before and what comes after.[6] The cumulative effect of his

---

5 See note 3.
6 The section Düntzer omits reveals both a shared intimacy and intensity of feeling between Goethe and Frau von Stein; see *CvST* 1:151 and cf. the text of Goethe's letter of 12 March 1781, quoted on p. 42. For some other examples of this critic's

biased account is to lend strong support to the very impression that Charlotte von Stein herself was so anxious to create and sustain right through from 1776 to 1788, when Goethe returned from Italy. The von Stein family granted Düntzer private access to the poet's letters to Charlotte in order to write his account of her life and her 'friendship' with Goethe, and the authority of these letters seemed so indisputable that Düntzer's account came to colour a great deal of what was subsequently written by others. Schmidt, Bode, Staiger, Fairley, Friedenthal, Viëtor, and Conrady, for example, have also presented a view of Frau von Stein that accords essentially with the image which she herself sought to project and foster: that of a sympathetic, profoundly humane, and dedicated friend who helped Goethe to find greater inner harmony and stability than in his earlier years.[7] However, such a view does not accurately reflect her dealings with him in Weimar up to 1786 and consequently leads to a distorted picture of how he wrote, for their relationship played a most important role in his literary productivity.

Goethe's letters to Charlotte von Stein have been accurately characterized by Karl Robert Mandelkow, who claims that they break through 'das Monologische subjektivistischer Ichaussage' and focus to the point of self-abnegation on the beloved as an all-important counterpart; Emil Staiger also rightly points out the way in which these letters illustrate

---

slanted selectivity see ibid. 75 (February–June 1777); also 156f. (3–4 August 1781); 159 (his reading of the poem 'Der Becher'); 242f. (21 August to 8 September 1785).

7 Erich Schmidt, 'Frau von Stein,' in *Charakteristiken*, 1886, 1901, 1:302–20; Bode, *Charlotte von Stein*, passim; Barker Fairley, 'Charlotte von Stein,' in *A Study of Goethe*, 1947, 97–104; Karl Viëtor, *Goethe*, 1949, 70f.; Richard Friedenthal, 'Die Schule der Frau von Stein,' in *Goethe: Sein Leben und seine Zeit*, 1963, 255–71; Karl Otto Conrady, *Goethe: Leben und Werk*, 1984, 1:338ff. A sketch of the work of earlier scholars on the same subject is given by Lena Voss, *Goethes unsterbliche Freundin, Charlotte von Stein*, 1921, 4ff. Walter Hof's book, 1979, *Goethe und Charlotte von Stein*, is the best contribution to our understanding of Frau von Stein's impact on Goethe's literary oeuvre to date, but the portrait that he paints of her is, like the others, too indulgent. The same tendency towards glorification of her noble qualities can be seen in Otti Lohss, 'Goethe und Charlotte von Stein,' 1986. As this manuscript was completed by mid-1990, it was not possible to take into account the work of Nicholas Boyle, *Goethe: The Poet and the Age* (Oxford, Oxford University Press, 1991). Boyle's view of Frau von Stein's role in Goethe's life is essentially traditional, however.

Goethe's seemingly instinctive desire not to falsify, in the sense of overplay through language, the reality of this particular love experience.[8] Both critics are right in regarding this body of writing as a clear expression of genuine openness and devotion on Goethe's part, for in Frau von Stein he believed he had found his ideal partner in love, a woman who embodied all that he sought, the first and only woman to whom he need add nothing from his own creative imagination. As he wrote to her in March 1782, for example: 'Ich habe mein ganzes Leben einen idealischen Wunsch gehabt wie ich geliebt sein mögte, und habe die Erfüllung immer im Traume des Wahns vergebens gesucht, nun ... find ichs endlich in dir auf eine Weise daß ich's nie verlieren kann ... Leb wohl du einzige in die ich nichts zu legen brauche um alles in dir zu finden' (P843).[9] In his eyes she was also a fully fledged mental and spiritual partner to whom he accorded a major role in what and how he wrote. His letters to Charlotte reflect this quite clearly and offer a valuable insight (albeit one-sided) into the relationship between them. However, they also do more. The striking similarity over a ten-year period between many parts of these letters and Werther's record of his life and love, above all in the second version of the novel, deserves some closer investigation if we are to pass valid judgment on the changes. Goethe did not in fact undergo in Weimar any rapid or constant process of inner development away from the passionate and tumultuous temperament reflected in his original *Werther*, as an examination of his relationship with Frau von Stein will show – a relationship that had been the dominant factor of his life in Weimar for more than ten years by the time he came to rewrite his first novel. It was a different Goethe who wrote the second *Werther*, but not the Goethe in whom we have believed for so long.

The similarity to which I have referred between the poet's letters to Frau von Stein and the text of his rewritten novel did not escape the attention of Adolf Schöll, who published these letters for the first time in 1848–51, long after the deaths of both writer and addressee. A few other scholars have also attempted in the past to establish some limited links between this private correspondence with Charlotte and the second version of *Werther*, but the fact is that none of these critics has

---

8 HA *Briefe* 1:641; Staiger 1:319f.
9 Cf. 18 August 1785 (P1432).

gone far enough and in more recent years their insights appear to have been lost altogether.[10] The more closely one looks at these letters and the revised novel, the more it seems that scholars may well have been closer over a hundred years ago to penetrating one of Goethe's deepest, best-kept secrets than they are today or have been for quite some time. Goethe did mature and develop a desire for useful activity in Weimar without a doubt, but he nevertheless remained a deeply tormented man on both the emotional and professional fronts, one who stayed on in Weimar only because he could not bring himself to face up to the emotional trauma of leaving, despite the recurring awareness that this would be the only way in which to save himself from continuing to live out the torment of Werther all over again.

That he had fled from one impossible love for a woman who was bound to another man, only to find himself in the throes of a similar, even more impossible love, was clear to Goethe from early on, as we see, for example, from a letter to Charlotte von Stein in June 1776 in which he enclosed this four-line poem:

Hier bildend nach der reinen stillen
Natur, ist ach mein Herz der alten Schmerzen voll
Leb ich doch stets um derentwillen
Um derentwillen ich nicht leben soll.[11]

At this early stage Goethe's awareness of his emotional situation was quite clear; he was, as he wrote to his beloved, 'des Herztheilens überdrüssig,' (P79) and wished he could settle for someone sweet and available, 'ein liebes Geschöpf ... und dann nichts weiter geliebt' (P79).

How true such a wish really was, particularly in 1776, must remain in doubt, however, when we consider the major role that *Werther* was to play throughout the relationship between Goethe and Frau von Stein. It seems possible, even probable, that the decision to rewrite the work in the way that he did was at least in part the result of his awareness – at times demonic and tormented, at times playful, at other

---

10 See Adolf Schöll, *Goethes Briefe an Frau von Stein*, 1883, 1885, 2:626f.; also Erich Schmidt, 'Aus der Wertherzeit,' in *Charakteristiken*, 1:288–301; Wilhelm Bode, 'Frau von Stein als Figur im "Werther," ' in *Stunden mit Goethe*, 1905–21, 6:215–19.
11 P77 (29 June 1776); 'Hier bildend ...': Goethe was sketching by the Ilm at the time of writing.

times exalted and devout – that he and Charlotte were living out a story that Fate had decreed he should first write before they ever met each other. Uncannily – although this has gone unremarked – various details concerning the beloved Lotte of Version One, details allegedly derived from a composite picture of Charlotte Buff and Maximiliane LaRoche, suddenly all fitted the reality of the new beloved. The dark eyes of Werther's first Lotte, for example, 'known' by contemporary acquaintances and subsequent scholars to belong to Maximiliane (Charlotte Buff had blue eyes), were the most striking feature of Charlotte von Stein; the original Lotte's family name was changed in the novel to begin with S, not B (for Buff), while the Weimar Lotte's surname did indeed begin with S both before and after marriage.[12] In addition, the silhouette of Lotte which meant so much to Werther had a mysterious counterpart in the significance for Goethe of the silhouette of an unknown Frau von Stein before he ever got to Weimar in 1775. Perhaps none of these details might in itself be very telling, were it not for the fact that Goethe had a marked tendency, particularly at this time, to place great weight on omens, the idea of Fate and the notion of metempsychosis. With *Werther* the vital link between Charlotte von Stein and himself on his arrival in Weimar, such details gain a new importance. The picture we have built up of Goethe's development in the first decade in Weimar is simply so inaccurate that his whole relationship with Frau von Stein needs to be looked at again in some considerable detail if we are to be able to examine objectively the experiences he had during the time in which he altered or added to the original text of *Die Leiden des jungen Werthers*.

Life, Love, and Writing 1775–89

January to November 1775

Before he ever got to Weimar in November 1775 as friend and appointee of the young duke, Karl August, Goethe had already made the acquaintance of Charlotte von Stein, a lady-in-waiting at the court. They had never met in person, but twice that same year he had come

---

12 Charlotte von Stein's maiden name was von Schardt.

across her in the form of a silhouette drawing and twice he had felt an immediate interest and attraction. Silhouette 'reading' was a favourite pursuit at the time because of the widespread popularity of the theories of Johann Kaspar Lavater on the relationship between physiognomy and traits of character and personality, and Goethe's first reading of Frau von Stein's silhouette showed a surprising degree of insight in its final phrase, even though on the whole it might seem in the light of subsequent events to have erred somewhat on the side of generosity: 'Festigkeit, gefälliges, unverändertes Wohnen des Gegenstandes, Behagen in sich selbst, liebevolle Gefälligkeit, Naivetät und Güte, selbstfließende Rede, nachgiebige Festigkeit, Wohlwollen, treubleibend, *siegt mit Netzen*'[13] (emphasis mine). Some weeks later he selected the silhouette of this same woman at random from a hundred or so offered to him for analysis by Johann George Zimmermann, a Swiss physician and writer and an admiring friend of Frau von Stein. This time he wrote below the drawing: 'Es wäre ein herrliches Schauspiel, zu sehen, wie die Welt sich in dieser Seele spiegelt. Sie sieht die Welt, wie sie ist, und doch durch das Medium der Liebe.'[14] Little did he know then how important his relationship with Frau von Stein would become, or how he would ultimately be led to revise this generous appraisal of her character at considerable emotional cost to himself.

Charlotte von Stein, for her part, was equally unaware of the major role that Goethe would play in her life from 1775 onward, despite her ardent desire to meet the author of *Die Leiden des jungen Werthers* long before he ever came to Weimar. To her express wish to do so in January 1775, Zimmermann responded in a cautionary tone: 'Mais pauvre amie, vous n'y pensez pas, vous désirez de le voir et vous ne savez pas à quel point cet homme aimable et charmant pourrait vous devenir dangereux.'[15] It was indeed to be a dangerous liaison for her, but perhaps even more so for Goethe, a liaison that would afford each of them heights and depths of joy and sorrow previously unknown to either.

By November 1775 Frau von Stein was almost thirty-three years old and had been unhappily married for eleven years to Gottlob Ernst

---

13 Petersen 1,1:xi
14 Ibid.
15 Bode, *Charlotte von Stein* 70

24 Werther's Goethe

Josias von Stein, a wealthy member of the landed gentry and *Oberstallmeister* at the court. Von Stein was a good-natured but superficial man of limited intellect, a man unsuited to meet the emotional or intellectual needs of a wife such as his.[16] Seven pregnancies in the eight years from 1764 to 1772 had produced four daughters and three sons, but only the sons survived infancy, and by 1775 Charlotte von Stein was an exhausted and deeply disappointed wife. Writing to Charlotte von Lengefeld in later years, she lamented her own life and the lot of woman in these terms:

> Von Tränen ermüdet schlief ich ein und schleppte mich wieder beim Erwachen einen Tag, und schwer lag der Gedanke auf mir, warum die Natur ihr halbes Geschlecht zu dieser Pein bestimmt habe. Man sollte den Weibern deswegen viele andere Vorzüge des Lebens lassen, aber auch darin hat man uns verkürzt, und man glaubt nicht, wie zu so viel tausend kleinen Geschäften des Lebens, die wir besorgen müssen, mehr Geisteskraft muß aufgewendet werden, die uns für nichts angerechnet wird, als die eines Genies, das Ehre und Reichtum einerntet.[17]

But whatever her unfulfilled mental and emotional needs, Frau von Stein was meticulous in the execution of her role as a married lady of the court and took care to uphold the fiction of wifely devotion wherever possible for others to see, despite her true feelings for her husband.[18] Intelligent and ambitious, her overriding concern in all things, like that of her parents before her, was the high regard of other people.[19] However, although she may have been a clever and calcu-

---

16 See Hof 38f.; Schöll, *Goethes Briefe* 1:6.
17 Petersen 1,1:xiif.
18 An example that illustrates my point can be found in Charlotte von Stein's letter of 18 June 1784 to her son Fritz, who was away in Eisenach with a group of people from the court, among whom were Goethe and her husband, Fritz's father. The relevant portion of the letter reads: 'Dein Bruder Ernst hat mich besucht; mit dem Geheimderath [Goethe] wirst Du wohl ein Gleiches thun, wenn der Eisenacher Aufenthalt ein Ende hat. Lebe wohl, gib Deinem Vater einen Kuß von mir und laß mich immer hören, daß Du wohlgezogen bist' (Düntzer, *CvSt* 1:219.) On her unhappy relationship with her husband, see ibid. 2:4. Letters to individuals were usually circulated throughout the group as a matter of course as soon as they arrived, and Frau von Stein could have anticipated Goethe's jealous reaction to this kiss for her husband.
19 Cf. Biedermann/Herwig 1:361 (Sophie Beckers Tagebuch, 2 March 1785); Düntzer, 'Goethes Eintritt in Weimar,' 1870, 3:40.

lating woman,[20] she was also possessed of more endearing qualities, as is shown by the fond esteem she enjoyed among many writers and thinkers of the day.[21] A certain prudishness and exaggerated spirituality, plus a tendency towards gloomy speculation, were undoubtedly facets of her personality,[22] but she was also witty, charming, well-read, and generally well-liked for her friendly immediacy in social intercourse.

Significantly, despite the enormous impact Goethe made on Charlotte von Stein through *Die Leiden des jungen Werthers* even before she met him, the only part of the novel that she found objectionable – even though many others were morally outraged at the work as a whole – was a lengthy section in the letter of 26 May where Werther deplores Philistinism in love, life, and art, defining it as an attitude of mind that dictates moderation and caution in response to all elemental power or passion. While caution and moderation may make for a good committee man, says Werther, they must destroy both the lover and the artist. The 'offending' passage concludes with these words:

O meine Freunde! warum der Strom des Genies so selten ausbricht, so selten in hohen Fluthen hereinbraust ... Lieben Freunde, da wohnen die gelaßnen Kerls auf beyden Seiten des Ufers, denen ihre Gartenhäuschen, Tulpenbeete, und Krautfelder zu Grunde gehen würden, und die daher in Zeiten mit Dämmen und Ableiten der künftig drohenden Gefahr abzuwehren wissen.[23]

That Frau von Stein felt personally offended by the assertions of this passage is clear from a letter she wrote to Zimmermann in early

---

20 See Henriette von Egloffstein: 'Memoiren,' in Biedermann/Herwig 1:396.
21 Cf. Knebel to his sister, 18 April 1788, in *Karl Ludwig Knebels Briefwechsel mit seiner Schwester Henriette 1774–1813*, ed. Heinrich Düntzer, 1858, 81; see also Zimmermann to Lavater (Hof 31f.) and Schiller to Körner, *Goethe in vertraulichen Briefen seiner Zeitgenossen*, compiled by Wilhelm Bode, rev. and ed. by Regine Otto and Paul-Gerhard Wenzlaff, 1982, 1:338; Tobler to Lavater (ibid. 268); subsequent references to this text appear as *Vertrauliche Briefe* followed by the volume and page number.
22 Düntzer, CvSt 1:269
23 All *Werther* references are taken from vol. 1 of *Werke Goethes*, prepared by Erna Merker, 1954. This volume contains both versions of the novel side by side, the first version (1774) on the left, the second (1786) on the right; hence references are given with the page number followed by L/R, L, or R as appropriate. Here 14L/R.

1775, but her reaction is less than surprising, given the way in which she chose to or felt obliged to lead her own life.²⁴ In rejecting Goethe's view of Philistinism, however, she was rejecting a fundamental and vital aspect of his thought and personality even before she met him, and although he might struggle valiantly in later years to alter his perspective and accept the need for a degree of renunciation in affairs of the heart – indeed, although he even at times declared that he had achieved her desired perspective – in the end there could be no real meeting of minds and hearts between them on the issue of life and love. 'Alles um Liebe' was the seal Goethe used on his letters to her from early 1776;²⁵ 'mäßig ist halb gelebt,' he wrote in his diary in April 1780;²⁶ 'Love is the A and O of everything' was the message of the poem he sent to her in June 1786 (P1588). What forced the two lovers apart in the end was the same gulf that had separated them before they ever met, for the very principles of life by which Charlotte von Stein lived were those that Goethe fundamentally deplored, based as they were on the need for society's approval and a deep-seated fear of all intensity of feeling as loss of control. This was not to become clear to him for a very long time, however, and even when he left for Italy almost eleven years after his first meeting with Charlotte, he was not yet the sadder and the wiser man that he would be forced to become on his return.

November 1775 to June 1789

Goethe arrived in Weimar wearing the costume of Werther and behaving as if he took delight in overturning all the rules of polite society.²⁷ Charlotte von Stein, though flattered by his eager attentiveness

---

24 'Er [Goethe] scheint zu glauben, ein Genie müsse auch ausschweifen, und ärgert sich über die Kerls, die am Ufer wohnen und sich bescheiden vor der Überschwemmung verpalisadieren. Folglich sind die großen Geister mit Verpalisadierung Seltenheiten; diese halbe Wahrheit aber könnte vor einen jungen Menschen gefährlich sein.' Zimmermann cites her letter in his reply of 19 January 1775, disagreeing with what she has to say (*Vertrauliche Briefe* 1:102).
25 See Petersen 1,2:555.
26 WA 3,1:115. WA is used to denote the 4-part, 133-vol. 'Weimarer Ausgabe,' published in Weimar, 1887–1919.
27 On Goethe's rather unruly behaviour see, for example, Biedermann/Herwig 1:177; cf. CvSt to Zimmermann (6 March 1776) *Vertrauliche Briefe* 1:166f. Düntzer tells us

in the early months of their acquaintance, soon had serious misgivings about him because of his wild behaviour: 'Es ist nicht möglich,' she wrote to Zimmermann in March 1776, 'mit seinem Betragen kommt er nicht durch die Welt! Wenn unser sanfter Sittenlehrer gekreuz'get wurde, so wird dieser bittere zerhackt! Warum sein beständiges Pasquillieren? Es sind ja alles Geschöpfe des großen Wesens, das duldet sie ja! Und nun sein unanständ'ges Betragen mit Fluchen, mit pöbelhaften, niedern Ausdrücken.'[28] Her disapproval and fundamental opposition to him are very clear in this letter: above all she deplores the bad influence she feels he is exerting on the young Duke, who now sees merit only in the rough and ready manners of the lower classes. 'Das ist nun alles von Goethen,' she goes on; 'Ich fühl's: Goethe und ich werden niemals Freunde. Auch seine Art, mit unserm Geschlecht umzugehn, gefällt mir nicht. Er ist eigentlich, was man coquet nennt, es ist nicht Achtung genug in seinem Umgang.'[29] But however much she may have disapproved of this man, it is clear that he held some sort of fascination for her, for just two months later she again wrote to Zimmermann about him, this time in a rather different tone: 'Mir geht's mit Goethen wunderbar. Nach acht Tagen, wie er mich so heftig verlassen hat, kommt er mit einem Übermaß von Liebe wieder. Ich hab zu mancherlei Betrachtungen durch Goethen Anlaß bekommen; je mehr ein Mensch fassen kann, deucht mir, je dunkler, anstöß'ger wird ihm das Ganze, je eher fehlt man den ruhigen Weg. Gewiß hatten die gefallnen Engel mehr Verstand wie die übrigen.'[30]

The year 1776 is most important for a variety of reasons, among them Frau von Stein's behaviour and attitude. Though constantly trying to adhere to the rules of court propriety and to dissuade Goethe from his tendency towards emotional self-indulgence, as she saw it, by early October she herself was caught in a conflict between the dictates of her conscience and her heart. The pleasurable anticipation she had felt in the prospect of getting to know Goethe, the poet and author, was already more than justified by the reality of his presence close to

---

(*CvSt* 1:9f.) that Goethe did not dress like Werther, but he is obviously mistaken; see Biedermann/Herwig 1:175, 176, 180, 388.
28 *Vertrauliche Briefe* 1:169
29 Ibid.
30 Ibid. 180 (10 May 1776)

her in Weimar: they read Shakespeare and Ossian together, he sent her poems, drama fragments, and included her in everything he was doing, wherever possible. Literary or quasi-literary pursuits evidently played an important part in the establishment of their relationship, for there are many references in Goethe's letters to Charlotte in 1776 to readings, rehearsals, or performances of works he has already begun or completed, as well as to others planned or written since his arrival in Weimar.[31] It must have seemed to both of them that theirs was a marriage of true minds to which an insuperable impediment had to be admitted, simply because of their situation. Indicative of Charlotte von Stein's inner conflict regarding her feelings for Goethe are these lines which she wrote in pencil on the back of an anguished letter he sent to her on 7 October 1776:

> Ob's Unrecht ist, was ich empfinde –
> und ob ich büßen muß die mir so liebe Sünde
> will mein Gewißen mir nicht sagen;
> vernicht' es, Himmel du! wenn mich's je könt anklagen.[32]

The reason for his anguish was that she had banned him from joining her at her country estate in Kochberg, where she spent almost two months. Why she did so, however, needs to be looked at in the context of their whole relationship as it had developed from almost the beginning of the year.

The profound, even passionate attachment that Goethe felt for Charlotte von Stein already in early 1776 is abundantly plain from the letters he wrote and from the poems he sent to her at that time. In these his mood ranges from joyous and serene to bitter and tormented, while he also shows a clear awareness of the similarities between his current situation and that of Werther, an awareness that is at times accepting, at others, despairing. Just to give three of the many examples available, allowing Goethe to speak for himself so that his style and tone are not lost: On 30 January he ends his third letter of

---

31 For example, *Egmont, Stella, Erwin und Elmire*: P8–10, P65. Also *Der Falke, Die Geschwister*: P84, P86, P100, P114. Reference is also made in Goethe's diaries to these works, as well as to *Claudine von Villa Bella* and *Die Mitschuldigen*; see Gräf 2,1:no. 140, 141; 2,3:no. 3212, 3213, 3215–17.
32 Petersen 1,2:568

the day to her with words that clearly recall a significant moment in *Werther*, well known to both of them: 'Adieu Engel, ich werde eben nie klüger, und muß Gott dancken dafür. Adieu. Und mich verdriessts doch auch dass ich dich so lieb habe und iust *dich*!' (P11).[33] By April the lightness of tone has disappeared:

> Warum soll ich dich plagen! Liebstes Geschöpf! – Warum mich betrügen und dich plagen und so fort – Wir können einander nichts seyn und sind einander zu viel – ... eben weil ich die Sachen nur seh wie sie sind, das macht mich rasend. Gute Nacht Engel und guten Morgen. Ich will dich nicht wiedersehn – Nur – du weisst alles – Ich hab mein Herz – Es ist alles dumm was ich sagen könnte ... (P42)

Agitation and a certain anger are in evidence in late May after a row between them; Charlotte von Stein has apparently assured him of her love but has also told him to stay away for the sake of preserving appearances at court, for the sake of the good opinion of 'the world' ('die Welt'):

> Wenn ich mit Ihnen nicht leben soll, so hilft mir Ihre Liebe so wenig als die Liebe meiner Abwesenden, an der ich so reich bin. Die *Gegenwart* im Augenblicke des Bedürfnisses entscheidet alles, lindert alles, kräfftiget alles. Der Abwesende kommt mit seiner Sprüzze wenn das Feuer nieder ist – und das alles um der Welt willen! Die Welt die mir nichts seyn kann will auch nicht dass du mir was seyn sollst – Sie wissen nicht was sie thun. Die Hand des Einsam verschlossnen, der die Stimme der Liebe nicht hört, drückt hart wo sie aufliegt. Adieu beste. (P57)

That Goethe's growing love for Charlotte soon became the chief focus of his emotional life and the effective cure for his unhappiness over the separation from Lili Schönemann which had preceded his arrival in Weimar can be seen from three letters he wrote, the first in December 1775 to Karl August, the second in April 1776 to Johanna Fahlmer, and the third in July 1776 to Frau von Stein. The text of his letter to Karl August reads:

---

[33] Note the similarity to Lotte's words to Werther during their penultimate meeting when she tells him that he only loves her because she belongs to someone else: 'Fühlen Sie nicht,' she asks, 'daß Sie sich betrügen, sich mit Willen zu Grunde richten? Warum denn mich! Werther! Just mich! das Eigenthum eines andern' (130L).

> Noch ein Wort eh ich schlafen gehe. Wie ich so in der Nacht gegen das Fichtengebürg ritt; kam das Gefühl der Vergangenheit meines Schicksaals, und meiner Liebe über mich, und sang so bey mir selber:
> Holde Lili warst so lang
> All meine Lust und all mein Sang
> Bist ach nun all mein Schmerz und doch
> All mein Sang bist du noch.[34]

By April his pain and longing for Lili were a thing of the past, for he wrote to his aunt: 'Von Lili nichts mehr, sie ist abgethan'[35] and in July he reacted as follows in a letter to Charlotte, on hearing the news of Lili's marriage: 'Gestern Nachts lieg ich im Bette schlafe schon halb, Philip bringt mir einen Brief, dumpfsinnig les ich – dass Lili eine Braut ist!! kehre mich um und schlafe fort. – Wie ich das Schicksal anbete dass es so mit mir verfährt! – So alles zur rechten Zeit – Lieber Engel gute nacht ...' (P75). Although Goethe claimed in later years that the greatest love of his life was Lili, whom he never forgot,[36] his own letters to Charlotte show that this was not the case. Lili may have been the beloved woman whom he most fondly called to mind in retrospect once the relationship with Frau von Stein was long past, with all the pain, disappointment, and disillusionment its ending brought, but there can be no doubt that his love for Charlotte was the more profound experience. Retrospective readjustments of this kind were by no means rare for the later Goethe, however.

The first major crisis in the relationship arose in September 1776. Frau von Stein forbade Goethe to go to Kochberg, where she spent about seven weeks from 9 September to 31 October. To make matters worse, she took Lenz along in his place as her English tutor, thus causing him double anguish. From her own pencilled confession of inner conflict already quoted above it seems likely that her decision was an attempt to sidestep the difficult, 'sweetly sinful' reality of her own feelings for Goethe, but no doubt it was also an attempt to cool his ardour and to avoid giving the wagging tongues of the court yet further cause for gossip. The torment her decision caused him is expressed in a letter he wrote to her on 10 September, the day after

---

34 HA *Briefe* 1:201
35 Ibid. 212
36 See Eckermann 621f. (5 March 1830).

her departure for Kochberg and two days after he had received her express command that he remain in Weimar:

> O Sie haben eine Art zu peinigen wie das Schicksaal, man kan sich nicht drüber beklagen so weh es thut. Er [Lenz] soll Sie sehn, und die zerstörte Seele soll in ihrer Gegenwart die Balsamtropfen einschlürpfen um die ich alles beneide. Er soll mit Ihnen seyn – Er war ganz betroffen da ich Ihm sein Glück ankündigte, in Kochberg mit Ihnen gehen, sie lehren, für Sie zeichnen, sie werden für ihn zeichnen, für ihn seyn. Und ich – zwar von mir ist die Rede nicht, und warum sollte von mir die Rede seyn – Er war ganz im Traum da ich's ihm sagte ... Ade. von mir hören Sie nun nichts weiter, ich verbitte mir auch alle Nachricht von Ihnen oder Lenz. Wenn was zu bestellen ist mag er's an Philip schreiben.   (P97)

Some hours later that same day he took up his pen once more to add the following:

> Lenz will nun fort, und ich hatte Bedencken Ihnen die vorhergehende Seite zu schicken, doch Sie mögen sehn wie mirs im Herzen manchmal aussieht, wie ich auch ungerecht gegen Sie werden kann ...   (P97)

Charlotte returned to Weimar briefly almost a month later, and the prospect of her second departure gave rise to this letter from Goethe (on the back of which she acknowledged her 'sweet sin'):

> Leben Sie wohl beste! Sie gehen und weis Gott was werden wird! ich hätte dem Schicksaal danckbar seyn sollen, das mich in den ersten Augenblicken da ich Sie wiedersah so ganz rein fühlen lies wie lieb ich Sie habe, ich hätte mich damit begnügen und Sie nicht weiter sehen sollen. Verzeihen Sie! Ich seh nun wie meine Gegenwart Sie plagt, wie lieb ist mirs dass Sie gehn, in einer Stadt hielt ichs so nicht aus ...   (P103)

On 28–29 October, when she had been away for almost seven weeks he wrote *Die Geschwister*, a play since acknowledged as an example of his covert revelation of his private life in his writings.[37] Wilhelm, the central character, is in love with Marianne, daughter of the dead Charlotte whom he also loved but could not marry because of adverse

---

37 See Adolf Schöll, 'Über Goethes Geschwister,' in *Goethe in Hauptzügen seines Lebens und Wirkens*, 1882, 68–97; also Conrady 1:332; Friedenthal 260f.

circumstances. In the course of the play he reads aloud his favourite letter from Charlotte – a letter thought to contain lines actually written by Frau von Stein to Goethe in 1776.[38] The relevant part reads: 'Mein Herz macht mir Vorwürfe; ich fühle, daß ich Ihnen und mir Qualen zubereite. Vor einem halben Jahr war ich bereit zu sterben und bin's nicht mehr' (HA 4:355). The dead widow, Charlotte, had found new meaning in life through her love for Wilhelm; through her love for Goethe Charlotte von Stein had done the same. She is evidently cast in the play not only as the dead Charlotte but also as her own daughter, Marianne, with whom Wilhelm is now in love, and who lives with him, believing him to be her brother. Writing this play undoubtedly helped Goethe during a period when he was suffering from the emotional isolation imposed on him by Frau von Stein, for not only did he joyously recall in it her confession of how much he meant to her, but he also adjusted his present reality to his own liking by creating a 'happy end' in which 'brother and sister' marry. The play's chief message is that the best outcome for love is marriage and not any mere brother-sister relationship, which is what Charlotte von Stein was ostensibly advocating for them at the time. Some months before, in April, Goethe had referred to this idea in letters and in a poem he had written for her ('Ach, du warst in abgelebten Zeiten / meine Schwester oder meine Frau'[39]), but by the time he came to write *Die Geschwister* in late October he was in no state of mind to be able to sustain thoughts of any such relationship with her. Evidently the play was his attempt to lessen the sense of torment he felt and hence a very personal document. While he allowed it to be performed in Weimar, the fact that he took much greater care of this manuscript than any other is indicative of his awareness of its confessional nature.[40] But although

---

38 Schöll, 'Goethes Geschwister' 94ff.; also Albert Bielschowsky, *Goethe: Sein Leben und seine Werke*, 1896, 1902, 1:303; Staiger 1:323
39 The lines are contained in the poem 'Warum gabst du uns die tiefen Blicke' (HA 1:122f.). Frau von Stein evidently objected to the notion of herself as Goethe's wife, for on 16 April, two days after sending her this poem, he wrote in response to a note from her: 'Adieu liebe Schwester weils denn so seyn soll' (P43). The poem was not published during Goethe's lifetime; it first appeared in print in 1848 with the publication of his letters to Frau von Stein.
40 On this point Erich Schmidt comments: 'Goethe that bis zum Druck sehr ängstlich mit der Handschrift, die ihm und der lieben Frau wie etwas Intimes verwahrt sein sollte' (Schmidt, *Charakteristiken* 1:313); see also Friedenthal 261.

writing the play may have effected a healing of the wounds Goethe felt as a result of Frau von Stein's seeming harshness towards him, it was a temporary and imperfect healing only. The enormous suffering he endured because of this incident is reflected for a long time in his letters to her and there can be no doubt that it left a deep wound that was slow to heal, if heal it did, for he referred to it again several times long after the relationship had stabilized.[41]

Charlotte returned to Weimar on 31 October, and just two days later Goethe wrote a poem for her with the title 'An den Geist des Johannes Sekundus,' in which he lamented his own wretchedness and made a plea for the restoration of his beloved's favours. While it is possible to regard this as an imitative poem – Goethe had read *Basia* (= kisses) by the sixteenth-century Dutch writer Jan Everard (Johannes Sekundus) just the day before – it seems altogether unlikely that it was intended as anything other than a light-hearted personal greeting for Frau von Stein, albeit one with a serious intent. It is a poem likely to amuse and shock its reader, particularly a reader with some awareness of poetic forms who feels herself addressed by the tormented author. It opens amusingly with an exaggerated flourish that becomes increasingly ludicrous as one reads on:

> Lieber, heiliger, groser Küsser,
> Der du mir's in lechzend athmender
> Glückseeligkeit fast vorgethan hast!
> Wem sollt ich's klagen? klagt ich dir's nicht!
> Dir, dessen Lieder wie ein warmes Küssen
> Heilender Kräuter mir unters Herz sich legten, ...   (P105)

Although the whole poem is something of a parody and an ironic self-caricature, it contains some very specific information and a very specific personal plea, and so I have emphasized in the lines that follow, those that were particularly relevant to Goethe's relationship and situation at the time of writing, lines whose underlying message was meant to appeal successfully to Frau von Stein. (Some of the unemphasized lines were likely to elicit a sense of shock, but no doubt this was also meant as a deliberate joke, a small act of loving retribution):

---

41 Cf. P107 (8 November 1776), P176 (6 July 1777), Goethe's diary, 22 August 1779 (WA 3,1:95), P445 (24 June 1780).

34 Werther's Goethe

> Ach wie klag ich dir's, dass meine Lippe blutet,
> Mir gespalten ist, und erbärmlich schmerzet,
> *Meine Lippe, die soviel gewohnt ist*
> *Von der Liebe süsstem Glück zu schwellen*
> Und, wie eine goldne Himmelspforte,
> Lallende Seeligkeit aus und einzustammeln.
> Gesprungen ist sie! Nicht vom Biss der Holden,
> Die, in voller ringsumfangender Liebe,
> Mehr mögt haben von mir, und mögte mich Ganzen
> Ganz erküssen, und fressen, und was sie könnte!
> *Nicht gesprungen weil nach ihrem Hauche*
> *Meine Lippen unheilige Lüfte entweihten.*
> *Ach gesprungen weil mich, öden, kalten,*
> *Über beizenden Reif, der Herbstwind anpackt.*
> Und da ist Traubensaft, und der Saft der Bienen,
> An meines Heerdes treuem Feuer vereinigt,
> Der soll mir helfen! Warrlich er hilft nicht
> *Denn von der Liebe alles heilendem*
> *Gift Balsam ist kein Tröpfgen drunter.*   (P105)

The following day a letter to his beloved Charlotte opens: 'Ich bitte Sie um das Mittel gegen die wunde Lippe, nur etwa dass ich's finde heute Abend wenn ich zurückkomme. Muss ich schon wieder um etwas bitten um etwas heilendes' (P106). There are several points to be made in connection with the poem: first, he *is used to* being kissed; second, he makes sure to let Charlotte know that he has kissed nobody else *since he last kissed her* ('Nicht gesprungen weil nach ihrem Hauche / Meine Lippen unheilige Lüfte entweihten'); and third, he laments the lack of 'Balsamtröpfgen' in the healing process of the love and attentiveness he is currently experiencing now that she has returned to Weimar ('Traubensaft,' 'Saft der Bienen' sound as if they refer to gifts she has sent to 'help' him). He had used the very same word ('Balsamtropfen') in his anguished and jealous letter to her about Lenz taking his place at her castle in Kochberg: 'Er soll Sie sehn, und die zerstörte Seele soll in ihrer Gegenwart die Balsamtropfen einschlürpfen um die ich alles beneide' (P97). 'Balsam' and the associated 'Balsamtropfen' appear to have belonged to their private code words, and Goethe uses the second word in both places to considerable effect – in the letter as a jealous attack on Charlotte for replacing him for eight weeks with Lenz, and in the poem to appeal to her for a restoration of favours. (The word 'Balsam' is also used in the same way to refer to kissing in the poem 'Der Becher,' sent to her in September 1781.[42]) In my view 'An den Geist des Johannes Sekundus' may well go some way towards explaining Charlotte's confession ('die mir so liebe Sünde') and why she banned Goethe from going to Kochberg, when many other members of the court were permitted to visit her during her stay there. The importance of this speculation will become clearer later on when we turn to an examination of the changes Goethe made to *Werther*, but both 'Johannes Sekundus' and *Die Geschwister* are important at this point for the way in which they illustrate how the author's emotional preoccupations formed the basis of material he wrote within the framework of a literary form; both also highlight his penchant for self-projection into characters of his own devising, and give an early indication of the playful obliqueness with which he expressed himself for the benefit of one particular reader who knew all his secrets. This is a characteristic that has ramifications for the interpretation of much that he wrote or rewrote from 1776 to 1789.

Surprisingly enough, the years 1776–80 were marked *not* chiefly by any growing serenity on Goethe's part, as we like to think, but by great swings of mood from joy to torment, largely as a result of Frau von Stein's criticism, doubt, or even apparent callousness, for she was often away from Weimar and often did not let him know of her plans. His outbursts of joy, of course, came in response to some sign of love or warmth on her part and were often more intense than their counterparts of rage, bewilderment, and hurt. A great many of Goethe's letters to Frau von Stein offer insight into the see-saw existence the poet led emotionally in Weimar, especially from 1776–80, but also well beyond that – in fact, right up to 1786, despite certain periods of relative harmony.

In January 1778, for example, his letters are loving but also defensive and biting – e.g., 'Es scheint ich soll wieder einmal fühlen dass ich Sie sehr lieb habe, und was ich Sie gekostet habe u.s.w. Dem sey wies wolle, ich mag und kan Sie nicht sehn' (P211). In February we see among notes expressing his love and happiness a glimpse of her inconsistency, his

---

42 See pp. 44f.

sharpness, and his ongoing search for a sign of love from her – as on the first of the month, for example: 'Es ist doch hübsch von Ihnen dass Sie den den Sie nicht mehr lieben doch mit eingemachten Früchten nähren wollen. Dafür danck ich. Obs gleich aussieht als wenn Sie mir Gerichte schickten damit ich nicht kommen solle sie bey Ihnen zu verzehren' (P216); and on the 18th, 'Ich dancke recht sehr dass Sie mir in meine Einsamkeit und Mangel, Frizzen und ein Frühstück schicken wollen. Wenn Sie mir was dazu von sich gesagt hätten wärs noch hübscher gewesen ...' (P219). April 1778 was an unsettled period in which there was friction once again: 'Ich weis sehr wohl wie Sie meine Picks track-tiren, dass es mir aber Ernst ist sehen Sie dadran dass ich nicht komme ob ich gleich gern käme. Adieu lieber Engel hier schick ich Ihnen Blumen. Wenn ich's übers Herz bringen kan so geh ich auf den Montag fort. Wenn man nicht sagen kan wie lieb man eins hat so scheints man wolle sich mit bösem helfen wenns im Guten nicht fort will' (P227).

The following month Goethe was travelling and in a highly negative frame of mind vis-à-vis society ('die Welt'): 'So viel kann ich sagen ie gröser die Welt desto garstiger wird die Farce und ich schwöre, keine Zote und Eseley der Hanswurstiaden ist so eckelhafft als das Wesen der Grosen Mittlern und Kleinen durch einander. Ich habe die Götter gebeten dass sie mir meinen Muth und grad seyn erhalten wollen biss ans Ende, und lieber mögen das Ende vorrücken als mich den lezten theil des Ziels lausig hinkriechen lassen ...' (P241). By June his longing to end his emotional torment is again clear, but contemplation of the pain he would have to endure, were he to leave Weimar, puts an end to all thoughts of action: 'Ich bin leider an Ihre Liebe zu fest geknüpft,' he writes to Frau von Stein, 'wenn ich manch-mal versuche mich los zu machen thut mirs zu weh da lass ich's lieber seyn' (P251). August and September letters reveal his love, her doubt, his dependence on her nearness, and his tendency towards jealousy (P270–6). Charlotte was away for several weeks in Kochberg during October and November, and his letters at that time reflect both his love and a sense of hurt at her failure to write, together with an impa-tience for her return to Weimar (P280–3). By December his sense of alienation from other people, including Charlotte von Stein, is quite extreme: '... zugefroren gegen alle Menschen,' he writes in his diary early that month, and with specific reference to Frau von Stein: '... sie kommt mir immer liebenswürdig vor, obgleich fremder. Wie die übrigen auch.'[43]

Two years later, in 1780, the same swings of mood prevail, though it is clear that she has by now been reciprocating his feelings of love for some time.[44] Here there are signs of sexual frustration in his letters, and not for the first time by any means, signs too of the same deep dislike for court circles already evident from 1776 onward. Defensiveness, irritation, and reproachfulness often mark his responses to Frau von Stein; yet all is not negative – far from it: 'Lieben Sie mich es ist mir zur Nothdurft worden,' he writes on 3 May (P419), followed two days later by a letter that ends with a rather bold pun on the name of her husband: 'Bleiben Sie mir nah und verzeihen Sie dass ich immer über mein eigenstes mit Ihnen rede, hätt ich Sie nicht ich würde zu Stein' (P420).

But 1780 was not a good year on the whole for Goethe, the lover. Despite the fact that tokens of lasting love were exchanged in June,[45] Frau von Stein's tendency to criticize and censure him whenever she saw fit to do so continued as before, causing him considerable pain. Several times he refers to his own inner turmoil in the course of this year, as at the end of June, for example, when he writes to her: 'Meine Seele ist wie ein ewiges Feuerwerck ohne Rast' (P447), or in September: 'Gott giebt mir zur Buse für meine eigne Sünden die Sünden andrer zu tragen. Und in meinem immer bewegten Zustand, beneid ich den

---

43 WA 3,1:72f.
44 For example, see P14 (February 1776), P84 (8 August 1776), P94 (1 September 1776), P116 (22 December 1776), P128 (16 February 1777), P167 (26 May 1777), P184 (6 September 1777), P191 (31 October 1777), P198 ('An den Mond,' November 1777), P251 (17 June 1778), P266 (7 August 1778), P305 (2 March 1779), P419 (3 May 1780), P443 (14 June 1780), P447 (30 June 1780: 'Eine Liebe und Vertrauen ohne Gränzen ist mir zur Gewohnheit worden. Seit Sie weg sind hab ich kein Wort gesagt, was mir aus dem innersten gegangen wäre').
45 Charlotte von Stein sent Goethe a ring engraved with the initials CS (13 June 1780), but he insisted on the insertion of a 'v' (for 'von') between them as CS were also the initials of Corona Schröter. He evidently regarded this ring as a special token of love (cf. note 73). As a further demonstration of his emotional commitment to her he sent her the gloves he had been given by the Masons, saying: 'Es [das Geschenk] hat ... das merckwürdige dass ich's nur Einem Frauenzimmer, ein einzigsmal in meinem Leben schencken kann' (P445, 24 June 1780).

der mich um etwas bittet und dem ich durch eine kleine Gefälligkeit seine Wünsche ausfüllen kan und selbst niemand habe der mir – doch will ich nicht ungerecht und undanckbar seyn ...' (P482). A visit he makes to Charlotte in Kochberg the following month evidently ends up on a painful note, for on his return to Weimar he writes:

> Was Sie mir heut früh zulezt sagten hat mich sehr geschmerzt, und wäre der Herzog nicht den Berg mit hinauf gegangen, ich hätte mich recht satt geweint. Auf ein Übel hauft sich alles zusammen! Ja es ist eine Wuth gegen sein eigen Fleisch wenn der Unglückliche sich Lufft zu machen sucht dadurch dass er sein Liebstes beleidigt. Und wenns nur noch in Anfällen von Launen wäre und ich mirs bewusst seyn könnte; aber so bin ich bey meinen tausend Gedancken wieder zum Kinde herabgesezt, unbekannt mit dem Augenblick, dunckel über mich selbst, indem ich die Zustände der andern wie mit einem hellfressenden Feuer verzehre.
>
> Haben Sie Mitleiden mit mir. Das alles kam zu dem Zustand meiner Seele darinn es aussah wie in einem Pandämonium von unsichtbaaren Geistern angefüllt, das dem Zuschauer, so bang es ihm drinn würde, doch nur ein unendlich leeres Gewölbe darstellte ... (P485)

Her failure to send some signal that he is in her thoughts wounds him, for he adds to this letter the following evening: 'Knebel, hofft ich, sollte mir etwas von Ihnen mitbringen, sonst hätt ich meinen Boten schon heute fortgeschickt. Nun nicht eine Zeile, nicht ein welckes Blat, nichts was Ihnen nichts gekostet hätte ... Gute Nacht, meine beste. Ach man weis nicht was man hat, wenn man gute Nacht mit Hand und Mund sagen kan' (P485). Two days later, on 13 October, he writes: 'Es ist wunderbaar und doch ists so, dass ich eifersüchtig und dummsinnig bin wie ein kleiner Junge wenn Sie andern freundlich begegnen. Gute Nacht Gold. Seit denen Paar Tagen bin ich noch nicht zur Ruhe gekommen als schlafend, das ist mir aber am gesundsten ... Ich bin wie eine Kugel die rikochet aufschlägt ...' (P486). And on his way to visit her in Kochberg about two weeks later he has the feeling that things are not yet right between them; his letter of 29 October 1780 reflects his sorrow at this and also an uncertainty regarding her feelings for him that makes him emotionally vulnerable and insecure:

> Ich weis nicht warum, aber mir scheint Sie haben mir noch nicht verziehen. Ob ich Vergebung verdiene weis ich nicht, Mitleiden gewiss.

> So gehts aber dem der still vor sich leidet, und durch Klagen weder die seinigen ängstigen noch sich erweichen mag, wenn er endlich aus gedrängter Seele Eli, Eli, lama asabthani ruft, spricht das Volck, du hast andern geholfen hilf dir selber, und die besten übersezzens falsch und glauben er rufe dem Elias.
>
> Nur keine Gedanckenstriche in Ihren Briefen mehr, Sie können versichert seyn dass ich sie immer mit dem schlimmsten ausfülle ... (P489)

Four days later, on 2 November, there are more signs of trouble, even though Goethe welcomes the direct expression of anger in what she now writes in preference to her earlier dissimulation and indifference: 'So einen bösen Vorhang mir Ihr Brief herunter wirft, und neue Nebel meine schönsten Aussichten decken [the prospect of her return to Weimar]; so ist mirs doch wilkommner als Ihr anfänglich gleichgültig thun, da Sie mirs ausreden und mich beruhigen wollten ...' (P490).

Clearly, the picture that these letters convey is not that of a Goethe at one with himself or with Frau von Stein even five years after his first arrival in Weimar, and a similar selection from 1782 will be looked at presently, so it surprises one to read the fiction adhered to by so many critics to the effect that the poet underwent a change of temperament in his early years in Weimar, turning his back on the emotional fireworks he had so glorified in his *Sturm und Drang* phase prior to 1775, and growing increasingly serene because of the influence of Charlotte von Stein. Again Düntzer seems to have had a hand in setting us on the wrong course: he draws on the letters Goethe wrote to Charlotte von Stein from his Swiss journey in the winter of 1779–80 to make the following observation, for example: 'Die Briefe, die er von der Reise schreibt, zeigen eine holde Innigkeit, keine Spur von der leidenschaftlichen Glut, der stürmischen Unruhe und peinigenden Sehnsucht, die seine Seele sonst bei jeder kurzen Trennung von ihr verzehrte.'[46] What Düntzer overlooks is the fact that these letters are not characteristic of those that often succeeded them, and therefore represent no real watershed of the kind he implies in Goethe's emotional life. But then he had already noted the same watershed about half a year earlier, at the point where the poet first began to write *Iphigenie*. For this critic the play is: '... eine dichterische Verklärung der

Beruhigung ... welche Charlotte endlich über den leidenschaftlichen Stürmer gebracht hatte ... die erste volle Frucht der glücklich durch den lindernden Einfluß ihres liebevollen Vertrauens in ihm erwirkten Veränderung.'[47] The mistake Düntzer clearly makes is to see the play as evidence of a change that had already taken place in Goethe once and for all by mid-1779.

Over a hundred years later and with the authority of this critic and others behind it, a similar error of judgment appears in *Der Weimarer Werther*, when Dieter Welz reads Goethe's diary entry of 7 August 1779 (expressing his dedication to 'die Idee des Reinen') as evidence of his rejection henceforth of all *Sturm und Drang* elements in his life and writings.[48] Admittedly, Welz falls into error with the help of the poet himself, as he uses a quotation from *Dichtung und Wahrheit* in order to substantiate his claims, but such errors are not uncommon in the scholarly literature on Goethe.[49] What we must realize, however, is that the poet's express desire for a regular and serene life filled with achievement was merely a recurring, unfulfilled wish that did not become a reality until well after the first Italian journey. It is quite wrong to take any one of the instances up to 1786 where Goethe formulates the wish for greater calmness and serenity of mind and heart, or even the assertion that he has achieved these, as evidence that he has now undergone a significant and lasting change of this kind. In early 1779 he began working on *Iphigenie*, and in late 1780 he began to write *Tasso*, but while both works were begun as a reflection of Goethe's devotion to Charlotte von Stein, the difficulties he had in completing the second, and the significant differences in mood and tone between the two completed dramas offer an important insight into the course of his emotional life in Weimar. Had *Tasso* been completed in early 1787 and *Iphigenie* in mid-1789 instead of the other way around, then perhaps we might be able to lend greater support to the theory of his growing calmness and moderation.

---

47 Ibid. 107
48 The diary entry deals with his dissatisfaction at the wildness of his past life and with what he has written so far. It then goes on: 'Möge die Idee des Reinen, die sich auf den Bissen erstreckt, den ich in Mund nehme, immer lieblicher in mir werden' (WA 3,1:94).
49 Welz 12f., also 40. Cf., for example, Konrad Burdach 68; Georg Lukács, *Faust und Faustus*, 1968, 29.

From 1777–80, as in 1776, Goethe was eager to include Frau von Stein in all that he wrote, rehearsed, or performed in, and as he began to draft or write new material her role became increasingly important. There are several references to his literary or dramatic activities in his letters to her in 1777 – references to existing works (*Erwin und Elmire, Die Mitschuldigen*[50]), as well as to a new play (*Lila*), and a new novel he was then planning (*Wilhelm Meisters theatralische Sendung*).[51] While 1778 was an unproductive year in terms of both writing and performance,[52] in 1779 Goethe began to write *Iphigenie*, and his intensive work on the new drama is reflected in his letters to Charlotte, as is her role as helpmate.[53] The following year he wrote *Die Vögel* (June–August) and began serious work on *Tasso* in November.[54] Whereas he and Frau von Stein had shared chiefly in the pleasure of readings and performances of his works in the earlier years, by 1779–80 they had begun to share in the writing of his new material, and her increased involvement can be seen from his correspondence with her at this time. Here are some examples from late November 1780, when he was working on *Tasso*:

> Lassen Sie mich meine beste Ihnen einen guten Morgen sagen, hierhaussen ist es wild und trüb, die Wolcken liegen der Erde und dem Geiste schwer auf. Doch ist unter der Hülle mein erster Ackt fertig geworden, ich mögt ihn gerne lesen, dass Sie theil an allem hätten was mich beschäfftigt ... (P494)

> Ihr gütigs Zureden und mein Versprechen [to continue working on *Tasso*] haben mich heute früh glücklich den IIten Ackt anfangen machen.

---

50 Cf. P122, P131, and accompanying notes (Petersen 1,2:570); also Gräf 2,1:no.760, 762, and 2,3:no.3218–20.
51 See P119, P120, P191, and notes (Petersen 1,2:569f., 575); also Gräf 2,3:no.2784, 2787, 2795; 1,2:no.1126, 1131.
52 There were two performances of *Der Triumph der Empfindsamkeit* (30 January, 10 February), one of *Erwin und Elmire* (27 February), and one of *Das Jahrmarktsfest zu Plundersweilen* (20 October); see Gräf 2,4:no.4333, 4334; ibid. 2,1:no.763; ibid. 2,3:no.3447. Goethe did little new writing in 1778 (*Sendung, Egmont*); see ibid. 1,2:no.1133, 1134, 1137–9; also ibid. 2,1:no.355–8.
53 See letters of February–March 1779: P301–9, P312. N.B. P306: 'Noch hab ich Hoffnung dass wenn ich d. 11ten oder 12ten nach Hause komme mein Stück fertig seyn soll. Es wird immer nur Skizze, wir wollen dann sehn was wir ihm für Farben auflegen.'
54 See P446–8, P450, P462, P464 (*Die Vögel*); P492–4, P496–9, P502, P503, P505, P508 (*Tasso*).

> Hier ist der 1ste mög er in der Nähe und bey wiederhohltem Lessen seinen Reiz behalten. Lassen Sie ihn niemand sehen ... (P496)
>
> Behalten Sie den Ackt wie Sie wollen, er wird mir erst lieb da Sie ihn lieben ... (P497)
>
> Geschrieben ist worden heute früh, wenig, doch stockts nicht. Behalten Sie den Antheil den ich offt leider einen Augenblick nicht fühle an dem was mich angeht und helfen mir leben. Und lassen mir den Glauben dass ich auch etwas zu Ihrer Zufriedenheit beytrage. (P499)

Just a few months later a significant change occurred on the emotional front, a change that ushered in a period of greater happiness and fulfilment that was to last, albeit with anguished interruptions similar to those of the previous five years, until the latter half of 1785:

> Meine Seele ist fest an die deine angewachsen, ich mag keine Worte machen, du weist daß ich von dir unzertrennlich bin und daß weder hohes noch tiefes mich zu scheiden vermag. Ich wollte daß es irgend ein Gelübde oder Sakrament gäbe, das mich dir auch sichtlich und geseztlich zu eigen machte, wie werth sollte es mir seyn. Und mein Noviziat war doch lang genug um sich zu bedencken ... (P596)

This avowal of lasting love is contained in a letter written by Goethe from Neunheiligen on 12 March 1781 in response to one he has just received from Charlotte, and from this point on there is an immediate increase in the references he makes to the beneficial effects her love is having on him.[55] March and April are a time of happiness, joy, gratitude, and exalted devotion for him, a time in which he begins to address his beloved as 'Lotte,' 'liebe Lotte' for the first time,[56] but already in May and June we again see in his letters reflections of Frau von Stein's criticism and possessiveness, which seem to occur fairly frequently from now on, in all probability because of her heightened sense of vulnerability.[57] Having evidently committed herself once

---

55 Cf. P600, P602, P606, P607, P609, P611, P613, P615, etc. (from 17 March 1781).
56 See P649. 'Liebe Lotte,' 'Lotte,' 'meine l.L.,' etc. were forms of address used by Goethe in his letters to Frau von Stein from May 1781 to March 1785. There are only three supposedly later occurrences before he left for Italy in September 1786 and these are of uncertain date.
57 For example, P666 (30 May), P672 (6 June), P684 (1 July), P686 (5 July), P701 (4 August), P711 (29 August), etc.

and for all to their love relationship, she needs constant reassurance from him about his commitment, as she lacks confidence regarding his total and exclusive devotion to her (P686, P711). Yet even at this essentially happy time the force of the continuing conflict within him is clear. From Ilmenau he writes, for example: 'Ich sehne mich heimlich nach dir ohne es mir zu sagen, mein Geist wird kleinlich und hat an nichts Lust, einmal gewinnen Sorgen die Oberhand, einmal der Unmuth, und ein böser Genius misbraucht meiner Entfernung von euch, schildert mir die lästigste Seite meines Zustandes und räth mir mich mit der Flucht zu retten; bald aber fühl ich dass ein Blick, ein Wort von dir alle diese Nebel verscheuchen kan ...' (P688).

But however much Goethe may have lamented Frau von Stein's doubts about the depth of his commitment to her in the late summer of 1781, within a few months such lamentation has given way to joy in the mutual exclusivity of their love. In early October he writes and sends to her this well-known poem, first published under the title 'An Lida' in 1789, long after his return from Italy:

> Den einzigen Lotte welchen du lieben kannst
> Foderst du ganz für dich und mit Recht.
> Auch ist er einzig dein. Denn seit ich von dir binn
> Scheint mir des schnellsten Lebens lärmende Bewegung
> Nur ein leichter Flor durch den ich deine Gestalt
> Immerfort wie in Wolcken erblicke,
> Sie leuchtet mir freundlich und treu
> Wie durch des Nordlichts bewegliche Strahlen
> Ewige Sterne schimmern.   (P728)

Goethe changed the name 'Lotte' in the first line to accord with the new title he gave the poem for publication; his intent, as usual, was to hide his real meaning from outsiders.

Although coded messages for Frau von Stein in works he wrote were nothing new by 1781, his awareness of the danger they represented had been heightened by a visit to the theatre at the end of September to see a play by Gotter (*Das öffentliche Geheimnis*).[58] However, despite all such heightened awareness, he continued to write as

---

58 Cf. P726 (1 October 1781). The plot of the play was very similar to Goethe's own real-life situation: Laura, lady-in-waiting to the princess, is engaged to Allessandro

before, for he greatly enjoyed playing with fire by means of his literary productions, in which he placed private messages for Charlotte von Stein and himself, knowing that these would remain hidden to others who read the works themselves or heard them read aloud. This had been true of *Die Geschwister* in 1776, true of a play (*Rino*) that Frau von Stein herself had written that same year, and it was equally true of other works besides, as I mean to show more fully later. A particularly good example of the high degree of conscious esotericism in Goethe's writing is the poem 'Der Becher,' sent to Charlotte in September 1781, when he was away from Weimar on official business. In a letter to her at that time he refers as follows to certain poems he has written, poems as yet unknown to her but due to appear shortly in the *Tiefurter Journal*: '... ich [ergötzte mich sinnend] an einigen Gedichten die ich in das Tiefurter Journal schicke von da aus sie erst meiner Besten die Cour machen sollen' (P725). The poems in question were 'An die Zikade' and 'Der Becher.' The latter did indeed appear in the *Tiefurter Journal* shortly afterwards, but under the deliberately misleading title 'Aus dem Griechischen.' Here is how it begins:

> Einen wohlgeschnitzten vollen Becher
> Hielt ich drückend in den beiden Händen,
> Sog begierig süßen Wein vom Rande,
> Gram und Sorg auf einmal zu vertrinken.
> Amor trat herein und fand mich sitzen,
> Und er lächelte bescheiden-weise,
> Als den Unverständigen bedauernd.
> 'Freund, ich kenn ein schöneres Gefäße,
> Wert, die ganze Seele drein zu senken;
> Was gelobst du, wenn ich dir es gönne,
> Es mit anderm Nektar dir erfülle?'
> O wie freundlich hat er Wort gehalten!
> Da er, Lida, dich mit sanfter Neigung
> Mir, dem lange Sehnenden, geeignet.
> Wenn ich deinen lieben Leib umfasse

---

but loves Federigo and is in turn loved by him. Unable because of their situation and circumstances to meet as they would like, the two lovers write to each other in a code language inaccessible to others, and in this way find expression for their love.

> Und von deinen einzig treuen Lippen
> Langbewahrter Liebe Balsam koste ...[59]

The poem concludes with a lengthy smokescreen of classical allusions to justify its published title, but the sensual message is clear enough.[60] Again the stimulus for writing is highly personal, the message also, but Goethe's literary talent has enabled him to conceal the esoteric meaning, which is exactly what he intended.

His joy at having at last convinced Frau von Stein of his love for her seems to have been complete by October 1781 (P728). From then on he was concerned to have the good opinion of other people – for her sake, not his own: 'Meine Seele ist an dich fest gebunden, deine Liebe ist das schönste Licht aller meiner Tage, dein Beyfall ist mein bester Ruhm, und wenn ich einen guten Nahmen von aussen recht schäze, so ists um deinetwillen daß ich dir keine Schande mache' (P733). In November he moved to the Frauenplan to be closer to her, and the prospect of his elevation to the ranks of the nobility was discussed officially for the first time.[61] Despite recurring ups and downs, everything seems to have been developing well between them now for nearly six months by this stage: they have a settled, even domesticated, routine in which each inquires almost daily about how the other has slept, they exchange food dishes, fruit, send items of clothing, and repeatedly arrange to be together, alone or in the company of other people. Characteristic of Goethe's constant attentiveness in the second half of 1781 are the following five notes written to his beloved in the course of twenty-four hours, during which he saw her several times:

> In der Hoffnung bald aufgeweckt zu werden legt ich mich nieder, und dancke nun für Ihr frühes Andencken. Ein Hemd kommt mit. Es ist

---

59 BA 1:346. (The poem is not in the HA.). BA is used to denote the 23-vol. edition of Goethe's works entitled *Goethe: Berliner Ausgabe*, 1972–8.
60 K.R. Eissler's Freudian conclusions about the meaning of this poem seem to me unnecessarily speculative. From the way in which Goethe used the term 'Balsam' in his letters to Frau von Stein, the poem might well refer simply to kissing. For Eissler's interpretation see *Goethe: A Psychoanalytic Study 1775–86*, 1963, 1:415ff.
Lena Voss (75ff.) offers a reading that reflects a more exalted view of Charlotte.
61 See P743 (18 November 1781). Düntzer attributes Goethe's move to the Frauenplan house to the urgings of Frau von Stein; see *CvSt* 1:161f.

Conseil und wenn ich nicht mit dem H[erzog] bleibe so folg ich Ihrer Einladung. (P712)

Danck für alles gute und liebe. Hier Trauben und Pfirschen. Vielleicht komm ich in die Zeichenschule. Adieu beste. Ich bin heut musikalisch und esse mit der S[chrötern], bin und bleibe doch aber ganz dein. (P713)

Wenn mich's zu hause lässt, so schick ich und lasse holen was mir das liebe anbietet. (P714)

Die Pfirschen sollen dich begrüsen, und ihr guter Geschmack erinnern daß ich dich liebe. Leb wohl meine beste. Und erhalte mir mein kostbaarstes. (P715)

Zahn wird heut Abend mit der Harfe kommen, die Schr[öter] auch. Willst du die Lieder hören so komm und bringe mit wen du willst. Etwa auch deine Mutter. Ich lasse beyde Häsgen und das Feldhuhn braten daß wir alle satt haben. (P716)

By December 1781 Goethe had become so secure in Frau von Stein's love that he was capable of a new attitude to her husband: 'Es wird mir recht natürlich Steinen gefällig zu seyn und ihm leben zu helfen. Ich bin es dir schuldig, und was bin ich dir nicht ieden Tag und den deinigen schuldig. Was hilft alle das kreuzigen und seegnen der Liebe wenn sie nicht thätig wird ...' (P762).

For her part, however, Frau von Stein remained ruled by her head in matters both large and small. Unable to forget the fear of censure should the truth of their relationship become known, for example, she refused to abandon the written use of the formal 'Sie,' despite the fact that she was well aware that Goethe found this wounding. In a letter of 12 December from Wilhelmsthal his sense of hurt erupted once more with great force:

Um Gotteswillen kein *Sie* mehr! – Wie hofft ich auf deinen Brief ich macht ihn zuletzt auf, und die *Ihnen*! er mag nun erst liegen ich muss *dich* erst aus diesen *Ihnen* wieder übersetzen. Zur Strafe schreib ich dir nichts von mir und meiner Liebe du sollst nur hören wie es andern geht und mir mit andern.

> Indess die andre Seite trocknete hab ich deinen Brief durchkorrigirt, und alle *Ihnen* weggestrichen. Nun wird es erst ein Brief. Verzeih dass ich die Kleinigkeit zu Etwas mache! ...   (P763)

The last sentence of this passage is particularly important for the insight it gives into the constellation of power within the relationship, for Charlotte von Stein knew very well by this time that her mode of address in letters to Goethe was of great consequence to him and so his apology seems out of place in its exaggerated modesty. The fact is that his love for her made him wish to please her at all times, rendering him vulnerable to her every whim, and she seems to have exploited this vulnerability right up to 1786 in an astonishing variety of ways, which ensured that she always retained the reins of power. Whether or not she had a deep-seated emotional need to do so – and sufficient indications exist to suggest that this was the case – she wielded control over Goethe in every aspect of his life in Weimar, including a great deal of his writing. It was a control to which he willingly subjected himself, however, because of his love for her.

With work continuing on *Iphigenie, Torquato Tasso, Elpenor,* and *Wilhelm Meisters theatralische Sendung*,[62] 1781 was a year of increased literary productivity, and Goethe's letters to Charlotte during this largely happy period reflect her ever-growing importance for his literary efforts. He writes, for example, on 25 March:

> An Tasso wird heute schwerlich gedacht werden. Mercken Sie aber nicht wie die Liebe für Ihren Dichter sorgt. Vor Monaten war mir die nächste Scene[63] unmöglich wie leicht wird mir sie ietzt aus dem Herzen fliesen ...   (P609)

And on 19 April:

> Da Sie sich alles zu eignen wollen was Tasso sagt, so hab ich heut schon soviel an Sie geschrieben daß ich nicht weiter und nicht drüber kann.   (P637)

---

62 *Iphigenie* (P550, P634); *Tasso* (P609, P635, P637–40, P646, P648, P653); *Elpenor* (P707). As Gräf points out (1,2:710f.), he was constantly working on the *Sendung* at this time also.
63 The scene referred to is thought to be Tasso's monologue, Act 2, Sc. 2; see Gräf 2,4:no.4132, note 3.

The following day he writes:

> Ich habe gleich am Tasso schreibend dich angebetet. Meine ganze Seele ist bey dir ... (P638)

And on 22 April:

> ... ich summirte in der stillen Nacht meine Glückseeligkeit und fand eine ungeheure Summe. Ich werde wohl am Tasso schreiben können ... (P639)

Most significant, however, is his note of 23 April, since it points to a clear division between the artist and the man:

> Diesen Morgen ward mirs sowohl daß mich ein Regen zum Tasso weckte. Als Anrufung an dich ist gewiss gut was ich geschrieben habe. Obs als Scene und an dem Orte gut ist weis ich nicht ... (P640)

A similar division becomes evident in many of his later writings and revisions, but it does not always reflect the happiness and sense of emotional well-being expressed here.

By the beginning of 1782 Goethe's letters to his beloved have taken on the air of those of an ardent, loving husband, albeit one who has not been married for very long. He writes more often than ever before;[64] his dependence on her and his desire to please are constant, his anxiety that she might cease to love him, recurrent. These letters are often serene, calm, and happy, but at times they also reveal anguish, fear, defensiveness, and vulnerability. On 9 April he writes from Kaltennordheim, for example: 'Über dein leztes Blat sind mir viel traurige Gedancken aufgestiegen, ich habe in einer Nacht recht bitterlich geweint da ich mir vorstellte daß ich dich verlieren könnte. Gegen alles was mir wahrscheinlich begegnen kann, hab ich ein Gleichgewicht in mir selbst, gegen *das einzige* nicht ...' (P856). The following day he writes from Ostheim: 'Ich schäme mich dir zu wiederhohlen, wie und wie immer ich an dich dencke. Du bist mir in alle Gegenstände transsubstanziirt ... ich bin weder abwesend noch zerstreut und doch immer

---

[64] The yearly breakdown of the notes and letters is as follows: 117 (1776), 91 (1777), 85 (1778), 168 (1779), 171 (1780), 240 (1781), 269 (1782), 152, (1783), 141 (1784), 161 (1785), 100 (January to September 1786).

bey dir und immer mit dir beschäfftigt ...' (P856). On 2 May he characterizes himself as 'deines ganzen Wesens eifriger Liebhaber ... und zugleich dein treuer Freund wie du ihn wünschen magst' (P865), and ten days later: 'Es ist gewiss meine Liebste, meine Sinne gehören dir so zu eigen, daß nichts bey mir ein kann ohne dir Zoll und Akzise zu bezahlen ... Wer dich gefunden hat weis warum er in der Welt ist' (P871).

Around 20 May 1782 Fritz von Stein went to live with Goethe, who was to be his new tutor; on 11 June the latter was raised to the nobility and took up the post of *Kammerpräsident*; on the 16th Charlotte von Stein took possession of the garden apartment he had so lovingly prepared for her: this was a settled and happy interval in the relationship. Yet only a month later the old situation arose again: Frau von Stein was angered by Goethe's behaviour (the specific reason for this is unclear), which provoked a series of tormented notes from him every day for almost a week. These begin on 19 July 1782 and they are sufficiently important for our understanding of the nature of the relationship to be given here at some length: 'Sage mir L. Lotte wie bist du aufgestanden? Sag mir ist es phisisch oder hast du etwas in der Seele was dich kränckt? Du glaubst nicht was mich dein Zustand gestern geängstigt hat. Das einzige Intresse meines Lebens ist daß du offen gegen mich seyn magst. Das Eingeschlossne halt ich nicht aus. Lebe wohl. Der deine' (P918). The following day he writes: 'Du hast mein Herz in Verwahrung und also brauchst du weiter nichts. Die Zeit wird ia wohl auch wieder kommen wo has deinige sich öffnet' (P919).

Evidently she sends him a cold or critical reply to this, for on the 22nd he responds with the first small signs of self-assertion: 'Ich will nicht überlastig seyn, aber nur so viel sagen daß ichs nicht verdient habe. Daß ichs fühle. Und schweige' (P920). A second note from him the same day lays claim to fair treatment from her for the first time: 'Ich schicke das Büchelgen nur zum Vorwande, denn du mußt mir noch ein Wort sagen, sonst hab ich keine Ruhe. Ich bin dir viel schuldig das weis ich wohl, aber du bist mir's auch. Laß mich nicht so' (P921). To this she obviously replies, for the next day (23rd) he writes: 'So war es denn Gott sey Danck ein Mißverständniß das dich dein Billett schreiben lies. Ich bin noch betäubt davon. Es war wie der Todt man hat ein Wort und keinen Begriff für so etwas ... Lebe wohl. Öffne mir dein Herz wieder. l. L.' (P922). Despite her somewhat more soothing reply on the 24th it is clear that the hurt she has inflicted on him remains profound. He responds the same day:

> Während daß ich schlief kam die Erquickung von dir, wie ich aufwache erhalte ich sie. Noch weis ich nicht wie mir ist, o daß der Zustand bald vorüber gehn möge. Es ist noch so heis, in einigen Stunden will ich kommen, will abwarten wo es hinaus will, mein ganzes Wesen ist in seinem innersten angegriffen. So tief deine Liebe drang und mir wohl machte so tief hat der Schmerz die Weege gefunden und zieht mich in mir selbst zusammen. Ich kan nicht weinen, und weis nicht wohin. Adieu verzeih mir. Dein Schmerz ist's der mich ängstigt. Wenn dir's nicht wieder mit mir wohl werden kann so geb ich auf eine freudige Stunde zu haben. (P924)

Later that day he writes again: 'Es wird hoff ich werden, noch sitze ich da und sehe vor mich hin, es ist mir so wie eine Leerheit in meinem ganzen Wesen. Tausen Danck für deine Liebe. Ich kann nichts zusammenbringen. Aengstige dich nicht du kannst alles. O Geliebte. Ich will kommen so bald ich nur kann' (P925). Only after she has replied again does he begin to recover his emotional equilibrium, but still traces of the profound hurt he has felt remain on the 25th: 'Ich habe lange geschlaften und gut, dein frühes Zettelgen empfängt mich und ist der erste Grus des neuen Tags. Mir ist um vieles besser, noch wie ein vom Blitz gestreifter fühl ich eine kleine Lähmung, die wird aber bald verschwinden wenn die einzige Arzeney angewendet wird. Wenn ich noch daran zurück dencke so graust michs wieder, und ich kann nicht eher ruhig werden, als biß ich für die Zukunft sicher bin' (P926).

Although everything seems to be restored to a happy footing by 27 July (P929), almost immediately he is hurt again, this time by her doubts of him (P933), and only on 5 August is his zest for life evident once more: 'Wie die Zeit vergeht, seitdem ich deiner Liebe gewiss bin ists wie gar keine Zeit' (P938). His delight in loving is paramount by the 23rd ('Was ich dir auch schreibe, will die Feder immer nur sagen: ich liebe! ich liebe!' (P956), and in the third note of the day on the 25th, after her departure for Kochberg with her children, the tone is again more fervent: 'So hab ich noch nie an dich geschrieben, so noch nie deine Entfernung gefühlt. Ich sehe dich unter den deinigen, bin in euch transsubstanziirt. *Liebe Lotte!* hab ich wieder zwanzigmal des Tages mit leisen Lippen ausgesprochen ...' (P957).

It has been necessary to present most of these notes in their entirety because of their characteristic quality of tone and because of the characteristic situation they reflect: suddenly in the middle of a settled and contented phase Goethe does something to arouse Charlotte von Stein's anger; he pleads with her to tell him what is wrong, she refuses to do so or responds in a coldly critical or self-justifying tone; the pain she causes him by her words, and by the attitude to him which they reveal, is enormous, lasting well beyond the time when she reassures him again by letter of her love. Repeatedly there is an element of punishment and retribution in Frau von Stein's behaviour whenever Goethe displeases her in some way, and it is this that is most wounding for him.[65] Nor does he forget such wounds, even though his joy in loving her returns. It seems likely that the row that broke out between the two was the result of Frau von Stein's suddenly hostile reaction towards Goethe one evening, followed up by a torrent of bitter reproaches about his whole conduct in their relationship, including the sphere of physical intimacy. Note the last part of his last letter during the period of anguish in July: '... noch wie ein vom Blitz gestreifter fühl ich ein kleine Lähmung, die wird aber bald verschwinden wenn die einzige Arzeney angewendet wird. Wenn ich noch daran zurück dencke so graust mich wieder, und ich kann nicht eher ruhig werden, als biß ich für die Zukunft sicher bin' (P926). The only real cure for his ongoing wretchedness is what he terms 'die einzige Arzeney': this evidently does not mean mere reassurance in words of her love for him, for we can tell from his letters of the previous few days that she has already written at least twice to tell him that she loves him, and so 'the only medicine' must refer to a rather more intimate reassurance – which would fully explain the sentence that follows: her rejection [of his attempted embrace?] has wounded him profoundly and has made him uncertain, so what he needs now is for her to apply the 'only medicine' that can cure his present wretched condition, help him overcome his horror at what has happened, and help him know

---

[65] His awareness of her habit of conscious punishment is shown in a letter he writes from Italy (20 December 1786): 'Noch ist kein Brief von dir angekommen, und es wird mir immer wahrscheinlicher daß du vorsäzlich schweigst' (P1620). See also P1652 (1 June 1789), cited on p. 69: 'Wo sollte da Vertrauen und Offenheit gedeihen, wenn du mich mit vorsätzlicher Laune von dir stießest ...'

where he stands for the future. The 'medicine' he appeals for here was in all likelihood the restoration of a certain intimacy that would reassure him of her love – her kisses, perhaps, by which his wound would be healed. It is an appeal reminiscent of that unhappy time in 1776 after her return from Kochberg with Lenz, when Goethe wrote to beg her for 'das Mittel gegen die wunde Lippe' (P106). Although the possibility I have raised cannot be proved beyond doubt and involves speculation one would obviously prefer not to bother with at all, I think the incident ought not to be overlooked, as Charlotte von Stein's behaviour during the years 1776–86 suggests that my reading of events here is more a well-founded likelihood than an outrageous and unjustified assault on her high moral sense. She was not always the calm, soothing, and sisterly confidante who assuaged the torment of Orest's soul, and we would do well to bear this in mind, for it appears to be reflected in the changes made to *Werther*. Despite the fact that I disagree with many of K.R. Eissler's exaggeratedly Freudian assertions about Goethe, I find that I must agree with what he concludes about Frau von Stein's repeated need for assurance from the poet of his responsiveness to her sexual attractiveness: 'It is probable that a woman of Charlotte von Stein's type, ... tested from time to time whether Goethe still harbored passionate feelings for her ... I assume she wanted chastity combined with periodic assurance that her feminine charms still kept the fire burning.'[66]

November 1782 was a time of stocktaking for Goethe. Reviewing the previous seven years since his first arrival in Weimar, he reasserted his increasing desire to please his beloved in everything, but he also felt that he had by no means achieved any real sense of clarity regarding his own person or his function in life. Looking over the letters he had received since 1772 (his first Werther-period), he wrote to Frau von Stein:

> Ich strich um mein verlassen Häusgen, wie Melusine um das ihre wohin sie nicht zurückkehren sollte, und dachte an die Vergangenheit von der ich nichts verstehe, und an die Zukunft von der ich nichts weis ... Seit einigen Tagen seh ich die Briefe durch die an mich seit zehen Jahren

---

66 Eissler 2:963

geschrieben worden, und begreife immer weniger was ich bin und was ich soll. Bleibe mir l. Lotte du bist mein Ancker zwischen diesen Klippen ... ' (P1008)

The following month his old longing to get away from Weimar but the impossibility of doing so because of his love for her came to the fore once again: 'Mich hält nur deine Liebe,' he wrote on 8 December, 'Fast mögt ich wünschen einmal durch fremde Lufft durchzugehen, und kann mich *doch* nicht von dir getrennt dencken' (P1029), and on the 24th: 'O liebe Lotte wenn ich dich nicht hätte ich ginge in die weite Welt ... Ich lebe nur in dir, die übrige Welt will nicht an mir hafften' (P1042). Even at this time, seven years after his first arrival in Weimar, he was a man torn inwardly between general displeasure at his life as an official of the court and passionate delight in his love for Charlotte von Stein, which he now knew for sure to be fully reciprocated.

Throughout 1782 Goethe's literary energies were devoted chiefly to *Wilhelm Meisters theatralische Sendung*.[67] Frau von Stein was by now important not only as his inspiration for writing or as a listener whom he wished above all to please, but as an active collaborator in his work process as well – which had considerable drawbacks, of course, if their relationship was troubled, as it was in July. Although Goethe had been working eagerly on his novel throughout the month of June, progress was halted for almost four weeks while he recovered from the serious upset of his row with Charlotte, to whom he had sent all that he had written of the novel so far on 2 July with these words: 'Hier l. Lotte überliefre ich dir meine ganzen Capitale, ich kann mich nun nirgends mehr vor dir verschliesen. Und übergebe mich dir aber und abermal zum Eigenthum ...' (P902). Only with the restoration of harmony by early August is there evidence of eager collaboration once again: 'Gegen deinen Kuchen kann ich dir nur Commisbrod schicken, aber Liebe gegen Liebe,' he writes on 9 August, 'Vielleicht schreiben wir diesen Nachmittag ein wenig' (P941); and the next day: 'Heute früh habe ich das Capitel im Wilhelm geendigt wovon ich dir den Anfang

---

67 Cf. (March to December 1782): P843, P874, P877, P895–8, P900–2, P941, P943, P956, P960, P980–2, P992, P995, P997, P998, P1000, P1002–4, P1022, P1043. In the letters there are also references to writing *Egmont* in March (P838, P839, P841, P843, P844), and to rehearsals or performances of *Die Fischerin* from June to September (P895, P901–3, P915, P916, P922, P970).

dicktirte. Es machte mir eine gute Stunde. Eigentlich bin ich zum Schriftsteller gebohren. Es gewährt mir eine reinere Freude als iemals wenn ich etwas nach meinen Gedanken gut geschrieben habe. Lebe wohl. Erhalte mir die Seele meines Lebens, Treibens, und Schreibens' (P943).

Work on the novel continued until the end of the year. In his letters to Charlotte there are many references to the progress he is making, references also to their writing together, and to her as the focus of his thoughts as he writes alone. Her pleasure and approval ensure his ongoing productivity, as he tells her again on 12 November: 'Nachdem ich heute früh das dritte Buch meines W[ilhelm] glücklich beschlossen grüse ich dich meine Liebe, mit der Versicherung daß meine größte Freude dabey ist, es dir vorzulesen und deinen Beyfall zu haben ...' (P1004).

The long-prevalent belief in Goethe's swiftly growing sense of inner calm and serenity as a result of Frau von Stein's influence from his first arrival in Weimar is evidently not borne out by his own intimate record of the period up to the end of 1782, and the years that followed were not markedly different, despite certain periods of happiness and contentment. Although his letters are full of expressions of his extreme need for and dependence on Charlotte, 1783 was a settled and harmonious time, apart from periods of yearning when Goethe was separated from her either because of his official duties or because of her visits to her estate in Kochberg, as, for example, in May, June, and September.[68] But again it is clear that there were ongoing difficulties in the relationship, for on 20 June Frau von Stein wrote of Goethe to her sister-in-law, Sophie von Schardt: '... mündlich ist nicht mit ihm zu sprechen, ohne daß wir uns beide weh thun ...'[69] However, by November 1783, the eighth anniversary of his arrival in Weimar, he seems to have achieved a new serenity: 'Meinem Lottgen muß ich zur Neuen Epoche guten Morgen sagen. Noch nie hab ich sie so angefangen. Möge es uns täglich wohler und ich dir täglich lieber werden, und wir recht lange so bleiben' (P1163). Yet life in Weimar remained very difficult for Goethe on all fronts apart from his love.[70] The only mi-

---

68 Cf. P1105, P1112–14, P1145, P1146, P1148, P1149.
69 Petersen 1,2:536
70 Cf. P1173 (23 November 1783): 'Sey wegen meiner unbesorgt denn alles was mir widerfährt freut mich, weil es mir um deinetwillen geschieht. Denn auch das

nor gathering cloud on this particular horizon is reflected in his increasing requests for more frequent signs from her that he is always in her thoughts.[71]

Work continued in 1783 on *Iphigenie* and the *theatralische Sendung*, and he took up *Elpenor* also.[72] Once again her encouragement was most important. As he wrote on 9 November: 'Deine freundliche Zusprache gestern Abend hat mich bewogen heute früh am Wilh[elm] zu schreiben und ich hoffe heute das vierte Buch zu endigen und gleich das fünfte anzufangen ...' (P1164). His hopes were realized three days later in the successful completion of Book Four (P1165).

Despite Frau von Stein's continuing anxiety about the discovery of their secret relationship,[73] January to May 1784 was a fairly settled period. As the prospect of his departure in June on a lengthy official journey draws closer, however, his letters display the old longing and torment, without evidence of any answering echo from Charlotte.[74] Goethe and she spent a great deal of time apart from June to October of this year, first one, then the other being away from Weimar for various reasons. What he writes to her from Eisenach in early June reflects his old discontent with the behaviour of the gentry, and disappointment at the seeming lack of fervour in her letters to him:

> Hier habe ich's gefunden wie es zu erwarten war. Die Hofleute klagen über Langeweile, über stehen, gehen, fahren, Staub, Hitze, Berge u.s.w.

---

entfernste duld ich weil du bist, und wenn du nicht wärst hätt ich alles lange abgeschüttelt. Du aber machst mir alles süse ...' See also Caroline Herder to J.G. Müller, 14 December 1783: 'Goethe leidet noch mehr als mein Mann' (Biedermann/Herwig 1:343); Wieland to Merck, 5 January 1784 (*Vertrauliche Briefe* 1:299).

71 He has been making such requests for a long time, as she is often less attentive than he would like, but they increase in frequency by December 1783; cf. P1182-4, P1186, P1188, P1191, P1193, P1195.

72 Cf. (*Iphigenie*) P1057, P1142; (*Sendung*) P1115, P1164, P1165; (*Elpenor*) P1067-9.

73 She was afraid that someone might discover her initials engraved inside the ring she had given Goethe and so she asked for it back. (See P1220, mid-February 1784; Düntzer, *CvSt* 1:208.) She gave him another ring to wear when he was away, but he greatly regretted the loss of the original, to which he seems to have attached almost the symbolic value of a wedding ring. Cf. P1223, 21 February; P1267, 5 June; P1268, 8 June; P1274, 20 June.

74 In referring to early May 1784, Düntzer says: 'Goethes steigende Leidenschaftlichkeit beunruhigte sie [CvSt] gewaltig, und doch konnte sie sich nicht zurückziehen, weil sie ihn dadurch noch mehr aufzuregen fürchten mußte.' See *CvSt* 1:213.

> Loben die Gegend auserordentl. und haben keinen Genuß davon ...
> Deine lieben Briefe sind angekommen, und ach ich bin deiner Gegenwart so gewohnt daß sie mir kalt vorkamen, daß ich erst wieder mich gewöhnen musste deiner Handschrifft eben den Sinn zu geben den die Worte von deinen Lippen haben. Schreibe mir ia recht fleisig und viel ... (P1268)

At this time we also see again his extreme yearning and need for her:

> Die Stunden die dein gehören bring ich alleine zu; so freundlich mir die Menschen sind kann ich doch nichts mit ihnen verkehren. Ich binn nun eingewöhnt und verwöhnt dir anzugehören und bin auf diesen Punckt abgeschnitten, das heist nach Lavaters Terminologie so gut wie wahnsinnig ... (P1269)

In general this is a period of intensified passion for Goethe in which he laments his own lack of inner calm (P1271). In a letter from Eisenach on 23 June he says that if he could only write one tribute to her, he would hew the following coded secret into the face of a rock:

> Was ich leugnend gestehe und offenbarend verberge
> Ist mir das einzige Wohl, bleibt mir ein reichlicher Schatz
> Ich vertrau es dem Felsen damit der Einsame rathe
> Was in der Einsamkeit mich was in der Welt mich beglückt. (P1275)

Hope, joy, fear, despair, and the unwelcome awareness of the need for concealment are all reflected in this long letter, but the dominant characteristic is an overwhelming sense of restlessness caused by his separation from her, and this increases as time goes on,[75] only to be met with doubt and jealousy on her part in early July (P1278), and with letters in French to which he replies in some considerable anguish on 18 August:

> Voiant ces caracteres barbares etrangers a mon coeur ce fut un tout nouveau sentiment pour moi, ces *Vous* me faisoit trembler et je tournai vite la feuille pour Voir s'il n'y avoit pas un mot de la langue cherie qui

---

75 Cf. P1277 (28 June): 'Nun wird es bald Zeit liebe Lotte daß ich wieder in deine Nähe komme denn mein Wesen hält nicht mehr zusammen, ich fühle recht deutlich daß ich nicht ohne dich bestehen kann ... Ich bin kein einzelnes kein selbstständiges Wesen ...'

m'est devenue tous les jours plus chere par les expressions du veritable sentiment dont tu l'enrichis ... (P1287) [No accents in the original text]

Whether or not her aim may have been to help him practise the language of the court of Braunschweig, where he was staying at the time, it is clear that she used French in the hope of moderating the tone of his letters.[76] Her ploy has about it the flavour of a reprise – in this case, of her controlling use of 'Sie' for such a long time in years gone by. Far from moderating his passion, however, the use of a foreign language seems to have had just the opposite effect, for his expression of yearning, need, and total dependence is merely intensified, as, for example, in this letter of 30 August which is distinctly reminiscent of the Werther of ten years before:

... mon amour pour toi n'est plus une passion c'est une maladie, une maladie qui m'est plus chere que la sante la plus parfaite, et dont je ne veux pas guerir ... Je n'ai d'autre souhait que de te plaire, de te rendre heureuse autant qu'il est en mon pouvoir, d'etre tous les jours plus digne de ta tendresse ... (P1290)

Just a few days earlier Goethe had sent Frau von Stein the following poem, once again expressing his awareness of his need to leave, to get away, but the impossibility of doing so because of his love for her:

Gewiss ich waere schon so ferne ferne
Soweit die Welt nur offen liegt gegangen
Bezwaengen mich nicht uebermaecht'ge Sterne
Die mein Geschik an deines angehangen
Dass ich in dir nun erst mich kennen lerne
Mein Dichten, Trachten, Hoffen und Verlangen
Allein nach dir und deinem Wesen draengt
Mein Leben nur an deinem Leben haengt. (P1288)

This is by now a very familiar expression of conflict, is it not? Goethe sent the verse to Charlotte with the following commentary, which emphasizes his total emotional dependence on her: 'Ah mon unique amie, chere confidente de tous mes sentiments que je me sens un besoin de te parler et de te communiquer mes reflexions. Tu m'as isolé

---

76 Düntzer offers the more indulgent explanation (CvSt 1:221).

dans le monde – je n'ai absolument rien a dire a qui que ce soit, je parle pour ne pas me taire et c'est tout ... Je finis par un vers allemand qui sera placé dans le poeme que je cheris tant [*Die Geheimnisse*, on which he was working] parceque j'y pourrai parler de toi, de mon amour pour toi sous mille formes sans que personne ne l'entende que toi seule' (P1288). Note the deliberate subterfuge. He is particularly fond of *Die Geheimnisse*, he says, because in it he will be able to speak of her and of his love for her in a thousand different ways *without anyone apart from her being aware of what he is really saying*. A great many similar messages were tucked away in much of what Goethe wrote in Weimar, as were messages of quite a different kind.

By late September 1784 he was again feeling the tension of the constraints imposed on him by the need for secrecy,[77] but the yearning he felt for Charlotte's nearness continued until late October when she at last returned from Kochberg. From then until the end of the year his every waking movement appears to have been determined in accordance with her wishes and her plans.[78] Despite his undoubted joy in her love, the relationship evidently remained quite out of balance, even at this stage.

As far as his writing was concerned, the most intensive period of work in 1784 was in August, when he was busy with *Die Geheimnisse* ('le poeme que je cheris tant'); he also began to write *Scherz, List und Rache*, and his collaboration with Frau von Stein on the *theatralische Sendung* continued.[79] As before, her positive response to his writing was a spur to continued effort; on 16 September, for example, he sent her a brief letter in which he referred to *Die Geheimnisse* in these terms:

---

77 See P1295 (20 September 1784): 'Nous faisons si bien notre devoir ma chere Lotte qu'a la fin on pourroit douter de notre amour ... je trouve tes raisons asses valables qui t'empechent de venir, et cependent je suis mecontent de toi et de moi que nous sommes si raisonnables.' [Accents missing in the original.] He goes on to lament the strain of not being able to talk about her as he would wish, even with his close friends.
78 Just one example: on 5 December Goethe asked Frau von Stein whether or not he should agree to the Duke's request to meet him in Frankfurt and travel back with him to Weimar. The letter he wrote declining the request is dated the following day. See P1326 and notes, 2,2:659.
79 Cf. (*Die Geheimnisse*) P1285, P1286, P1290, P1292; (*Scherz, List und Rache*) P1286; (*Wilhelm Meister*) P1271, P1272, P1279, P1297, P1308.

'Daß dir mein Gedicht so lieb ist, wird mich anfeuern es fortzusetzen, wie mir es möglich ist ...' (P1292).

Although Goethe had long disliked many aspects of his social and working life in Weimar, his dislike reached a new high point in April/May 1785.[80] On the emotional front, however, the early months of 1785 were happy and contented; his letters to Frau von Stein show a loving attentiveness, also the same eagerness as before for them to be together constantly, and the same profound yearning for her if he is obliged to be away from Weimar. But there is also a new quality in evidence – a settled, almost routine, tone when they are not separated, despite his constantly recurring declarations of love. These Frau von Stein seems to have begun to take for granted, for Goethe writes in lamentation on 10 May: 'Du schreibst mir gar nicht mehr wenn ich dich nicht auffordre ... ' (P1413). By this stage their game-playing in matters both large and small, overt and covert, has been extended for quite some time to include playing at marriage and joint parenthood,[81] but great clouds are looming now. By the middle of the year Goethe is suffering from severe nervous strain, which manifests itself as extreme irritability. The old volatility has not been eradicated even yet, it seems.[82]

From July to August 1785 he spent several pleasant weeks in Karlsbad with Charlotte von Stein and Knebel, returning to Weimar on the 21st, but by the time of his return an irrevocable change had taken place that was to alter the course of his love relationship: Duke Karl August had discontinued the custom of having the household officials dine at court.[83] From then on Josias von Stein was to dine at home,

80 Cf. CvSt to Knebel 20 April 1785 (*Vertrauliche Briefe* 1:313f.). Her solution to Goethe's difficulties is a religious one: she believes he must adopt the attitude of Christ on the cross. See also Knebel to Herder, 7 May 1785: 'Sein [Goethe's] reifendes Gefühl für das, was menschlich ist, nimmt ihm nachgerade alle Freude seines politischen Zustandes' (Biedermann/Herwig 1:363).
81 Their 'first girl child' was a goddaughter (Charlotte Wilhelmine) born to Wieland and his wife in early 1776; see Wieland to Gleim, 22 March 1776 (ibid. 1:195). Their ongoing role as 'parents' was of course played out from early on through Frau von Stein's own young son, Fritz.
82 Cf. Knebel to his sister, 24 June 1785 (*Vertrauliche Briefe* 1:315).
83 Bode, *Charlotte von Stein* 263. See also Herder to Knebel, 28 August 1785, in Johann Gottfried Herder, *Briefe: Gesamtausgabe 1763–1803*, 1977–88, 5:135.

severely curtailing the freedom of intimacy that his wife and Goethe had so long enjoyed. Petersen sums up the sudden change in circumstances well: 'Die traulichen Stunden des Zusammenseins sind gestört. Die ungesunde Basis der Beziehungen wird jetzt erst fühlbar; eine neue Wertherstimmung stellt sich ein.'[84]

Frau von Stein was away in Kochberg for six weeks from the beginning of September, and nothing Goethe could write concerning his need for her, his sense of total isolation in the world, or his longing for her return, could make her shorten her stay or even induce her to write more often in response to his constant pleadings.[85] This was yet another very difficult time for him, but he tried to fill it by working on his 'Wilhelm,' as always in order to be able to offer her the pleasure of hearing him read it aloud and discussing it with him. November was a calmer month, but by early December Goethe was showing signs of frustration at the difficulty in finding time together, undisturbed by others: 'Hier dein Brief und der meinige, schicke mir beyde wieder zurück. Diesen Abend bin ich bey dir du beste, ich hoffe wir werden ungestörter seyn' (P1476). By 30 December the frustration was even greater: 'Wann werden wir wieder ruhige Abende und gesellige Tage zusammen leben?' (P1499). The answer to this question was to be 'never,' although Goethe was unaware of it at that point.

Throughout 1785 the link between his literary productivity and his emotional life is again highlighted in his letters to Charlotte. In early June, for example, when all is going well between them, he also seems to be fairly confident about making good progress on his new novel: 'An Wilhelm habe ich fortgefahren vielleicht thut er diesmal einen guten Ruck. Ich dencke immer dabey an die Freude die ich dir damit machen werde ...' (P1423). Two weeks later a poem that he has written for inclusion in his novel is sent to her as the expression of his sorrow and yearning in anticipation of her departure for Karlsbad ('Nur wer die Sehnsucht kennt, / Weiß was ich leide'). He sends her this poem on the day she leaves, with the brief observation: 'Hierbey ein Liedgen von Mignon aus dem sechsten Buche. Ein Lied das auch nun mein ist' (P1428). Progress on the novel was halted during July and August

---

84 Petersen 1,1:xxxiv. Goethe's 'Werther' mood is already referred to in a letter he wrote to the Duke on 17 August; see HA *Briefe* 1:481.
85 See P1440–9 (11 September to 10 October).

while Goethe was in Karlsbad, but resumed again during September and continued fairly steadily until almost the end of the year.[86] Given his penchant for writing himself into his works, and for using these as a means of transforming unpalatable realities into scenarios more to his own liking, it seems probable that he again took to writing at this point as a means of protecting himself from the pain of his new life without Lotte, now that his opportunities for spending time alone with her were greatly reduced. What more likely than that he should again have offset his current unhappiness by means of his writing, just as he had done by writing *Die Geschwister* when he was so unhappy ten years before? Then he had 'resolved' his own misery by providing a happy ending to the problems of Wilhelm and Marianne in the play; now he worked on the story of another Wilhelm and Mariane, the central characters of his new novel. We know that the original ending to *Wilhelm Meisters theatralische Sendung*, like that of *Die Geschwister*, was to be a happy marriage,[87] and up to the end of 1785 there was no mention by Goethe of any qualms or doubts about the completion of this tale. Such doubts would only arise for the first time about half a year later, when he was no longer hopeful that he and Charlotte might again be able to enjoy that sense of intimacy and togetherness they had known from 1776 to 1785.

What makes such a speculation about Goethe's work on *Wilhelm Meister* in late 1785 even more well-founded is the fact that in November he began to write a new operetta, *Die ungleichen Hausgenossen* and continued to work on it avidly for several months.[88] Never completed, this work is both a playful and not-so-playful assault on others as well as himself (in the guise of the poet Immersüß, companion of a baroness who is unhappily married to a man who loves horses and hunting in the manner of Josias von Stein); it too displays obvious links with Goethe's own situation at the time of writing; it too was meant to end up happily for all concerned after a period of considerable emotional turmoil. Significantly, however, the baron and baroness

---

86 Cf. P1437, P1439, P1440, P1443, P1448, P1449, P1463–5, P1480, P1484 (1 September to 12 December).
87 Recounted to Ludwig Tieck by Goethe's mother in 1806 (Gräf 1,2:730)
88 See (November 1785 to April 1786) P1463, P1484, P1485, P1520, P1521, P1550, P1553, P1557, P1567.

were to be restored to a state of marital harmony, rather than the baroness and the poet.[89]

In much the same way as the previous year had drawn to a close, 1786 opened with unfulfilled longings on Goethe's part for a restoration of lost freedom, intimacy, and sense of togetherness with his beloved. His notes to Charlotte reveal this quite clearly, for on the first day of the year he writes to her from only a very short distance away in Weimar: 'Guten Morgen Geliebte. Ich bleibe zu Hause und richte mich ein. Gebe uns der Himmel ein gutes Jahr. Ich liebe dich herzlich, *bleibe mir wenn auch iezt getrennter als sonst, das mir offt fast zu schweer wird*. Lebe wohl. ich bin dein' (P1501, emphasis mine). Two days later he is trying to find a way to see her on his own ground rather than on hers: 'Wie wäre es wenn m. liebe diesen Nachmittag gleich nach Tische zu mir käme? ... Auf den Abend lüd ich die Imhof und Herders. Wie sehr wünscht ich wieder einmal ein Paar Stunden mit dir zu seyn' (P1502). There is a rather disconsolate air about some of his notes to her around this time, such as the one written on 15 January: 'Ich freue mich deines Gruses, und schicke dir ein Frühstück. Wie gern wäre ich bey dir und thäte was ich zu thun habe in deiner Nähe ...' (P1511). One senses in what he writes the following day a growing tension and anguish, even though he has been at her house or in her company several times in the course of the previous two weeks: 'Hier schicke ich die Zeitungen und einen Brief des Prinzen. Gingst du wohl um zwölfe spazieren? Es ist zwar ein wenig Wind. Ich kann es kaum mehr ertragen so von dir getrennt zu seyn' (P1512).

---

[89] For an outline of the plot see BA 4:705ff. (cf. note 59). An aria Goethe wrote for the Baroness in Act 2 obviously reflects his own sense of loss and withdrawal at the time:

  Ach wer bringt die schönen Tage,
  Jene Tage der ersten Liebe,
  Ach – wer bringt nur eine Stunde
  Jener holden Zeit zurück.

  Leise tönet meine Klage,
  Ich verberge Wunsch und Triebe,
  Einsam nähr ich Schmerz und Wunde,
  Traure mein verlornes Glück.

Ibid. 351f. He reworked these lines slightly for publication as a poem under the title 'Erster Verlust' in 1789.

Werther, Goethe, and Charlotte von Stein 63

Throughout January to May we find Goethe at times on the defensive because of signs of neglect from Frau von Stein, at times happy, at others disappointed, while her role as the dominant partner seems more firmly in place than ever.[90] But things are changing now. No longer does he avail himself of every conceivable opportunity to spend time with her at her home, no doubt because of her husband's presence. It is almost as if he can enjoy a greater closeness to her while writing than while being with her under the unsatisfactory circumstances that have prevailed since the previous August. A note he sends her on 12 March reads: 'Daß ich dich nicht besuche wirst du nicht tadeln wenn ich dir sage daß mich ein guter Geist anweht und ich an Wilh[elm] schreibe ...' (P1548). And on the 21st: 'Ich bleibe nur zu Hause um dir Freude zu machen. Die Operette [*Die ungleichen Hausgenossen*] und Wilhelm rucken zusammen. Du musst mich recht lieb haben. Heute ess ich beym Herzog und nach Tafel besuche ich dich. Abends schreibe ich wieder und hoffe Donnerstags dir und Herders etwas zu lesen' (P1553). The importance of his writing is clear here, as in his letter of a week later, but in this we also see how uncertain of her he has become, how tentative about assuming that she loves him: 'Wie befindet sich meine beste. Es war mir gestern eine rechte Freude dich vergnügt bey mir zu sehn. *Es schien mir auch als wenn du mich recht lieb hättest.* Heute hab ich viel zu thun, gehe auch gegen Abend zur Herzoginn Mutter. Dann seh ich dich wenigstens einen Augenblick, ich möchte gern an meinen Werckgen schreiben' (P1557, emphasis mine). On the same day Charlotte von Stein wrote to Knebel, remarking with a certain amusing acidity on how busy Goethe was with his writing: 'Goethe ist wohl und vergnügt hier wieder angekommen [from Jena, where he had been staying with Knebel] und pinselt immerfort an seinen Prometheusschen Menschen, die er sich schafft und gut und bös seine Lieblinge sind.'[91]

There are also some traces of hurt here and there in Goethe's letters to Frau von Stein at this time, which seem to spring from what he perceives as her dwindling attentiveness.[92] His hopes for a period of renewed togetherness in Karlsbad in July are the ray of light in May

---

90 Cf. P1504, P1516, P1532, P1539, P1545, P1546, P1552, P1560, P1564, P1575.
91 *Vertrauliche Briefe* 1:319
92 See P1546, P1563, P1564 (10 March to 9 April 1786).

and June, but this is a time when he withdraws into silence, which clearly upsets Charlotte von Stein, who knows that taciturnity is never a good sign in him.[93] As Goethe himself was to declare with regard to the matter of silence some thirteen years later: 'Schweigen gebührt dem Menschen, der sich nicht vollendet fühlt. Schweigen geziemt auch dem Liebenden, der nicht hoffen darf, glücklich zu sein.'[94]

From the beginning of the year he had spent more time than usual on his writing, with work on *Die ungleichen Hausgenossen* proceeding at almost fever-pitch in January; on the 24th he wrote to Frau von Stein, for example: 'Wahrlich bin ich an der Operette kranck, denn ich habe schon heute früh daran schreiben müssen' (P1520). He continued to work on it through March and April, while from March to May he was again busy with the *Sendung* and again evidently eager to please her with what he was writing.[95] In late May, however, we find him expressing doubts about his novel for the first time: 'An Wilhelm hab ich geschrieben und bey ieder Seite hoffe ich auf die Freude sie dir vorzulesen. Einige Sorge habe ich doch für dieses Buch' (P1578). It would appear that he had only now begun seriously to doubt the feasibility of the novel as originally planned.

During this period he was also reworking his existing material for a new edition of his collected works to be published by Göschen. 'Diese Dinge durchzugehen und wieder in mir zu erneuern,' he wrote to Charlotte from Ilmenau on 16 June, 'macht mich halb fröhlich halb traurig. Wenn ich nicht müsste ich thät es nicht' (P1585). A new acquiescence in whatever she thinks best, rather than the old outrage or lamentation at plans she may have that do not fit in with his wishes, is now clear, however; the resignation she has preached for so long and which he has never before been able to accept fully as the right response to difficulties is reflected in his letter of 25 June after she

---

93 Cf. CvSt to Sophie von Schardt, 7 October 1784 (Petersen 12,2:539); to Charlotte von Lengefeld, 30 January 1786 (ibid. 542); to Knebel, 10 May 1786 (ibid.).
94 *Der Sammler und die Seinigen*, 6th letter, HA 12:87. For more on the subject of 'schweigen' in Goethe's life and works see Victor Lange, 'The Metaphor of Silence,' in *Goethe Revisited*, 1984.
95 See (*Die ungleichen Hausgenossen*) P1550, P1553, P1557, P1567; (*Wilhelm Meisters theatralische Sendung*) P1548, P1549, P1553, P1557, P1578–80, P1601.

refuses his request that she delay her departure for Karlsbad: 'Thue meine Liebe was und wie dir's recht ist und es soll mir auch so seyn. Behalte mich nur lieb und lass uns ein Gut, das wir nie wiederfinden werden, wenigstens bewahren, wenn auch Augenblicke sind wo wir dessen nicht geniessen können. Ich korrigire am Werther und finde immer daß der Verfasser übel gethan hat sich nicht nach geendigter Schrifft zu erschiesen ...' (P1587).

Shortly before she leaves for Karlsbad he sends her a poem from Valentin Andreas's *Chymische Hochzeit*, whose implicit message is the same as the motto on the seal he used on his letters to her from early 1776: 'Alles um Liebe.'[96] For him love is still paramount, it seems, however restrained his public behaviour may have become since the early days. However, obliged to remain in Weimar to await the birth of the ducal baby, he is unable to join Charlotte in Karlsbad as early as planned. He continues to prepare his writings for publication and has the unhappy experience of finding many of his old emotions rekindled. 'Ich bin von tausend Vorstellungen getrieben, beglückt und gepeinigt,' he writes to her on 9 July, 'Da ich meine alte Schrifften durchgehe, werden auch viel alte Übel rege. Es ist eine wunderbare Epoche für mich, in der du mir eben fehlst' (P1591).

During this time he secretly decided to go to Italy.[97] On 25 July he left Weimar for Karlsbad, having already made certain arrangements with Seidel for a lengthy period of absence, and on the 27th he arrived in Karlsbad to join Frau von Stein until 14 August. On the 13th he wrote to Seidel: 'Noch hat sich nichts zugetragen, das mich an Ausführung meines Plans hindern könnte. Gegen Ende des Monats werde ich die Reise antreten ...'[98] It is not altogether clear whether his plans were firm or tentative before he left Weimar, or whether his time in

---

96 For the text of the poem see P1588 (28 June); cf. notes, Petersen 2,2:681f. A commentary is offered by Joseph Strelka in *Esoterik bei Goethe*, 1980, 33–43.
97 Cf. references to a forthcoming journey in his letter to Jacobi, 12 July 1786 (WA 4,7:243); also to Karl August, 24 July 1786 (ibid. 253f.); to Knebel, 13 August 1786 (WA 4,8:1). Goethe's letter of 9 July cited above also reflects his negative attitude to administrative duties (P1591). A stronger indictment by him of the Weimar administration is to be found in the report of the *Wegebaudirektion* of the same date; see Goethe's 'Bericht vom 9.vi.1786 über die Tätigkeit der Wegebaudirektion in den Jahren 1784/85 (B9261),' in *Jahrbuch der Goethe-Gesellschaft* 6 (1919): 273–80.
98 WA 4,8:2

Karlsbad was to be a test to see if his relationship with Charlotte von Stein might be restored to its former footing.[99] In any case, nothing has happened, as he says, to prevent him from leaving. On 14 August he accompanied Frau von Stein as far as Schneeberg (on the way to Kochberg), where he remained for two days before returning to Karlsbad. By the 22nd his work on *Werther* ('mein schweerstes Pensum') was finished (P1597). The first intimation he gave her of his forthcoming journey was in a letter written the following day. Here he begins by discussing his work on *Iphigenie*, saying he hopes to finish it within the week; he then goes on: 'Und dann werde ich in der freyen Welt mit *dir* leben, und in glücklicher Einsamkeit, ohne Nahmen und Stand, der Erde näher kommen aus der wir genommen sind ...' (P1597). By 30 August his impatience to be away is growing (P1599). What he writes to her on 1 September is highly significant, however:

> Nun noch ein Lebewohl von Carlsbad aus, die Waldner soll dir dieses mitbringen; von allem was sie erzählen kann sag ich nichts; das wiederhohl ich dir aber daß ich dich herzlich liebe, daß unsre letzte Fahrt nach Schneeberg mich recht glücklich gemacht hast und daß deine Versicherung: daß dir wieder Freude zu meiner Liebe aufgeht, mir ganz allein Freude ins Leben bringen kann. Ich habe bisher im Stillen gar mancherley getragen, und nichts so sehnlich gewünscht als daß unser Verhältniß sich so herstellen möge, daß keine Gewalt ihm was anhaben könne. Sonst mag ich nicht in deiner Nähe wohnen und ich will lieber in der Einsamkeit der Welt bleiben, in die ich ietzt hinausgehe ... (P1600)

The last several lines of this passage tell their own story: (i) Charlotte has told him that she *once more* takes delight in his love – a comment that only makes sense in the wake of a period where he has known or sensed that this was not the case; (ii) he has suffered a great deal but has felt it necessary to keep his real feelings bottled up for some time past; (iii) he has a clear idea of how he wants their relationship to be and is not willing to make do with less. As he says, if it

---

[99] It seems unlikely that he might have feared the imposition of new duties that could delay his departure, as he had already secured the Duke's permission to take a lengthy break, albeit without disclosing his intended destination.

cannot be as he wants, then he would prefer to be far away from her on his own. Given that his frustration with life in Weimar goes back almost a decade by this time and that he has been able to cope with it all because of his love for her, at least until late 1785, there is no reason to believe that had their relationship remained as fulfilling for him as it had been from 1781 to 1785 he would have done anything at this point about his desire to leave. But now everything is out of joint and the old Werther-problematic exists again in even more agonizing form. The constant hurt and frustration he must endure in being relegated to second place behind her husband, whom he knows she does not love, means that staying in Weimar is impossible.

It seems quite likely that he may have conceived his journey to Italy initially as a therapeutic measure that would enable him to escape the emotional strain caused by being expected to make constant concessions to the primacy of the von Stein marriage, likely too that he hoped the escape would restore him to full health and strength and help the establishment of that kind of unassailable love relationship he wanted and Frau von Stein herself had so long advocated.[100] But the escape therapy can have had no immediate good effect on him as far as coming to terms with his pent-up anguish and frustration was concerned, for in a letter from Rome some five months later on 21 February 1787 his old feelings suddenly erupt again for the first time in years and with considerable force:

> An dir häng ich mit allen Fasern meines Wesens.[101] Es ist entsetzlich was mich oft Erinnerungen zerreisen. Ach liebe Lotte[102] du weist nicht welche Gewalt ich mir angethan habe und anthue und daß der Gedancke dich nicht zu besitzen mich doch im Grunde, ich mags nehmen und stellen und legen wie ich will aufreibt und aufzehrt. Ich

---

100 This is borne out by many of his letters from Italy, November 1786 to mid-June 1787. Cf. in particular P1611 (7 November), P1616 (2 December), P1621 (29 December), P1627 (17 January 1787), P1635 (18 April), P1636 (25 May), P1637 (8 June).
101 He had used almost exactly this same wording in a letter to Frau von Stein on 15 November 1785 (P1467), but it first occurred in Bk. 1, ch. 17 of *Wilhelm Meisters theatralische Sendung*, completed in January 1778; there we are told of Wilhelm's gradually increasing amorousness and Mariane's charmingly weak resistance (BA 9:303). The passage was omitted in the *Lehrjahre*.
102 Goethe had not used this form of address to Frau von Stein for almost two years by this point; see note 56.

> mag meiner Liebe zu dir Formen geben welche ich will, immer immer – verzeih mir daß ich dir wieder einmal sage was so lange stockt und verstummt. Wenn ich dir meine Gesinnungen meine Gedancken der Tage, der einsamsten Stunden sagen könnte ... Leb wohl. Ich bin heute konfus und fast schwach ... (P1634)

This was written only after he had received the first letter from Charlotte since his departure in which she again told him she loved him – words that *he* had not been able to bring himself to write from the beginning of September until the beginning of December.[103] It was not until several months later, in June 1787, that he at last gave vent to his sense of the accumulated tension of recent years: 'Wie das Leben der letzten Jahre wollt ich mir eher den Todt gewünscht haben und selbst in der Entfernung bin ich dir mehr als ich dir damals war' (P1637).

The relationship appears to have been doomed, however, from the point at which Goethe took over from Frau von Stein the active responsibility for his own well-being and began to dictate terms for their life together. Her behaviour in the wake of his departure and on his return to Weimar nearly two years later is proof of that, but I shall not deal with it here since it has no bearing on the rewritten *Werther*.[104] Let me cite just one final passage from the letter he wrote which sealed the break. Written in June 1789, a full year after his return to Weimar and during the last phase of his work on *Tasso*, the significance of which will be dealt with later, it shows how long Goethe was capable of waiting before expressing his resentments. The catalyst was a letter from Frau von Stein in which she objected to his affair with Christiane Vulpius.[105] His pent-up resentment is only now unleashed:

---

103 P1616 (2 December): 'Der Grund aller meiner Freude ist darinn daß ich dir es wieder sagen kann und werde.'
104 Apart from her cold and vengeful behaviour after Goethe's return, she wrote a play in 1794 (*Dido*) in which she attacked him for his faithlessness, self-indulgence, glibness, and falsity; cf. note 12, chapter 3.
105 She had left the letter for him in Weimar before departing for Ems on 5 May, having found out about his relationship with Christiane in March. As he writes in the letter quoted here (28 June), he has had to wait to reply because he did not want to hurt her even more. Obviously he was extremely angry on reading what she had to say.

Leider warst du, als ich ankam, in einer sonderbaren Stimmung und ich gestehe aufrichtig: daß die Art wie du mich empfingst, wie mich andre nahmen, für mich äusserst empfindlich war. Ich sah Herdern, die Herzoginn verreisen, einen mir dringend angebotnen Platz im Wagen leer, ich blieb um der Freunde willen, wie ich um ihrentwillen gekommen war und mußte mir in demselben Augenblick hartnäckig wiederhohlen laßen, ich hätte nur wegbleiben können, ich nehme doch keinen Theil an den Menschen. u.s.w. Und das alles eh von einem Verhältniß die Rede seyn konnte das dich so sehr zu kräncken scheint.

Und welch ein Verhältniß ist es? Wer wird dadurch verkürzt? Wer macht Anspruch an die Empfindungen die ich dem armen Geschöpf gönne? Wer an die Stunden die ich mit ihr zubringe?[106]

... Aber das gestehe ich gern, die Art wie du mich bißher behandelt hast, kann ich nicht erdulden. Wenn ich gesprächig war hast du mir die Lippen verschloßen, wenn ich mittheilend war hast du mich der Gleichgültigkeit, wenn ich für Freunde thätig war, der Kälte und Nachläßigkeit beschuldigt. Jede meiner Minen hast du kontrollirt, meine Bewegungen, meine Art zu seyn getadelt und mich immer *mal a mon aise* gesetzt. Wo sollte da Vertrauen und Offenheit gedeihen, wenn du mich mit vorsätzlicher Laune von dir stießest ... (P1652)

The recriminations in this letter have the ring of truth about them, for this was the way in which Charlotte von Stein had always tended to treat Goethe if ever he displeased her, as I have tried to show. The difference of course is that he is now wholly aware of it for the first time and no longer willing to tolerate her attempts at total control. His ideal woman has turned out to be less Frau Minne than Frau Welt in back view, if I may draw on an extreme metaphor from the Middle Ages, for it is she who has betrayed all the tenets of love that she initially nurtured in him, she who has responded to his acute need for escape with many acts of spitefulness and revenge.[107] On the back

---

106 These lines are generally taken by scholars as explicit proof that there had never been any physical intimacy between Goethe and Frau von Stein; the most recent example is to be found in Conrady 1:492. All that they prove, however, is that at the time of writing no such intimacy existed. This had certainly been the case since August 1786 at least, almost three years earlier.
107 During his first months in Italy, for example, she wrote him several recriminatory

of this letter, unlike that of early October 1776 where she had acknowledged her feelings for him as 'die mir so liebe Sünde,' she registered her horror with the exclamation: 'O!!!' Frau von Stein's control was finally over for good and she was speechless.

---

notes and letters designed to wound him (cf. P1619, P1620, P1623); she also wrote threatening to break off correspondence with him and to ask for the return of the letters that she had written to him over the years.

2
Writing and Rewriting 1776-90

Throughout his first decade in Weimar Goethe wrote above all for one specific reader, Charlotte von Stein, sending to her and discussing with her almost everything he was working on as soon as it was completed. She, for her part, was not only an eager and interested helpmate, but also something of a benevolent taskmaster who constantly urged him on to sustain and increase his literary productivity.[1] Scholars tend to view these years as unproductive in a literary sense because of the lack of significant works published between 1776 (*Stella*, written before Goethe went to Weimar) and 1787 (*Iphigenie*, completed in Italy); they also tend to attribute Goethe's flight from Weimar to his intense frustration as a writer swamped by a round of frustrating official duties that kept him from exercising his greatest talent. However, although he might well have written a great deal more if he had not been laden down with other heavy responsibilities, the fact is that these years *were* highly productive from a literary point of view. Publication dates, as we know, are notoriously unreliable indicators of the actual period of most intense creativity, and to measure Goethe's literary output by such a yardstick is simply to falsify his record as a writer. Apart from a large number of slight, 'occasional' pieces, he also either conceived or substantially wrote many of his major works during these years: e.g., *Wilhelm Meisters theatralische Sendung* (1777–86), *Egmont* (1778–87), *Iphigenie* (1779–87), *Tasso* (1780–9), a great many lyric poems, including some of his best,[2] and the second, final version of *Die Leiden des*

---

1 Cf. Düntzer *CvSt*, passim; also Schmidt, *Charakteristiken* 1:302.
2 In terms of Goethe's lyric production 1789–95 were much leaner years than 1776–86; cf. BA 4:926–9. The poems written between 1775 and 1786 are usefully collected together in chronological order in *Goethe: Sämtliche Werke nach Epochen*

jungen Werthers (1781–6). The only major drama already conceived and begun that he did not work on at this time was *Faust*, but for that and subsequent major works he needed first the intellectual and personal experiences that came only after 1788. It is not my intention to look here at all of what Goethe wrote during the years 1776–89, as this would lead too far afield from the examination of *Werther* that I mean to pursue, but simply to establish certain fundamental characteristics in his writing during this period, to consider his interest in *Werther* prior to its reworking in 1786, and to see what changes he made to other works at or around the same time. In this way I hope to gain a firm base from which to show that the changes he made to his first novel follow a pattern evident also in his treatment of other existing material.

Literary Game-playing

As I have said before, Goethe's relationship with Frau von Stein determined a great deal of what and how he wrote during his first ten years in Weimar, and it is worth looking again briefly at 1776 with this in mind, for his ongoing game of literary self-revelation and self-concealment was established very early and lasted at least until after he returned from Italy. It certainly was still his dominant writing principle when he began to rework *Werther* in the months before he left. Frau von Stein engaged in the same game – indeed, it may well be that she was the one to initiate the whole process of literary game-playing which Goethe engaged in so avidly in Weimar, for it was she who first wrote a play that involved both of them. Her play bore the title *Rino* and was written in mid-1776, by which time Goethe was already bombarding her with tumultuous avowals of love, although only she and he were aware of this. The name of the central character is taken from the Ossian passage which Werther and Lotte read together and by which they are both so overwhelmed,[3] and Frau von

---

seines Schaffens, ed. Karl Richter in co-operation with H. Göpfert, N. Miller, and G. Sauder, 1985ff., here 2,1:7–110. From a perusal of these poems it is clear that Goethe's lyric productivity during this decade was by no means of inferior quality, as is often believed.

3 137L/R. See note 23, chapter 1.

Stein's play, which comprises only three short scenes, takes the form of a discussion among four society ladies on the subject of this young man, Rino, who has much of the air of a Werther about him and is the darling of them all. Rino himself appears only briefly in the first scene, but Frau von Stein's casting of the roles is important for the hidden message she wishes to convey: Rino is to be played by Goethe, the four ladies by Countess Anna Amalia, Fräulein von Göchhausen, Frau von Werthern, and Charlotte von Stein herself. She is the sceptic among the four, the one who admits her interest but claims that poor Rino cannot help but fall in love with and pay court to all and sundry. Clearly, the play has two levels of meaning, the one eso-, the other exoteric. Outwardly to its actors and audience it represents nothing more than a playful tribute to the new darling of the Weimar court, but behind that lies a secret message from Charlotte von Stein to Goethe which only he could understand, given that his already ardent courtship was a deep secret known only to the two of them. Through her text she offers him a hidden and flirtatious challenge along these lines: 'You say you love me and I have all these letters to prove it, but I'm quite sure you behave this way with every woman. I understand it. Poor dear, I know you just can't help yourself.'[4] Precisely such daring, such playing with fire while taking care to wrap oneself in asbestos, was irresistible to Goethe, who repeatedly engaged in the same process himself during the years before the break. I shall come back to this presently, but for now, let me just quote two highly significant lines from Frau von Stein's play. Referring to Rino (Goethe), she has this to say in her own chosen role as Gertruth:

---

4 Gertruth, the character played by Frau von Stein, summarizes her feelings about Rino to her three friends as follows:
   Er hat mir wohl so mancherley gesagt,
   Daß, hät ich es nicht reichlich überdacht,
   Ich wär stolz auf sein Beyfall worden.
   Doch treibt ihn immer Liebe fort,
   Ein neuer Gegenstand an jedem neuen Ort.
   Die schönern Augen sind gleich sein Orden,
   Vor die muß er manch treues Herz ermorden;
   So ist er gar nicht Herr von sich,
   Der arme Mensch, er dauert mich.
The whole play is reprinted in Schöll, *Goethes Briefe* 1:398–400; here 400.

> Gleichgültig ist er mir eben nicht,
> Doch weiß ich nicht, ob er oder Werther mir spricht.'[5]

Written in jest as a somewhat arch, backhanded compliment to Goethe, these lines also contain a good deal of truth, for it was not primarily Goethe, the man, whom Charlotte von Stein was so eager to meet when he first arrived in Weimar, but Goethe, the poetic creator of Werther. By her own admission she was so carried away by his novel when she first read it that she was depressed for a whole week,[6] so when the character she creates for herself in her own play says she does not know whether she is responding to the real Rino (Goethe) or to Werther, she is to be taken quite seriously, despite her attempt to present this as a teasing joke. Such role confusion was to last a long time and undoubtedly constituted a major component in the development of the relationship between Goethe and herself, a confusion seemingly fostered by both of them in the beginning and only finally destroyed with the major break in 1786, which came just a matter of days after the second version of the novel was completed.

But if Frau von Stein initiated the game of revelation and concealment, Goethe was both able and only too willing to carry it further. In August 1776 he wrote *Der Falke*, in which the central female figure (Giovanna) was a composite of his past and current loves, Lili Schönemann and Charlotte von Stein. Writing to Charlotte on 8 August he had this to say:

> Ich hab an meinem Falcken geschrieben, meine Giovanna wird viel von Lili haben, du erlaubst mir aber doch dass ich einige Tropfen deines Wesen's drein giesse, nur so viel es braucht um zu tingiren. dein Verhältniss zu mir ist so heilig sonderbaar, dass ich erst recht bey dieser Gelegenheit fühlte: es kann nicht mit Worten ausgedrückt werden, Menschen können's nicht sehen. (P84)

One doubts that he would have altered his plans even if she had refused him permission to write her into the character of Giovanna, but she did not object and so the literary game-playing gained momentum. It was fun, first and foremost, but it was to become increas-

---

5 Ibid. 398
6 See the reply from Zimmermann to CvSt in *Vertrauliche Briefe* 1:97f.

ingly important for Goethe to have this kind of safety valve for expressing what his situation required him to suppress or even deny. As we shall see, he often either drew on existing works or invented new ones in order to present 'openly' in his writings his innermost thoughts or wishes without fear of discovery by anyone other than Frau von Stein. From her he wanted to conceal nothing; to her he felt he could never reveal his inner self fully enough.

In late October 1776 he wrote *Die Geschwister* as an outlet for his own pent-up emotions, and less than a month later it was performed before a sizeable audience. The play could be understood for what it was only by Charlotte – an assertion of the inadequacy of the brother-sister relationship she was promoting between herself and Goethe and an exhortation to allow their love to take a more natural course. At the same time it was a highly flattering declaration of love and devotion, with particular secrets tucked away in it, secrets (quite apart from the inclusion of the actual text of one of her own letters) that only she could decipher. Take, for example, the following lines of a monologue by Wilhelm early in the play, spoken before his supposed sister (Marianne) comes on the scene:

WILHELM: ... O Marianne! wenn du wüßtest, daß der, den du für deinen Bruder hältst, daß der mit ganz anderm Herzen, ganz andern Hoffnungen für dich arbeitet! – Vielleicht! – Ach! – Es ist doch bitter – Sie liebt mich – ja, als Bruder – Nein, pfui! das ist wieder Unglaube, und der hat nie was Gutes gestiftet. – Marianne! ich werde glücklich sein, du wirst's sein, Marianne! (HA 4:353)

Or the following words of Marianne to Wilhelm, whom she believes to be her brother:

MARIANNE: ... Siehe, ich fühle mehr Vergnügen, bei dir zu sein, als Dank für deine mehr als brüderliche Sorgfalt. Und nach und nach nahmst du so mein ganzes Herz, meinen ganzen Kopf ein, daß jetzt noch etwas anders Mühe hat, ein Plätzchen drin zu gewinnen ... (ibid. 367)

The happy end, which brings the revelation that they are indeed free to marry, is expressed like this:

WILHELM (*ihr um den Hals fallend*): Du bist mein, Marianne!
MARIANNE: Gott! was ist das? – Darf ich dir diesen Kuß zurück geben? – Welch ein Kuß war das, Bruder?

WILHELM: Nicht des zurückhaltenden, kaltscheinenden Bruders, der Kuß eines ewig einzig glücklichen Liebhabers. (*Zu ihren Füßen*): Marianne, du bist nicht meine Schwester! Charlotte war deine Mutter, nicht meine. (ibid. 368)

As the inclusion of Charlotte's letter would indicate, Frau von Stein was cast by Goethe both in the role of the dead widow (Charlotte) and of her daughter, Marianne, whom Wilhelm loves for her own sake as he had once loved her mother, whom circumstances had made it impossible for him to marry. There can be no doubt that Charlotte von Stein would have picked up the hidden messages and tributes meant specially for her in the passages just cited, but to the remainder of the audience the play was bound to be nothing more than a pleasant little romantic interlude, just as Charlotte's own play *Rino* earlier that same year was ostensibly nothing more than an ironic tribute to the court's new darling, while to Goethe it was a covert encouragement to courtship, as we have seen. A similar kind of double message was placed in *Lila* (1777/8). On the surface this was merely an amusing, didactic *Singspiel* that offered remedies for wifely hysteria and superstition, but beneath that surface it contained several overt and covert references to Goethe's own experiences and attitudes: its good-natured, though mocking, portrayal of Josias von Stein (Graf Altenstein) as an affable dolt obsessed by horses, for example,[7] and its expression of the tension felt by a lover at being unable to express his love openly. The following passage, though written later when Goethe revised the work for publication, mirrors exactly the playwright's own situation at the time of first writing. Notice how even the use of 'du' on the part of the man and of 'Sie' on the part of the woman is retained here:

FRIEDRICH: Nur einen Augenblick, meine Beste! Welche Qual, dir so nahe zu sein und dir kein Wort sagen zu können! Dir nicht sagen zu dürfen, wie sehr ich dich liebe! Hab ich doch nichts anders als diesen einzigen Trost! Wenn mir auch *der* geraubt werden sollte –
ALMAIDE: Entfernen Sie sich, mein Freund! Es sind viele Beobachter auf allen Seiten.
FRIEDRICH: Was können sie sehen, was sie nicht schon wissen: daß unsre Gemüter auf ewig verbunden sind.

---

7 See P119 and notes, Petersen 1,2:569f.; also the play itself (BA 4:181–214).

ALMAIDE: Lassen Sie uns jeden Argwohn vermeiden, der unser unwürdig wäre.
FRIEDRICH: Ich verlasse dich! Deine Hand, meine Teure!   (BA 4:208)

Again this passage would have had no particular meaning for anyone in the audience apart from Frau von Stein (Friedrich is Graf Altenstein's son, Almaide the *sister* of Baron Sternthal, who was played by Goethe), but the fact that he included such messages to her in works to be performed before others indicates the extent to which she had a role to play in a great deal of what he chose to write and also in how he chose to express it.

A different example of literary game-playing can be found in *Jery und Bätely*, another musical drama written in late 1779 but not performed in Weimar until six months later because of a delay in the composition of the music. According to Goethe in March 1780, this work was quite simply 'eine kleine Operette, worin die Akteurs Schweizerkleider anhaben und von Kas und Milch sprechen werden. Sie ist sehr kurz und bloß auf den musikalischen und theatralischen Effekt gearbeitet' (WA 4,4:187). There can be little doubt that most of his audience saw just precisely this in the evening's entertainment, yet the purpose behind its writing was in reality a different one, as was the author's state of mind close to the time of original composition. The letter in which he first tells Charlotte von Stein about the operetta on 3 January 1780 begins as follows:

> So ziehen wir an den Höfen herum, frieren und langeweilen, essen schlecht und trincken noch schlechter. Hier iammern einen die Leute, sie fühlen wie es bey ihnen aussieht und ein fremder macht ihnen bang ... Hab ich Ihnen schon geschrieben, dass ich unterweegs eine Operette gemacht habe? *Die Scene ist in der Schweiz, es sind aber und bleiben Leute aus meiner Fabrick* ...
>
> Den sogenannten Weltleuten such ich nun abzupassen worinn es ihnen denn eigentl. sizt? Was sie guten Ton heisen? Worum sich ihre Ideen drehen ...?   (P362, emphasis mine)

Just over two weeks later he wrote to Kayser, who was originally intended to supply the music for the play: 'Den Charakter des Ganzen werden Sie nicht verkennen; leicht, gefällig, offen, ist das Element, worinn so viele andre Leidenschaften, von der innigsten Rührung biss zum ausfahrendsten Zorn u.s.w. abwechseln. Edle Gestalten sind in die Bauernkleider gesteckt, und der reine einfache Adel der Natur soll in einem wahren angemessenen Ausdruk sich immer gleich bleiben ...'[8] Indeed the play has to do in a significant sense with the glorification of the peasant, while seeming only to afford light amusement to the ladies and gentlemen of the court. Important for any consideration of how Goethe wrote at this time, however, are those passages which again speak only to Frau von Stein. The story is very simple: Jery is deeply in love with Bätely, but she is so used to his devoted homage that she does not realize her good fortune. With the arrival of his friend Thomas who (deliberately) offends all the proprieties of courtship by his instant and aggressive advances, she comes to value Jery as he deserves, and in the end the two are united. The playful yet dangerous message is again multi-faceted, including words of the utmost love and devotion from Jery to which Bätely responds with only desultory interest. All of this amounts to a cleverly concealed self-parody on Goethe's part, but one that ultimately makes the very important point for him, i.e., that he and Charlotte belong together. Here are some examples of passages that suggest a specific though covert appeal to Frau von Stein:

JERY: Du wirst an vielem Übel schuld sein. Schon so oft hast du mir den
Kopf so toll gemacht, daß ich dir zum Trutz eine andre nehmen wollte.
Und wenn ich sie nun hätte, und wäre sie gleich müde, und sähe immer
und immer: das ist nicht Bätely! ich wär auf immer elend.
BÄTELY: Du mußt eine Schöne nehmen, die reich ist und gut; so eine wird
man nimmer satt.
JERY: Ich habe *dich* verlangt und keine Reichere noch Bessere.
Ich verschone dich mit Klagen,
Doch das eine muß ich sagen,
Immer sagen: dir allein
Ist und wird mein Leben sein.
... (BA 4:231f.)

Later in the play the following amusing exchanges take place between Bätely and her impulsive, outrageous suitor, Thomas, exchanges in

---

8 HA *Briefe* 1:292f.

which Goethe seems to parody his own 'peasant' behaviour towards Charlotte in the past, as well as her reactions:

BÄTELY: Mir springt im Schmerze
  Der Wut mein Herze,
  Fühle mich, ach!
  Rasend im Grimm
  Und im Grimme so schwach!
THOMAS (*kommt wieder*):
  Gib mir, o Schönste,
  Nur freundliche Blicke,
  Gleich soll mein Vieh
  Von dem Berge zurücke!
BÄTELY: Wagst, mir vors Angesicht
  Wieder zu stehn?
THOMAS: Liebchen, o zürne nicht,
  Bist ja so schön!
BÄTELY: Toller!
THOMAS: O süßes,
  O himmlisches Blut!
BÄTELY: Ach, ich ersticke!
  Ich sterbe für Wut!   (ibid. 240)

However, in the end, with Jery hurt in a struggle with Thomas on her account, Bätely is filled with remorse and sees the error of her ways; thus the path to their dual happiness is prepared. Again we have evidence of playful wish-fulfilment in Goethe's writing:

BÄTELY: Rede, aber rede treulich,
  Sieh mir offen ins Gesicht!
  Findest du mich nicht abscheulich?
  Jery, aber schmeichle nicht!
  Der du ganz dein Herz geschenkt,
  Die du nun so schön verteidigt,
  Oft wie hat sie dich beleidigt,
  Weggestoßen und gekränkt!
  Hat dein Lieben sich geendet,
  Hat dein Herz sich weggewendet,
  Überlaß mich meiner Pein!

> Sag es nur, ich will es dulden,
> Stille leiden meine Schulden;
> Du sollst immer glücklich sein.
> JERY: Es rauschen die Wasser,
> Die Wolken vergehn;
> Doch bleiben die Sterne,
> Sie wandeln und stehn.
> So auch mit der Liebe,
> Der treuen, geschicht:
> Sie wegt sich, sie regt sich,
> Und ändert sich nicht.
> (*Sie sehen einander an, Bätely scheint bewegt und unschlüssig.*)
> JERY: Engel, du scheinst mir gewogen!
> Doch ich bitte, halt die Regung
> Noch zurück, noch ist es Zeit!
> Leicht, gar leicht wird man betrogen
> Von der Rührung, der Bewegung,
> Von der Güt und Dankbarkeit.
> BÄTELY: Nein, ich werde nicht betrogen!
> Mich beschämet die Erwägung
> Deiner Lieb und Tapferkeit.
> Bester, ich bin dir gewogen,
> Traue, traue dieser Regung
> Meiner Lieb und Dankbarkeit!
> JERY: Verweile!
> Übereile
> Dich nicht!
> Mir lohnet schon gnüglich
> Ein freundlich Gesicht.   (ibid. 247f.)

While this piece of writing may seem to be utterly trivial and of interest only in terms of the musical drama as a historical genre, it nevertheless does help, I believe, to illustrate the kind of private, concealed games Goethe enjoyed playing with much of what he wrote.

Similar in terms of its esoteric message, but rather different as far as its purpose was concerned, was *Die Vögel*, written in the summer of 1780 with a wistful look backward to the journey to Switzerland a few months before. Goethe and Karl August had stolen away in late

1779 disguised as the two chief characters who appear in the play, Treufreund and Hoffegut (BA 5:653). Their chief reason for going was dissatisfaction with life at the Weimar court, and this satire wickedly assails the false values that make them both feel so ill at ease there. Fallen among a group of hostile birds, the two friends are obliged to think up a strategem to win these over, and much of what they have to say is a bold, though implicit, attack on Weimar society. Take, for example, their series of responses to the question from an owl as to what kind of town they would really wish to live in:

HOFFEGUT: So eine Stadt, wo vornehme Leute die Vorteile ihres Standes mit uns geringern zu teilen bereit wären.
SCHUHU: He!
TREUFREUND: Eben eine Stadt, wo die Regenten fühlten, wie es dem Volk, wie es einem armen Teufel zumute ist.
SCHUHU: Gut!
...
TREUFREUND: Eine Stadt, wo Enthusiasmus lebte, wo ein Mann, der eine edle Tat getan, der ein gutes Buch geschrieben hätte, gleich auf zeitlebens in allem freigehalten würde.
SCHUHU: Sind Sie ein Schriftsteller?
TREUFREUND: Ei wohl!
SCHUHU: Sie auch?
HOFFEGUT: Freilich! wie alle meine Landsleute. (BA 5:410)

Pretending, for reasons of self-protection, that he and Hoffegut are themselves birds, hence outsiders in human society, Treufreund (played by Goethe) describes as follows how they have managed to thwart that society's attempt to impose its false standards on them:

TREUFREUND: Sie glaubten, uns zahm gemacht zu haben, weil wir, durch den Hunger gebändigt, nicht mehr wie anfangs hackten und krallten, sondern Mandelkerne und Nüsse aus den Händen schöner Damen annahmen und uns hinter den Ohren krauen ließen ... Aber vergebens! Wir, im Herzen wie Hannibal oder ein Rachsüchtiger auf dem englischen Theater, ungebeugt durch die Not, ohne Dank gegen tyrannische Wohltäter, schmiedeten einen doppelten, heimlichen, großen Anschlag – unserer Freiheit und ihres Verderbens ... Was uns täglich in die Augen fiel, war ihre Einbildung und ihre Albernheit, ihre Untüchtigkeit, etwas vorzunehmen, ihr Müßiggang, ihre plumpe Gewalttätigkeit und ihr ungeschickter Betrug. Ach! – seufzten wir so oft in der Stille – soll dies Volk, so unwürdig, von der Erde genährt zu werden, die ihnen durch den Diebstahl des Prometheus verräterisch zugewandte Herrschaft so mißbrauchen und sie den urältesten Herren, dem ersten Volke, vorenthalten!   (ibid. 419f.)

The fact is that the entire play, in spite of its silly plot, is a sustained assault on the values of those who assembled to watch its performance in August 1780 at the Ettersburger Liebhabertheater, an assault in which Goethe delighted and for which he boldly claimed praise and applause from his audience in a covertly audacious epilogue that laid any potential blame for offence at the door of Aristophanes (ibid. 429f.). Literary creativity of this kind allowed him to express and hence defuse some of the irritation and frustration that he felt as a result of life in Weimar without fear of discovery or reprisal. As he wrote in later years of another work in which he had secretly lampooned many of those around him at the court (*Das Jahrmarktsfest zu Plundersweilen*), only very few members of his audience became aware of the hidden assault on them that this entertaining work represented. In Goethe's words: 'Unter allen dort auftretenden Masken sind wirkliche, in jener Sozietät lebende Glieder, oder ihr wenigstens verbundene und einigermaßen bekannte Personen gemeint; aber der Sinn des Rätsels blieb den meisten verborgen, alle lachten, und wenige wußten, daß ihnen die eigensten Eigenheiten zum Scherze dienten' (HA 9:595).

Quite a different piece of writing from either *Die Vögel* or *Das Jahrmarktsfest*, but one that again appears to reflect Goethe's need to commit his inner state to paper within a literary framework, is an opera fragment that he began to write in late 1795 or early 1796. This time the concealed emotions were of a far from playful nature, and although the work falls outside the period under immediate consideration, it is worthwhile to consider it nevertheless as an example of how the poet used his writing as means of giving vent to pent-up feelings, in this case feelings of negativity and anger. The fragment I am referring to is *Der Zauberflöte zweiter Teil*, of which Knebel had the following to say in a letter to Böttiger on 8 December 1800: 'Goethe hat in seinem zweiten Teil der "Zauberflöte" feine und stechende Hieroglyphen gemalt.'[9] Max Morris has already shown that the barbs Knebel refers to here are directed against Charlotte von Stein, whose hatred of Goethe and Christiane Vulpius is reflected in the behaviour of the Queen of the Night towards Tamino and Pamina.[10]

As Morris points out, a fourth child (Karl) was born to Christiane and Goethe on 30 October 1795, but lived less than three weeks. Frau von Stein's *Dido* had been circulating in Weimar for about eleven months by that time, and it was no secret that the play was a vicious attack on Goethe. In his *Zauberflöte* the Queen of the Night has ordered that the baby son of Pamina and Tamino be snatched away from them at birth and placed in a golden coffin to be brought to her, but her forces of darkness are foiled in their attempt to bear the coffin away, so all they can do is to hold the child prisoner for her. The forces of life prevail, however; Tamino and Pamina successfully overcome the threat of water and fire to penetrate to the tomb of their baby son, enabling him as the genius of life (Euphorion-like) to fly to freedom. Thus the Queen of the Night is defeated. The following are several relevant quotations from the text that demonstrate how she is depicted:

DIE KÖNIGIN (*in den Wolken*):
Wer ruft mich an?
Wer wagt's, mit mir zu sprechen?
Wer, diese Stille kühn zu unterbrechen?
Ich höre nichts – so bin ich denn allein!
Die Welt verstummt um mich, so soll es sein.[11]

...

MONOSTATOS: In solcher feierlichen Pracht
Wirst du nun bald der ganzen Welt erscheinen;
Ins Reich der Sonne wirket deine Macht.
Pamina und Tamino weinen;
Ihr höchstes Glück ruht in des Grabes Nacht.

---

9 Gräf 2,4:501, note 1
10 Max Morris, 'Frau von Stein und die Königin der Nacht,' in *Goethe-Studien*, 1902
11 BA 4:360; cf. the original version of these lines, which points even more clearly to Frau von Stein at this time:
   Wer ruft mich an! Wer wagt es, ohne Grauen
   Das Angesicht der Königin zu schauen,
   Die tiefen Schmerz in ihrem Busen trägt.   (ibid. 390)

KÖNIGIN: Ihr neugeborner Sohn, ist er in meinen Händen?
MONOSTATOS: Noch nicht, doch werden wir's vollenden;
   Ich les es in der Sterne wilden Schlacht.
KÖNIGIN: Noch nicht in meiner Hand? was habt ihr denn getan?
MONOSTATOS: O Göttin, sieh uns gnädig an!
   Im Jammer haben wir das Königshaus verlassen.
   Nun kannst du sie mit Freude hassen. (BA 4:361)
   ...
[Tamino and Pamina have just successfully passed over the water.]
TAMINO: Meine Gattin, meine Teure,
   O wie ist der Sohn zu retten?
   Zwischen Wasser, zwischen Feuer,
   Zwischen Graus und Ungeheuer
   Ruhet unser höchster Schatz.
   (*Sie gehen durchs Feuer.*)
PAMINA: Einer Gattin, einer Mutter,
   Die den Sohn zu retten eilet,
   Macht das Wasser, macht das Feuer,
   In der Gruft das Ungeheuer,
   Macht der strenge Wächter Platz.
[The Queen of the Night appears in a cloud.]
KÖNIGIN: Was ist geschehen!
   Durch das Wasser, durch das Feuer
   Drangen sie glücklich und verwegen.
   Auf, ihr Wächter! ihr Ungeheuer!
   Stellet mächtig euch entgegen
   Und bewahret mir den Schatz.
DIE WÄCHTER (...):
   Wir bewahren, wir bewachen
   Mit Speer und Löwenrachen,
   O Göttin, deinen Schatz.
TAMINO UND PAMINA (*hervorkommend*):
   O mein Gatte, mein Geliebter,
   Meine Gattin, meine Teure,
   Sieh, das Wasser, sieh, das Feuer
   Macht der Mutterliebe Platz.
   Ihr Wächter, habt Erbarmen!

KÖNIGIN: Ihr Wächter, kein Erbarmen!
  Behauptet euren Platz!
TAMINO UND PAMINA:
  O weh! o weh uns Armen!
  Wer rettet unsern Schatz?
KÖNIGIN: Sie dringen durch die Wachen,
  Der grimmige Löwenrachen
  Verschlinge gleich den Schatz!
(*Die Wolke zieht weg. Stille.*)
DAS KIND (*im Kästchen*):
  Die Stimme des Vaters,
  Des Mütterchens Ton,
  Es hört sie der Knabe
  Und wachet auch schon.
  ...   (ibid. 385f.)

However little we may think either of this work itself or of the clear traces of Goethe's anger and desire for revenge that it contains, it nonetheless adds to our awareness of how very personal his approach to creative writing was. This approach seems to have been the same whether he was engaged on a masterpiece or on a more trivial work, and the secrets he expressed in what he wrote took many different forms, as I have tried to show. 'Wir, ... ungebeugt durch die Not, ohne Dank gegen tyrannische Wohltäter, schmiedeten einen doppelten, heimlichen, großen Anschlag – userer Freiheit und ihres Verderbens' – says Treufreund in *Die Vögel* in proud defence of his strategem to preserve his own inner freedom while preventing the world at large from encroaching on his inner being. And so thought Goethe, the author. Writing offered him this freedom, not simply because it afforded him an escape route inward from other people's rules and constraints, but more importantly, because it provided him with a means through which to lend outer form and substance to his innermost thoughts and feelings. While the act of writing in itself enabled him to experience a sense of inner liberation, the public reading or performance of his works offered him a sweet sense of domination over all that oppressed him. To write was for Goethe to exploit a particular means of ordering and expanding his own perceived reality in the manner that pleased him best or relieved him most, and he repeatedly made use of his literary talent for these purposes. The fact that we find so many hidden (and 'forbidden') personal messages of various kinds for one specific reader or listener as well as covert attacks on people or situations he found oppressive or intolerable offers ready proof that this was so.

But of course it goes without saying that he also did a great deal more at the same time, and precisely therein lies an aspect of his genius that has so far gone unappreciated. I have chosen to deal briefly with these particular works as examples of how Goethe used his writing as a secret outlet for various serious and playful ideas because these plays (with the exception of the *Zauberflöte*) were either made ready for publication before he left for Italy or were among those he took with him for revision or completion, and I mean to look presently at how he reworked other material in or around 1786 before going on to examine in detail the changes he made to *Werther*.

Much more significant in this connection than the examples I have cited so far are *Iphigenie* and *Tasso* because of their lasting high quality as works of literature. Both of these plays also contain a great number of personal messages or revelations despite all subsequent revisions in Italy and Weimar, and it is important to register the fact that both the personal and aesthetic spheres are interwoven in each of the respective final versions (albeit with unequal felicity), for a similar interweaving seems to lie at the heart of the changes to *Werther* also. Like the novel, *Iphigenie* and *Tasso* exemplify, both in their early and reworked form, Goethe's need for self-revelation and self-concealment. Although not completed until 1787 and 1789, the two plays were conceived and begun in 1779 and 1780 respectively, but what casts a most interesting light on their protracted composition is the degree to which the author's personal need to express his love for Frau von Stein increasingly came to predominate over his judgment as an artist at least at one stage, so that in April 1781 – the emotional turning-point of the relationship was in March – he could confess: 'Ich habe gleich an Tasso schreibend dich angebetet. Meine ganze Seele ist bei dir ... Als Anrufung an dich ist gewiss gut was ich geschrieben habe. Obs als Scene und an dem Ort gut ist weis ich nicht.'[12]

As we are aware, he later rejected what he had written of *Tasso* at

---

12 See above, p. 48.

this time and had great difficulty in transforming it into what we now know as the final version, but his subsequent change of heart vis-à-vis his original *Tasso* is less important than the fact that he could not bring himself to scrap the play altogether, persisting instead in his attempt to rewrite it until he felt it could be given up for publication. What is surprising is the fact that not only aesthetic but also highly personal considerations seem to have played a role in determining the point at which he felt willing to declare a work finished. Goethe almost never wrote anything of even a semi-literary nature without claiming it back subsequently from the person he had sent it to in order to publish it either just as it was or in a reworked form. It was as if he regarded what he wrote as a continuing part of himself, lent to others perhaps for a time, but always essentially his own property. Even Frau von Stein was no privileged exception as far as ownership rights were concerned, for not even she was allowed to regard all of the poems and letters he sent her as her own: on the back of a four-line poem he sent to her in June 1778, for example, she wrote in vain protest: 'Ich geb nichts gern wieder was ich von Ihnen habe' (P252). A full four years later he wrote another poem to her with these same four lines as his starting-point – a typical and oft-repeated practice for Goethe.[13]

Examples of this kind abound throughout his letters to Charlotte and would be of little further interest to us were it not for the light they shed on how he wrote and hence for the potential insight they offer into a deeper understanding of the rewriting of *Werther*.[14] While the unvarnished narrative of Goethe's love relationship with Charlotte

---

13 See P968, mid-September 1782, and notes to P252, Petersen 1,2:587.
14 For example, in March 1780 he asked her to return the personal letters he had written to her on his journey to Switzerland, September 1779 to January 1780; a public reading followed two days later (see P391). He also published many of the poems he had originally written and sent her in various letters – for example, an untitled poem written and sent by him on 15 September 1780 was published that year in the *Tiefurter Journal* under the title 'Ode'; it was subsequently republished in 1789 with the new title 'Meine Göttin' (see P480 and notes, Petersen 1,2:611); another poem with no title, sent to her on 5 April 1782, was reclaimed for publication 19 November 1783 under the title 'Das Göttliche' (see P852 and P1169, also notes, Petersen 1,2:641 and 2,2:644). While writing his private travel diary for Frau von Stein in September 1786, he already laid claim to it in advance for later publication purposes, telling her that she was to replace all the 'du' forms with 'Sie' and remove anything she regarded as too personal for other eyes to see; Erich Schmidt, *Tagebücher und Briefe Goethens aus Italien an Frau von Stein und Herder*, 1886, 8.

von Stein may provide us with a clearer picture of the emotional background to the writing of Version Two, we must not overlook the fact that the specific changes he made also bear the stamp of his own particular mode of literary production. Several things are important here: his elephantine memory in general;[15] his emotionalism and inability to forget traumatic events of the past;[16] the need he felt to set his own personal record to rights by reworking old material to his own satisfaction; the pleasure he often derived in this period from leading all but selected readers astray through what he wrote, while providing himself with an outlet for his own thoughts and feelings – all of these have had a clear impact on the revised *Werther*, as I mean to show. Of the many significant literary tasks Goethe undertook in Weimar up to September 1786, rewriting his first novel was the only one he completed, and this fact alone gives Version Two a unique place in his work. By preceding him to Weimar in 1775 and paving the way for the most profound love relationship he ever had, Version One already had a unique place in his life. It was to be several years before he felt the urge to turn his attention to the novel once again, but it was long before the decisive summer of 1786.

Werther 1776–86

It was not until Goethe had already been in Weimar for over eighteen months that he first had occasion to glance through a copy of his own *Werther*. Although he had been acutely and painfully aware throughout 1776 of the similarity of his current emotional situation with that

---

15 Perhaps the most striking example of Goethe's astounding power of memory is this: at the end of December 1779, in the company of Seckendorf, he wrote a series of trivial poems as a New Year's greeting for eight ladies of the court. Some forty-six years later he recalled the incident in a conversation with Kanzler von Müller. See Petersen 1,2:590.

16 Cf., for example, p. 33 and note 41, chapter 1; also Goethe's emotionalism as reflected in his reactions to revisiting the Hermannsteiner Höhle, where he had been with Frau von Stein – see P84 (8 August 1776), P474 (6 September 1780); note too how he was capable of bursting into tears at the thought of a situation he was planning to write into *Wilhelm Meister*, P441 (6 June 1780). There is also repeated evidence in his letters of his tendency to review and relive his past joys and sorrows – cf. P107 (8 November 1776), P193 and P194 (7 and 8 November 1777), P491 (7 November 1780), P999 (7 November 1782), etc.

in Wetzlar several years before,[17] by early 1777 one significant difference had become clear: his new beloved, though married and therefore unattainable as Charlotte Buff had been, was bound to her husband only by legal and social, not emotional, ties. As early as February 1776 he had already had the first intimation that Charlotte von Stein reciprocated his feelings in some measure at least, and a year later he was sufficiently used to a sense of reciprocity to be able to write of sharing with her the inner disquiet that the folly ('Thorheit') of their love brought to both of them (P128). Seen in this context it seems less than surprising that he should have found his own earlier novel 'new and strange' on cursory perusal in April 1777.[18] Yet his awareness of the unfortunate similarity between his past and present situation was not far from the surface, as the following quatrain, sent at this time, makes clear:

> Was mir in Kopf und Herzen stritt,
> Seit manchen lieben Jahren!
> Was ich da träumend jauchzt und litt
> Muss wachend nun erfahren.   (P154)

This was a tormenting thought that was to occur to Goethe again and again, but from 1777–81 he seems to have found sufficient cause for joy in his relationship with Frau von Stein to avoid total self-identification on a constant basis with his own tragic hero. In November 1779, for example, when asked by a group of admirers if he would be writing more works like his first novel, his instant reaction was: 'Gott möge mich behüten, dass ich nicht ie wieder in den Fall komme, einen zu schreiben und schreiben zu können' (P355). In April 1780 he read the novel through from beginning to end for the first time since publication six years before and reacted with wonderment.[19]

Despite the fact that he was well used to having Frau von Stein tell him that she loved him by early 1781, it was only after their relation-

---

17 Cf. P42, P48, P57, P72, P77, P79, P81, P82, P84, P94, P103 (April to October 1776).
18 P153 (28 April 1777): 'Gestern hab ich einen wunderbaaren Tag gehabt, habe nach Tisch von ohngefähr Werthern in die Hand gekriegt, wo mir alles wie neu und fremd war. Bin noch Nachts ausgeritten ...'
19 Goethe's diary of the time reads: 'd. 30 las meinen Werther seit er gedruckt ist das erstemal ganz und verwunderte mich' (WA 3,1:116). The same day he wrote in a note to Frau von Stein: 'Ich lese meinen Werther!' (P415).

ship seemed to be established on a secure footing once and for all by May of that year that he began to cast her as his 'Lotte,' 'liebe Lotte,' 'liebste Lotte,' and this continued until 1785, which suggests that during this period he did not expect their relationship to end in sorrow reminiscent of Werther. Already by the middle of 1781 he seems to have gone some considerable way towards overcoming the fear that his old fate as the tragic victim of an impossible love might be about to repeat itself with his new leading lady. Whereas he and Frau von Stein had read Ossian together in 1776, acting out the bitter-sweet roles of the old Lotte and the old Werther, five years later they worked eagerly together on an Italian version of the novel in the hope of restoring the flavour of the original to the new translation.[20] However, even at this time (six years after going to Weimar and more than seven since the first publication of *Werther*) Goethe was capable of experiencing the old anguish of Wetzlar and Frankfurt days and of expressing it in much the same terms,[21] although he had established at one point a clear distance between himself and the tragic, lovesick youth whose creation had become such a burden to him.[22]

The idea of rewriting his first novel does not seem to have occurred to him until November 1782, by which time he was writing to Charlotte as 'du süser Traum meines Lebens, du Schlaftrunk meiner Leiden' (P1014). On the very same day that he wrote these words to her he also wrote to Knebel with the news that he was planning to begin work on his novel again: 'Meinen Werther hab ich durchgegangen und lasse ihn wieder ins Manuscript schreiben, er kehrt in seiner Mutter Leib zurück du sollst ihn nach seiner Wiedergeburt sehen. Da ich sehr gesammelt bin, so fühle ich mich zu so einer delikaten und gefähr-

---

20 Goethe found that the whole tale had become incomprehensible because it had lost 'de[n] glühende[n] Ausdruck von Schmerz und Freude, die sich unaufhaltsam in sich selbst verzehren ...' (P763). Their collaboration on the work continued until the end of the year; see P765, P773.
21 Cf. Eissler 1:540: 'At any time, apparently, Werther could take over in Goethe ...' On p. 542 Eissler writes of the poet's relapse into the style of *Werther* in his letter of 12 December 1781 (P763).
22 Goethe's inner distance to the problems of Werther during 1781 is evidenced by the ironic portrait he included of himself in *Das Neueste von Plundersweilen*, written that year. There he presents himself as an author physically burdened down by the corpse of Werther and followed by a crowd of melancholy young men; see BA 5:439f.

lichen Arbeit geschickt.'²³ It is not difficult to see why he conceived the task of rewriting at this point as 'delikat und gefährlich' – 'delikat' because of its connections with other people, 'gefährlich' because of what it reveals about himself and because of the emotions it is still capable of arousing within him.

Undoubtedly the best-known of all the references Goethe made to rewriting *Werther* is the one contained in a letter to Kestner of 2 May 1783, in which he says that he has been working on the novel again in order to elevate it by a few notches, though without touching what has already met with such a sensational response; among other things, it has been his intention, he says, to alter the figure of Albert so that the reader will react more fairly to him.²⁴ This letter, I believe, has done almost as much to lead scholars astray on the subject of the second version of *Werther* as Düntzer has done on the subject of Charlotte von Stein, but I prefer to leave my reasons for this assertion until later, until after we have had the chance to look at and evaluate the changes actually made in Version Two. What we do know for certain is that Goethe was at work on his new *Werther* in May and June of 1783, for on 24 June he sent Frau von Stein an English translation as well as his own current revised version of the novel in manuscript form; clearly, the thought of a parallel between his new Lotte and the old held no terrors for him at that point, for he wrote: 'Hier liebe Lotte endlich den Werther, und die Lotte die auf dich vorgespuckt [sic] hat ...' (P1118).

Although Goethe's letters to Charlotte von Stein from 1783 to 1786 show many similarities to those of the original *Werther*,²⁵ there are no further explicit references to reworking the novel until mid-1786 when

---

23 HA *Briefe* 1:415
24 The relevant portion of this letter reads as follows: 'Ich habe in ruhigen Stunden meinen Werther wieder vorgenommen, und denke, ohne die Hand an das zu legen was so viel Sensation gemacht hat, ihn noch einige Stufen höher zu schrauben. Dabey war unter banderm meine Intention Alberten so zu stellen, daß ihn wohl der leidenschaftliche Jüngling, aber doch der Leser nicht verkennt ...' (ibid. 425).
25 There are too many examples for an extensive list to be given here, but the very weight of their number over many years bears out my claim that Goethe had never quite shed his inner affinity with Werther by the time he embarked on his Italian journey. For some appreciation of the obsessive, Werther-like quality of his love for Charlotte von Stein, for example, cf. (1783) P1130, P1148, P1159, P1170, P1180; (1784) P1267, P1269, P1272, P1277, P1288; (1785) P1369, P1379, P1429, P1440, P1467, P1498; (1786) P1512, P1564, P1588. Some overlooked links between *Werther* and *Tasso* (1789) are examined in chapter 4 of this study.

for a period of several months the poet felt caught up in a turmoil of emotions caused by going over his old material. We can assume it was at this time that he wrote the end of the farmhand's story and made most of the changes in the so-called Editor's Report[26] – changes which resulted not only in a new and more favourable picture of Albert, seen from an objective standpoint, but also in a new and less favourable picture of Lotte, seen from that same standpoint. Bearing in mind the personal trauma Goethe had been undergoing increasingly from 1785 onward, and the repeated need he felt to commit his emotional life to paper in one form or another, it is unthinkable that he should have undertaken the alterations and additions to *Werther* without reference to his lengthy relationship with Charlotte von Stein. The changes he wrought in the novel were not primarily the result of deference to high society's linguistic norms, nor an act of fair-mindedness specifically to Kestner, nor yet of concern for other suffering lovers who might misguidedly emulate Werther's suicide. These changes seem to have sprung primarily from Goethe's need for self-justification, and from the need to purge his heart and soul of a weight of suffering greater than he could bear and more agonizing than he could express in his everyday life. In the rewriting of *Werther* he appears to have engaged in a more profound process of simultaneous self-revelation and self-concealment than ever before, and by so doing to have prepared the way for an emotional self-liberation that would not only be augmented during his years in Italy but would also colour his experiences there. In order to understand and evaluate the basis for these beliefs we must of course look very closely at the substance of the changes he made to his original *Werther*, but first it will be useful to consider the changes he made to other works around the same time, for the principles behind the reworking were similar in all of them and underline the extraordinary strength of the link between the life he lived and his whole process of literary production.

Other Works Revised 1786–9

An examination of what Goethe wrote or rewrote on the basis of his experiences or state of mind at the time of writing may perhaps seem

---

26 A tentative dating of the rewritten parts is offered by Seuffert in WA 1,19:327–34.

an all-too-familiar approach, outmoded and bankrupt, intellectually disreputable, the haven of inferior scholars. It is an approach that can prove surprisingly fruitful, however, as is amply demonstrated by the recent book by Albrecht Schöne to which I referred in my Introduction, on three well-known and long-misread texts by Goethe.[27] By drawing on the poet's letters and diaries at the time 'Harzreise im Winter' was written in 1779, for example, Schöne has shown that despite Goethe's own claim in 1821 that the central figure of the poem was Friedrich Plessing, in reality that central figure was none other than the author himself. Conscious obfuscation of a text for the purpose of self-protection – this was a principle that Goethe often adhered to,[28] and it is a principle we should not overlook in approaching the task of interpretation and criticism any more than we should overlook his conscious habit of placing personal secrets in the works that he was writing at any given time, in the sure knowledge that they would not be perceived, let alone understood, by the majority of those who read these works or saw them performed. It seems to me that the failure to take account of both these characteristics has led to many rather doubtful readings even in the recent past.

Of the ten works contained in the first four volumes of the new edition published by Göschen in 1787 only *Iphigenie auf Tauris* was not completed before Goethe left Karlsbad in September 1786. The form of this drama still displeased him, but the other works were ready in his view for presentation to the public, even though he hesitated to submit his dedicatory poem 'Zueignung' until mid-January of the following year. A declaration of 'readiness' was often very difficult for the poet to make, prone as he was to continue reworking his existing material,[29] but these works were now 'ready': seven dramas first written between 1769 and 1780, 'Zueignung' first written in 1784 at the time when he was working on *Die Geheimnisse* as a hidden avowal of love for Frau von Stein, and *Die Leiden des jungen Werthers* which had preceded him to Weimar in its original form in 1774. The contents of the four volumes were as follows, with dates of original composition and subsequent reworkings shown in parentheses, not including 1786:

27 See Introduction, note 14.
28 See Schöne 37; also Riemer 1:246; WA 4,11:121.
29 Cf. HA 9:572; here Goethe recalls Merck's early scorn at his constant rewriting.

Vol. 1: 'Zueignung' (1784)
    Die Leiden des jungen Werther(s) (1774, 1782, 1783)
Vol. 2: *Götz von Berlichingen* (1771, 1773)
    Die Mitschuldigen (1769, 1769, 1780–3)
Vol. 3: *Clavigo* (1774)
    [*Iphigenie auf Tauris* (1779, 1780, 1781)]
    Die Geschwister (1776)
Vol. 4: *Stella* (1775)
    Die Vögel (1780)
    Der Triumph der Empfindsamkeit (1777, 1778–9)

Interestingly, despite the range and variety of these works, the original stimulus to write each one had been the same in every case apart from *Iphigenie* – the author's need to escape from a sense of suffocation or inner torment – and yet *Werther* alone underwent any substantial change in content for final publication. *Die Mitschuldigen*, for example, was his response to the oppressiveness of bourgeois society in Frankfurt in 1769; it was a play written 'um mir Luft zu verschaffen' (HA 9:285), in much the same way that *Die Vögel* was written in 1780 in response to life at the Weimar court. In the case of *Götz* too, a very different kind of drama, Goethe recalled that writing the work had offered him a sense of release and inner expansion (ibid. 536), and we have every reason to believe his comments on both plays from what we ourselves have so far seen of how he wrote. Similarly, *Clavigo, Werther, Stella*, and *Die Geschwister* all reflected the poet's own personal reactions to the emotional torment of his various loves – Friederike Brion, Charlotte Buff/Maximiliane LaRoche, Lili Schönemann, Charlotte von Stein. At times he seems to have found escape through wish-fulfilment, at others through self-castigation: in *Stella* and *Die Geschwister*, for example, he provided himself with the 'happy end' that reality denied him, but in *Clavigo* this was not the case. Here his chief aim was not the pursuit of his own fondest dreams, but rather of his own 'redemption' through a cathartic act of facing up to his own guilt and moral failure – a purging of the mind and heart by self-indictment and self-flagellation through the act of writing. As Goethe himself wrote, referring to this play: 'Zu der Zeit, als der Schmerz über Friederikens Lage mich beängstigte, suchte ich, nach meiner alten Art, abermals Hülfe bei der Dichtkunst. Ich setzte die hergebrachte poetische Beichte wieder fort, um durch diese selbstquälerische Büßung einer innern Absolution würdig zu werden' (ibid. 521f.).

By working on *Die Laune des Verliebten* in 1768 he had also been able to come to terms with his own responsibility for the rupture of an earlier love relationship, albeit without the same guilt; there too he had done penance by writing and so effected his own emotional cure.[30] Given that he used his literary talent in such various ways not once, but many times, and that the source he claimed for all his literary endeavours was to be found in his own feelings and experiences, it is clear that the act of writing had a real, existential importance for him, quite apart from enabling him to play games of various kinds with, for, or against, other people. That this was so he emphasized again and again – let me cite just one important example of how he expressed himself on the matter in retrospect:

> Verlangte ich ... zu meinen Gedichten eine wahre Unterlage, Empfindung oder Reflexion, *so mußte ich in meinen Busen greifen*; forderte ich zu poetischer Darstellung eine unmittelbare Anschauung des Gegenstandes, der Begebenheit, so durfte ich nicht aus dem Kreise heraustreten, der mich zu berühren, mir ein Interesse einzuflößen geeignet war ...
>
> Und so begann diejenige Richtung, von der ich mein ganzes Leben über nicht abweichen konnte, nämlich dasjenige, was mich erfreute oder quälte, oder sonst beschäftigte, in ein Bild, ein Gedicht zu verwandeln und darüber mit mir selbst abzuschließen, um sowohl meine Begriffe von den äußeren Dingen zu berichtigen, als mich im Innern deshalb zu beruhigen. Die Gabe hierzu war wohl niemand nötiger als mir, den seine Natur immerfort aus einem Extreme in das andere warf. Alles, was daher von mir bekannt geworden, sind nur Bruchstücke einer großen Konfession ...[31] (Emphasis mine)

We know the last sentence of this statement from *Dichtung und Wahrheit* so well and have seen it applied so clumsily to Goethe's various works for such a long time that it has lost much of its impact, but in fact the whole passage ought to be taken very seriously indeed, for a

---

30 Ibid. 284: 'Ja, ich wäre vielleicht an diesem Verlust [of Kätchen Schönkopf] völlig zugrunde gegangen, hätte sich nicht hier das poetische Talent mit seinen Heilkräften besonders hülfreich erwiesen.'
31 Ibid. 282f.; cf. 536.

close scrutiny of his works in their various stages of completion up to 1790 bears out all that he says here. By writing he evidently felt able to free himself of unwelcome emotions, to clarify the situation in which he found himself, and by so doing to go forward continually to a new, unburdened present. He did this, it seems, not only when first writing, but also when rewriting each of his works in the period up to 1790. Whether or not he altered substantially what he found there seems to have depended in every case on the degree of emotional endorsement he could bring to his existing material at the point of re-engagement with it, just as the writing of the original itself had been in the first instance a creative manifestation of his inner life at the point of initial composition. Surprising though it may seem, rewriting in the years up to 1790 was by no means necessarily synonymous with the artistic improvement of any given work; nor can we even be altogether sure that the latter was always Goethe's chief concern when he turned his attention for a second or third time to something he had written earlier. That personal concerns dominated much of his writing can be seen, for example, from a comparison of the two versions of *Götz*, written in 1771 and 1773 respectively. As Rudolf Käser has recently shown, the altered second version of the play denies to both reader and audience the possibility of understanding the motivation of the characters, which had been clear in the original.[32] In the 1771 version the theme of the quest for self played a central role, holding much of the psychological action together, but by 1773 other concerns of greater interest to Goethe obscured this theme in the rewriting, to the detriment of the work as a whole. In Käser's view, the play was altered in accordance with the altered self-understanding of the author at the time of rewriting. This is a claim that seems well-founded, not merely because of the critic's persuasive arguments, but because the same is true not only of *Götz* but of many other works as well, among them *Werther* and *Tasso*.

But why should *Werther* alone of the ten works Goethe revised in 1786 have undergone any recent significant change in substance in the course of rewriting? The seven other works he took with him to Italy and either completed during his stay there or within a year after his

---

[32] Käser 177

return to Weimar seem to offer certain pointers that can perhaps help us to find an answer to this question. The following is a list of those works in order of completion, with the dates of original composition and subsequent reworkings up to 1786 shown in parentheses:

Iphigenie auf Tauris (1779, 1780, 1781)
Egmont ([1775], 1778–9, 1781–2)
Erwin und Elmire (1773–5)
Claudine von Villa Bella (1774–5)
Torquato Tasso (1780–1)
Lila (1776, 1778)
Jery und Bätely (1779)

When Goethe actively confronted the task of preparing these remaining works for publication in December 1786, he again saw the whole process of rewriting, completing, or polishing his existing material as necessitating a re-entry into earlier phases of his life. This had been his experience when working on *Werther* half a year earlier, an experience that would have to be repeated many times over if he were to succeed in completing the task he had set himself. Significantly, it was this aspect of the work that lay before him that he emphasized most, rather than the need to approach his works as a literary critic for whom objective criteria must be paramount. Clearly, his own awareness of the link between what he had written and how he had felt at the time of first writing was very strong, so strong, indeed, that in order to set about reworking anything he felt obliged to relive in his mind the experiences and emotions of his past. That other (untargeted) people might conceivably register this link was evidently not what he expected, as a comment in a letter to Charlotte von Stein of 13–16 December 1786 illustrates:

> Ich las Tischbeinen meine Iphigenie vor die nun bald fertig ist. Die sonderbare, originale Art wie dieser das Stück ansah und mich über den Zustand in welchem ich es geschrieben aufklärte, erschröckte mich. Es sind keine Worte wie fein und tief er den Menschen unter dieser Helden Maske empfunden. (P1619)

The letter continues with a melancholy reflection on the task that now lies ahead of him:

> Setzest du nun dazu daß ich gezwungen bin an meine übrige Schrifften zu dencken, und zu sinnen wie ich sie enden und stellen will und daß ich dadurch genötigt werde in tausend vergangne Situationen meines Lebens zurückzukehren ... so wirst du dencken können in welcher Lage ich mich befinde.

It was in this letter that he had replied to Frau von Stein's reproaches, her threat of silence, and her demand that he return to her everything that she had written to him. Its opening lines illustrate the state of mind he was in at that point – loving, reassuring, hurt, disbelieving, and regretful, and yet hopeful that things would still right themselves between them:

> Könnt ich doch meine Geliebteste, jedes gute, wahre, süße Wort der Liebe und Freundschafft auf dieses Blat faßen, dir sagen und versichern daß ich dir nah, ganz nah bin und daß ich mich nur um deinetwillen des Daseyns freue.
>
> Dein Zettelchen hat mich geschmerzt aber am meisten dadrum daß ich dir Schmerzen verursacht habe. Du willst mir schweigen? du willst die Zeugniße deiner Liebe zurücknehmen? Das kannst du nicht ohne viel zu leiden, und ich bin schuld daran. Doch vielleicht ist ein Brief von dir unterwegs der mich aufrichtet und tröstet, vielleicht ist mein Tagebuch angekommen und hat dich zur guten Stunde erfreut. Ich fahre fort dir zu schreiben dir das merckwürdigste zu melden und dich meiner Liebe zu versichern ... (P1619)

He completed *Iphigenie* without any significant change in content just one month later and began work on *Egmont*, which was to be finished by September. In August he wrote to the Duke: 'Daß ich meine ältern Sachen fertig arbeite, dient mir erstaunend. Es ist eine Rekapitulation meines Lebens und meiner Kunst, und indem ich gezwungen bin, mich und meine jetzige Denkart, meine neuere Manier, nach meiner ersten zurückzubilden, das was ich nur entworfen hatte, nun auszuführen, so lern ich mich selbst und meine Engen und Weiten recht kennen.'[33] What he is saying here is that reading his old works and recognizing the differences that exist between how he once thought and felt compared with how he now thinks and feels, enables

---

33 HA *Briefe* 2:63

him to get to know himself better. He regards his literary works as a revelation of himself both as a man and as a writer, in other words, and he rereads them as his own autobiography. That he should eventually turn to autobiographical writing with ever-increasing attentiveness once he began to experience deep ongoing disappointment with the reception of his works was merely an extension of the urge he felt from early on to commit every significant experience to paper by incorporating it into some kind of literary creation through which he engaged in an ongoing search for his own inner standing ('Selbstbesinnung').[34] Writing was always his means to self-expression and self-creation; what would later be added in a manner rather different from that of his earlier works was the conscious securing of the self from the false or unwanted judgment of others by means of ostensibly frank, but in reality often misleading, commentary.

Iphigenie had already been written/rewritten three times, though never published, before Goethe took it with him to Italy.[35] What is of prime interest here is the fact that in preparing the final version his chief concern was with changes in form rather than content, for he made considerable changes in the content of other works, and not always for the better. Throughout all three earlier versions of the play he had also made only minor changes in content,[36] and the final rewriting was simply a transformation of the prose version into verse. Seemingly, the original vision at the heart of what he had written still had validity for him when he came to complete this work for publication.

The artistic superiority of the final version of *Iphigenie* over its predecessors is beyond all question, as is its artistic wholeness, but the same cannot be maintained about *Torquato Tasso*, which presented Goethe with enormous difficulties in the rewriting and was not finally completed until July 1789, over a year after his return to Weimar. Whereas *Iphigenie* had undergone little change in terms of content, *Tasso* was almost com-

---

34 Fascinating insights into Goethe's growing, and ultimately almost all-encompassing, need to present the record of his own life through what he wrote are provided by two very different recent books; see Käser, *Die Schwierigkeit, ich zu sagen*, 1987, and Stefan Koranyi, *Autobiographik und Wissenschaft im Denken Goethes*, 1984.
35 For the earliest examination of these three versions see *Die drei ältesten Bearbeitungen von Goethes Iphigenie*, ed. Heinrich Düntzer, 1854.
36 Ibid. 369; also Heinrich Meyer, *Goethe: Das Leben im Werk*, 1951, 226; Schmidt, *Charakteristiken* 1:314

pletely rewritten, and substantial changes were also made to the other works he revised for publication between January 1787 and July 1789, the respective completion dates of the two major dramas. These other works were *Egmont, Erwin und Elmire,* and *Claudine von Villa Bella. Lila* and *Jery und Bätely*, reworked once the task of finishing *Tasso* was over, showed little change in content from their original versions.

Although only *Egmont, Erwin, Claudine,* and *Tasso* were extensively rewritten, all of the works Goethe took with him to Italy were revamped to a greater or lesser degree in terms of style or form, with their original prose being transformed into verse in every case apart from *Egmont* and *Jery und Bätely*.[37] Why was some of the plot material changed and some not? The answer seems to lie in the place that writing had in Goethe's life and in the important function it fulfilled for him. What an examination of the substantive changes in both his major and minor works of this period suggests is that in writing he found both the means of giving covert expression to his own experiences wherever these were positive or enjoyable, and the means of providing a covert corrective to whatever seemed to him oppressive, unpalatable, or simply out of date in what he had already written. The act of rereading became an act of reliving the past from the perspective of his personal present, in other words, while that of rewriting became an act of backward and forward 'correction' from that same perspective. At times the changes were playfully self-denigrating, at times strongly self-justifying, at others accusatory, but in every case except *Tasso* they reflected a clear and logically secured optimism in terms of the eventual outcome of the plot.

Originally written in prose with occasional verse passages, both *Erwin* and *Claudine* were first designated 'ein Schauspiel mit Musik' but later transformed entirely into verse under the designation 'ein Singspiel.' The differences between the first and second versions were so substantial, however, that a contemporary critic wrote on the publication of the plays in volume 5 of the Göschen edition in 1788: 'Diese beyden Stücke erscheinen hier in so veränderter Gestalt, daß sie fast für ganz neu gelten können.'[38] Both plays were first written in the

---

37 The prose form of *Egmont* was retained and existing verse passages in *Jery und Bätely* were rewritten in prose (BA 7:887f. and BA 4:689).
38 6 September 1788, *Gothaische gelehrte Zeitungen*; see Julius Braun, *Goethe im Urtheile seiner Zeitgenossen*, 1883–5, 2:22.

pre-Weimar period and we know that both originally reflected Goethe's love relationship with Lili Schönemann. In the rewriting, however, they came to incorporate significant aspects of his relationship with Frau von Stein, which only a comparative study of the different versions can make clear.

Already in January 1786 Goethe was planning to make considerable changes to the two plays (WA 4,7:168), but it was not until early 1788 that he managed to complete these to his satisfaction, having already finished *Iphigenie* and *Egmont* in January and September of the previous year. Whereas *Iphigenie* presented a view of woman as a sisterly priestess of purity, moderation, and truth, *Egmont* – to the dismay of those left behind in Weimar – glorified a feminine capacity for love and passionate devotion that refused to count the cost. The changes made to *Erwin* and *Claudine* reflect something of the same altered notion of the feminine ideal also, for a new female character was introduced into both plays, a woman for whom love is all and whose attitude acts as a foil to the behaviour of the existing central female figures, Elmire and Claudine. Both of these latter wound their respective lovers by reticence or seeming indifference, but in the end each comes to see the error of her ways and actively atones for her past behaviour, with the result that all difficulties are happily resolved. From the changes he made, it seems as if in rewriting these two dramas Goethe was again doing what he had done in *Die Geschwister* (1776), namely, using his creative literary talent as an outlet for formulating, wallowing in, facing up to, and in the end 'fixing' the reality of his own life as he perceived it, so that in the course of his writing existing inner dissonances were transformed into the kind of harmonies he greatly preferred.

In the two plays love is presented initially as problematic and a source of anguish, but eventually blissful happiness is achieved in both. The changes made to the early part of *Erwin und Elmire* result in a picture of unhappy love more reminiscent of Goethe's experiences in Weimar than in Frankfurt, for the central female character is greatly altered to seem more brooding and reflective, rather older than in the original, more aware of her unjust behaviour towards the lover she has caused to flee, and more actively involved in atoning for her past callousness towards him. In addition, an important theme in Version One (and in the relationship with Lili) is taken out of Version Two, namely, the unnaturalness of a 'superior' upbringing and the demands it imposes on a youthful suitor. This theme had been central to Elmire's exchanges with her mother (Olimpia) in the original, but the mother is now removed altogether from the play, as is Bernardo, a fatherly figure who had dealt benignly with Elmire's coquettish behaviour and brought about the reconciliation of the two unhappy lovers. Replacing Olimpia and Bernardo are two quite different, new characters (Valerio and Rosa) for whom, as for Erwin and Elmire, the path of true love does not run smoothly. Erwin has been forced to flee from the world because of Elmire's coldness and scorn before the beginning of the play's action, and Valerio is soon forced to flee because of Rosa's jealousy. Both men have good reasons for leaving: both women are guilty of unloving behaviour and must atone for it before they can be happily reunited with their lovers. A look at several parts of the new text will render the flavour of these changes and their relevance to the events of Goethe's own recent emotional past at the time of rewriting. Reflections of Charlotte von Stein in the new Elmire character seem altogether unmistakable in the terms of the relationship with Goethe that we have looked at already.

A newly written opening scene that takes place between Valerio and Rosa, for example, presents the following exchange, in which they discuss the plight of their friend, Elmire, whose failure to show her love for Erwin has driven him away:

ROSA: Doch laß uns auch an unsre Freundin denken.
    Ich sehe sie am Fenster nicht, auch nicht
    Auf der Terrasse. Bleibt die Arme wohl
    An diesem schönen Tage still bei sich
    Verschlossen? oder wandelt sie im Walde
    Gedankenvoll, betrübt, allein?
VALERIO: Sie ist
    Wohl zu beklagen. Seit der gute Jüngling,
    Der sie so sehr geliebt, und dem sie selbst
    Sich heimlich widmete,
    Durch Kälte, scheinende Verachtung viel
    Gequält, zuletzt es nicht mehr trug und fort
    In alle Welt, Gott weiß wohin, entfloh,

> Seitdem verfolgt, und foltert der Gedanke
> Ihr Innerstes, welch eine Seele sie
> Gequält, und welche Liebe sie verscherzt.
> ROSA: Sie kommt. O laß uns mit ihr gehen, sie
> Mit fröhlichen Gesprächen unterhalten.
> ... (BA 4:37)

These lines, while having a new expository function in the play, also sum up Goethe's own case for fleeing from Weimar and Charlotte von Stein. Erwin, like his creator, is a lover who has been driven away by the coldness and seeming rejection of his beloved, and in these lines we see something of the anguish projected onto Elmire because of her maltreatment of him, anguish which Goethe no doubt partly regretted and partly relished in his imagination on account of the past few years of misery that he had endured because of Frau von Stein's behaviour towards him. The scene, as I have said, was specially written for the new version of the play in 1787–8.

When Elmire herself thinks back on what she has lost in causing Erwin to leave her, she is a very different person from the one she was in the original. While there are evident similarities between the portrayal of the first and the second Elmire, the changes reflect certain differences in Goethe's experiences of Lili and of Charlotte von Stein; again they offer the author the opportunity to paint a picture of his suffering beloved in a way that he must have both regretted and relished at one and the same time:

(Version I – Elmire: Lili)

> ELMIRE (*allein*): Liebste, beste Mutter! Wieviel Eltern verkennen das Wohl ihrer Kinder und sind für ihre dringendsten Empfindungen taub; und diese Mutter vermöchte mir nicht zu helfen mit all dem wahren Anteil an meinem innersten Herzen. Wo bin ich? Was will ich? ... Armer Erwin! Sie wissen nicht, was ihn quälte, sie kannten sein Herz nicht! – Weh dir, Elende, die du ihn zur Verzweiflung brachtest! Wie rein, wie zärtlich war seine Liebe! War er nicht der Edelste von allen, die mich umgaben, und liebt ich ihn nicht vor allen? Und doch konnt ich ihn kränken, konnte ihm mit Kaltsinn, mit anscheinender Verachtung begegnen, bis sein Herz brach, bis er, in dem Überfall des heftigsten Schmerzens,

seine Mutter, seine Freunde und ach! vielleicht die Welt verließ –
Schrecklicher Gedanke! er wird mich ums Leben bringen.   (ibid. 13)

(Version II – Elmire: Charlotte)
VALERIO: Im Busen eines Freundes widerhallend
　　Verliert sich nach und nach des Schmerzens Ton.
ELMIRE: Ich lausche gern dem schmerzlichen Gesang,
　　Der wie ein Geisterlied das Ohr umschwebt.
ROSA: Die Freuden andrer locken nach und nach
　　Uns aus uns selbst zu neuen Freuden hin.
ELMIRE: Wenn andre sich ihr Glück verdienen, hab
　　Ich meine Schmerzen mir gar wohl verdient.
　　Nein, nein! Verlaßt mich, daß im stillen Hain
　　Mir die Gestalt begegne, die Gestalt
　　Des Jünglings, den ich mir so gern entgegen
　　Mit seiner stillen Miene kommen sah.
　　Er blickt mich traurig an, er naht sich nicht,
　　Er bleibt von fern an einem Seitenwege
　　Wie unentschlossen stehn. So kam er sonst,
　　Und drang sich nicht wie jeder andre mir
　　Mit ungestümem Wesen auf. Ich sah
　　Gar oft nach ihm, wenn ich nach einem andern
　　Zu sehen schien; er merkt' es nicht, er sollt
　　Es auch nicht merken. Scheltet mich, und scheltet
　　Mich nicht. Ein tief Gefühl der Jugendfreuden,
　　Der Jugendfreiheit, die wir nur zu bald
　　Verscherzen, um die lange, lange Wandrung
　　Auf gutes Glück, mit einem Unbekannten
　　Verbunden, anzutreten – dies Gefühl
　　Hielt mich zurück, zu sagen, wie ich liebte.
　　Und doch auch so! Ich hätte können zärter
　　Mit dieser guten Seele handeln. Nur
　　Zu nah liegt eine freche Kälte neben
　　Der heißesten Empfindung unsrer Brust.   (ibid. 39f.)

Observe how much more reflective and mature the new Elmire has become, aware of the transitoriness of youth's joys, and hesitant to risk the commitment that acknowledging the love she feels for Erwin would entail. All of this points to a hidden, but personally liberating, self-justification by Goethe of his secret flight from Weimar, as does another newly written passage for Version Two which makes the link with Frau von Stein even clearer, seen from the author's perspective of 1787–8 when the play was being completed in Italy for publication; here, after the singing of Erwin's song 'Das Veilchen' (already present in the original), in which a young girl unwittingly tramples down a little violet, symbol of an unknown lover, Elmire responds in these terms:

ELMIRE: Und dieses Mädchen, das auf seinem Wege
   Unwissend eine Blume niedertritt,
   Sie hat nicht schuld; ich aber, ich bin schuldig.
   Oft hab ich ihn, ich muß es doch gestehn,
   Oft hab ich ihn gereizt, sein Lied gelobt,
   Ihn wiederholen lassen, was er mir
   Ins Herz zu singen wünschte; dann wohl
   Ein andermal getan, als wenn ich ihn
   Nicht hörte. Mehr noch, mehr hab ich verbrochen.
VALERIO: Du klagst dich streng, geliebte Freundin, an.
ELMIRE: Weit strenger klagt mich an des Treuen Flucht.
ROSA: Die Liebe bringt ihn dir vielleicht zurück.
ELMIRE: Sie hat vielleicht ihn anderwärts entschuldigt.
   Ich bin nicht bös geboren; doch erst jetzt
   Erstaun ich, wie ich lieblos ihn gemartert.
   Man schonet einen Freund, ja man ist höflich
   Und sorgsam, keinen Fremden zu beleid'gen;
   Doch den Geliebten, der sich einzig mir
   Auf ewig gab, den schont ich nicht und konnte
   Mit schadenfrohen Kälte den betrüben.[39]

Valerio's attempts to comfort Elmire give rise to jealousy in Rosa, jealousy so strong that it drives Valerio away to join Erwin in leading

---

[39] BA 4:40f. Originally Elmire had sung the song and Bernardo had reassured her as follows: 'Das wäre denn nun wohl recht gut und schön, nur seh ich kein End in der Sache. Daß Sie, mein Fräulein, ein zärtliches, liebes Herz haben, das weiß ich lange. Daß Sie es unter dieser gleichgültigen, manchmal spottenden Außenseite verbergen können, das ist Ihr Glück; denn es hat Sie doch von manchem Windbeutel gerettet' (ibid. 17). In Version Two there is no such indulgent excuse for Elmire's behaviour.

the life of a hermit. This new sub-plot also has unmistakable echoes of certain unhappy experiences Goethe had had with Charlotte von Stein, as we see from what Valerio has to say to Elmire on the subject of his beloved:

VALERIO: Sie bleibt mir ewig wert; doch fürcht ich stets,
    Sie macht mich elend, denn die Eifersucht
    Nagt ihre Brust wie eine Krankheit, die
    Wir nicht vermögen auszutreiben, nicht
    Ihr zu entfliehen. Oft, wenn sie die Freuden,
    Die reinsten, mir vergällt, verzweifl' ich fast,
    Und der Entschluß, sie zu verlassen, steigt
    Wie ein Gespenst in meinem Busen auf. (BA 4:45)

Exactly this had been Goethe's experience repeatedly for many years after 1781, up to late 1785, when the *Oberstallmeister* was installed, for the first time since Goethe's arrival in Weimar, as the most important man in the von Stein household. In the play, when the three friends meet up again, Rosa accuses both Valerio and Elmire of betrayal, to which Valerio responds in terms reminiscent of Goethe's past reactions to Charlotte's jealousy:

VALERIO [to Rosa]:
    So ist es denn nicht möglich, daß du dich
    Bemeistern kannst? doch ach, was red ich viel!
    Wenn dieser falsche Ton in einem Herzen
    Nun einmal klingt und immer wieder klingt,
    Wo ist der Künstler, der es stimmen könnte?
    In diesem Augenblick verwundest du
    Mich viel zu tief, als daß es heilen sollte.
    Wie? Diese redliche Bemühung eines Freundes,
    Der Freundin beizustehen, die Erfüllung
    Der schönsten Pflicht, du wagst sie zu mißdeuten?
    Was ist mein Leben, wenn ich andern nicht
    Mehr nutzen soll? Und welches Wirken ist
    Wohl besser angewandt, als einem Geist,
    Der, leidenschaftlich sich bewegend, gern
    Sein eignes Haus zerstörte, zu besänft'gen?

> Nein! Nein! ich folge jenem Trieb, der mir
> Schon lang den Weg zur Flucht gezeigt, schon lange
> Mich deiner Tyrranei auf ewig zu
> Entziehen hieß. Leb wohl! Es ist geschehn!
> Zerschlagen ist die Urne, die so lang
> Der Liebe Freuden und der Liebe Schmerzen
> In ihrem Busen willig faßte; rasch
> Entstürzet das Gefühl sich der Verwahrung
> Und fließt, am Boden rieselnd und verbreitet,
> Zu deinen Füßen nun versiegend hin.   (ibid. 47)

What is most striking about Valerio's reproaches here is the level of deep resentment they reveal towards his beloved because of her jealousy and attempts at total control, a resentment matched in all of the works rewritten between 1787 and 1789 only by Tasso's furious outburst against the Princess after she has rejected his embrace, as we shall see. Through Valerio's reactions to Rosa's jealousy we are given a second valid reason for the sudden flight of a lover, and it seems quite probable that in writing these lines Goethe was again giving vent to his own past anguish and justifying his own past decision to leave – which is of greatest importance in any examination of how he wrote for the way in which it demonstrates his capacity to write himself into various roles in the one work. This is a feature of his writing that we will see again in other literary creations both major and minor, including *Werther*.

So much for what seems to have been Goethe's pain and self-justification as expressed in the play. What follows is the happy resolution of both. Rosa and Elmire pursue their anguished lovers in order to put everything to rights, but the happy end is not as immediate as in Version One; both men first exploit their sense of satisfaction at the remorse shown by their respective errant lovers, and again in the newly written scene between Valerio and Rosa there is a certain flavour of delightful self-vindication for the man, as well as the imminent prospect of putting everything to rights as he would like:

ROSA: Kannst du nicht besänftigt werden?
   Bleibst du still und einsam hier?
   Ach, was sagen die Gebärden,
   Ach, was sagt dein Schweigen mir?

Hast du dich mit ihm verbunden,[40]
Ist dir nicht ein Wort erlaubt;
Ach, so ist mein Glück verschwunden,
Ist auf ewig mir geraubt.
VALERIO: Du jammerst mich, und doch vermag ich nicht,
Betrübtes Kind, dir nun zu helfen. Nur
Zum Troste sag ich dies: Noch ist nicht alles,
Was du zu fürchten scheinst, getan; noch bleibt
Die Hoffnung mir und dir. Allein ich muß
In diesem Augenblick den Druck der Hand
Und jeden liebevollen Gruß versagen.
Entferne dich dorthin und setze dich
Auf jenen Felsen; bleibe still und nähre
Den festen Vorsatz, dich und den Geliebten
Nicht mehr zu quälen, dort, bis wir dich rufen.
ROSA: Ich folge deinen Winken, drücke nicht
Die Freude lebhaft aus, daß du mir wieder
Gegeben bist. Dein freundlich-ernstes Wort,
Dein Blick gebietet mir; ich geh und hoffe. (BA 4:57)

The happy end already provided for Erwin and Elmire in Version One is retained almost verbatim in Version Two, with the only changes being those necessitated by the substitution throughout the play of Valerio and Rosa for Bernardo and Olimpia. Thus seeming coldness and aloofness turn into evident loving fervour, love triumphs over jealousy, and both couples live happily ever after. What we are dealing with here is of course an ancient topos, while the introduction of the two extra voices is a direct result of Goethe's study of the *opera buffa*, but he had a special talent for recognizing in traditional forms and topoi the means for lending expression to his own experience. What the various changes to this play achieve in essence is to add weight to the sufferings of the male lovers who have been badly treated by the women they love and to vindicate their decision to flee from the world. It is up to the women who have wronged them to make amends, for the men themselves are blameless. The faults of the

---

40 The word 'ihm' here refers to Erwin, whom Rosa mistakes for the wise hermit she and Elmire have come to see in order to seek advice; the line thus means: 'If you too have taken up the life of a hermit ...'

two women are not rated equally, however. From the text it is clear that Rosa's jealousy, intolerable and destructive though it may be, is seen by Erwin as an excess of love, which only throws the coldness of Elmire into even greater relief.[41] Implicit in his reaction to Valerio's unhappy plight is the idea that the hell of jealousy is vastly preferable to the hell of cold indifference, which mirrors Goethe's own experiences as recorded progressively in his letters to Frau von Stein from 1784 to 1786.[42] And so the new version of *Erwin und Elmire* seems to have offered Goethe the chance to review his past, lament his suffering, justify his eventual reaction, and put everything to rights on paper. That the wounds of his own past were not far from his mind when he was rewriting the play in Italy can be seen from the following lines that he wrote at the time:

> Hier sitzt in ewig neuer Pein
> Erwin, bis ihm das Herze bricht;
> Denn ach, Elmire denkt nicht sein,
> Und ach, Bernardo hilft ihm nicht.   (WA 1,11:426)

Similar rewritten passages are to be found in *Claudine von Villa Bella*, on which Goethe was also working during the winter of 1787–8. Here too his more recent hopes and unhappy experiences in love seem to find their expression, taking the place of the old. Although we must always be careful about accepting his own later comments on anything he has written, what he has to say about the play in the *Italienische Reise* (3 November 1787) is fully borne out by the changes he actually made in Version Two: ' "Claudine" ist nun in der Arbeit,' he writes, 'wird sozusagen ganz neu ausgeführt und die alte Spreu meiner Existenz herausgeschwungen' (HA 11:432). In rewriting this play Goethe removed the figure of Don Sebastian, an older family friend, as he had

---

[41] Cf. BA 4:54; here Erwin says to Valerio, who has just told him that he was forced to flee from Rosa because of her jealousy: 'So verscheuchte dich / Ein allzu großes Glück von ihrer Seite.'

[42] While Goethe may have suffered because of Frau von Stein's possessiveness and jealousy (cf. P665, P666, P672, P701, P711), he came to rejoice in this as evidence of her love for him (cf. 'An Lida' [P728]). However, from September 1785, after Josias von Stein had been restored to his own evening table, Goethe became increasingly hurt and disappointed at Charlotte's growing inattentiveness towards him; see, for example, P1440, P1442, P1444, P1446, P1449, P1473, P1503, P1528–30, P1539, P1546.

removed Bernardo from *Erwin*; the central female character is again made more mature, more self-possessed than in the original, and needs no older counsellor. Just as Rosa had been newly introduced into *Erwin* as an embodiment of the incautious, unreflective, and uncalculating woman in love, despite her jealousy, so Lucinde is introduced into *Claudine*, replacing two other cousins, Camilla and Sibylla. Whereas Claudine is given to concealing her love for Pedro, Lucinde, the model of a woman whose love knows no bounds or restraint, is only too eager to reveal her love for his brother, Rugantino. In Version Two the original love triangle involving Claudine and the two brothers is altered to present instead two pairs of lovers; and again, as in the revised *Erwin* as well as the original *Jery und Bätely* of 1779, the two leading men of the reworked *Claudine* represent two very different kinds of lover – one sensitive, vulnerable, discreet, and struggling with the lack of open response from his beloved (Pedro), the other more demanding, boisterous, and daring (Rugantino). Through the new character, Lucinde, we learn more of Claudine's reticent behaviour towards the man she loves, through her too, more of a woman's spontaneous joy in loving and of the will to risk danger for the sake of her love. This acts as encouragement and support for Claudine, helping her to gain the resolve to pursue her absent lover. Again, as in the new *Erwin*, it is the women who now actively bring about the happy end, putting themselves at some risk both physically and emotionally in order to do so – a projected male version of Utopia, as it were.

As with many of Goethe's rewritten poems, the second version of this play is generally considered less good than the first, having lost its old liveliness and force,[43] and even Goethe's own first production of 1795 was unenthusiastically received, which disappointed him greatly.[44] But perhaps his critics were not altogether wrong in their

---

43 For example: 'Dabei [in the reworking] verlor die zweite Fassung den hinreißenden Schwung, den der Stürmer und Dränger Goethe dem Werk verliehen hatte.' While acknowledging the time and effort invested in the formal, operatic aspects of the work and in its suitability for setting to music, the commentator goes on to say, 'Crugantino, jetzt Rugantino genannt, hat das Echte, Lebensvolle verloren'; see BA 4:670. Erich Trunz shares the view that the original was superior to the reworked version – HA 4:543; similarly Staiger (2:43), who also finds the original *Erwin* better than the final version of 1788.
44 BA 4:674f.

negative reactions, for the changes here, as in so many places elsewhere, appear to have had more to do with the author's need to create and re-create himself on paper, updating the record of his inner life through what he wrote, more to do with his need to engage in self-clarification and the creation of inner harmony through projected wish-fulfilment, than with any primary urge to improve an existing work from an artistic point of view. Evidently his ability to function as an artist was on occasion impeded by his need to satisfy more personal demands at the same time. This casts an interesting light on how he wrote and why that has important ramifications for any critical response to his reworked material.

A close comparative reading of the two versions of *Claudine* points to an updating of the work along the lines dictated by Goethe's experiences with Charlotte von Stein, the difficulties of his recent past, and his remaining hope for a happy outcome in the future. Let me offer just one example in which the major ideas correspond to his own emotional circumstances past and present at the time of rewriting, though cloaked in details that do not correspond exactly with reality. In the following passage Pedro is explaining to Claudine that he must leave her to resume the search for his roguish, disinherited brother, Rugantino, to whom he nobly wishes to restore half of their father's estate:

PEDRO: ...
  Mein Herz bleibt hier; und wenn ich eilen muß,
  So eil ich gern, um schnell zurückzukehren.
  Ich sage dir kein Lebewohl; kein Ach
  Sollst du vernehmen: denn du siehst mich bald
  Und würdiger vor dir. Und was ich bin,
  Was ich erlange, das ist dein. Geliebte,
  Ich dränge mich zur Gnade nicht für mich!
  Nimm deinem Freunde nicht den sichern Mut,
  Sich deiner wert zu machen. Der verdient
  Die Liebe nur, der um der Ehre willen
  Im süßen Augenblicke von der Liebe
  Entschlossen-hoffend sich entfernen kann.
  ... (*Ab.*)
CLAUDINE: Er flieht! Doch ist das nicht das letzte Wort;

> Ich weiß, er wird vor Abend nicht verreisen.
> O werter Mann! Es bleiben mir die Freunde,
> Das teure Paar, zu meinem Trost zurück,
> Die holde Liebe mit der seltnen Treue.
> Sie sollen mich erhalten, wenn du gehst,
> Und mich von dir beständig unterhalten.
>> Liebe schwärmt auf allen Wegen;
>> Treue wohnt für sich allein.
>> Liebe kommt euch rasch entgegen;
>> Aufgesucht will Treue sein.   (BA 4:132f.)

Not only is there again a seeming justification of Goethe's own decision to flee from Weimar in Pedro's words, but the speech also reflects what he himself maintained in his letters from Italy to Frau von Stein, namely, that his greatest wish in the time they were apart was to become increasingly worthy of her and more the person she wanted him to be.[45] In addition, the link that he made in his mind between the play and his own emotional life is revealed by the fact that he sent her the last four lines from the excerpt above in a letter of late 1787 when he was working on it.[46] Given his ongoing habit of writing specially for her, their close literary collaboration of more than a decade, and their mutual delight in literary game-playing, this is clearly yet more evidence of how inextricably linked Goethe's literary creativity and his emotional life remained in 1788.

Nowhere is the closeness of this link better exemplified than in the history of his failed attempts to complete *Tasso* while he was in Italy. We have already looked at several of his comments on the drama from mid-1781 when he was excited by the progress he was making on it, and we have seen the importance for him of investing what he was writing with the emotions he felt for Frau von Stein, an importance so great that he was altogether unsure that what he had written was in the right place or even made for a good scene in the play.[47] Of only

---

45 Cf., for example, (1786) P1611 (7 November), P1616 (2 December); (1787) P1623 (6 January), P1627 (20 January), P1635 (18 April), P1636 (25 May), P1637 (8 June).
46 Frau von Stein in turn sent the poem to Charlotte von Lengefeld (28 December 1787) as a salve to her wounded pride; the whole court and everyone associated with it knew she had been deserted by Goethe; see Petersen 1,2:546.
47 See above, p. 48.

one thing was he certain at that point, namely, that his writing was a successful expression of his deep love and devotion to her. By the time he came to tackle the completion of the work, however, a great deal had changed in his emotional life, and progress was no longer easy – indeed, it became more and more difficult as the months, then years, went by. In early 1787, when he completed the transformation of *Iphigenie* into verse, he foresaw no major difficulties with *Tasso* (P1627), but a year later this was no longer the case. He had lost that inner relationship to what he had written that was so vital to him in all that he produced. As he wrote jokingly, though not without a clear barb, to Charlotte von Stein on 10 January 1788, having just completed *Erwin und Elmire*: 'Wenn es mit der Fertigung meiner Schriften unter gleichen Konstellationen fortgeht, so muß ich mich im Laufe dieses Jahres in eine Prinzessin verlieben, um den "Tasso," ich muß mich dem Teufel ergeben, um den "Faust" schreiben zu können, ob ich mir gleich zu beiden wenig Lust fühle.'[48] He found no princess, however, and finishing the play became increasingly problematic for him,[49] being only finally completed a year and a half later, after the break with Charlotte had been sealed for all time.

Ever since its first publication in 1790 *Tasso* has been regarded as

---

48 HA 11:476 and note, 668. Of this part of the *Italienische Reise* ('Zweiter römischer Aufenthalt'), not reworked and published until 1829, Goethe said to Eckermann: 'Meine gedruckte "Italienische Reise" habe ich, wie Sie wissen, ganz aus Briefen redigiert. Die Briefe aber, die ich während meines zweiten Aufenthaltes in Rom geschrieben, sind nicht der Art, um davon vorzüglichen Gebrauch machen zu können; sie enthalten zu viele Bezüge nach Haus, auf meine weimarischen Verhältnisse, und zeigen zu wenig von meinem italienischen Leben. *Aber es finden sich darin manche Äußerungen, die meinen damaligen* INNEREN *Zustand ausdrücken*. Nun habe ich den Plan, solche Stellen auszuziehen und einzeln übereinanderzusetzen und sie so meiner Erzählung einzuschalten, auf welche dadurch eine Art von Ton und Stimmung übergehen wird' (Eckermann 310, emphasis mine, apart from the word 'inneren' which is emphasized in the original). This passage is interesting for the light it sheds on the weight he lends to revelations of his own inner state as the leaven of what he is writing.

49 Cf. 1 February 1788: ' "Tasso" muß umgearbeitet werden, was da steht, ist zu nichts zu brauchen, ich kann weder so endigen noch alles wegwerfen. Solche Mühe hat Gott den Menschen gegeben!' (HA 11:516); 28 March 1788 to Karl August: 'Ich wünsche, das angefangene Stück, wo nicht zu endigen, doch weit zu führen, eh ich zurückkomme. Hätte ich es nicht angefangen, so würde ich es jetzt nicht wählen ...' (Gräf 2,4:no.4174); see also October 1788 to Knebel (ibid.:no.4182, 4186); December 1788 to Herder (ibid.:no.4190); February 1789 to Karl August (ibid.:no.4197); June 1789 to Frau von Stein (P1653).

a problem play, and not without justification. As an anonymous critic asked in a perceptive review of the new drama when it first appeared:

> ... wie kann eine Handlung geendigt heißen, bey welcher uns noch so viel zu fragen übrig bleibt? Ist Tasso nun von seiner Liebe geheilt, oder ist er auf ewig ein unglückliches Opfer seiner Leidenschaft? ... Werden die Gesinnungen, die er in der letzten Scene äußert, unveränderlich in seinem Herzen bleiben? Wird sein Mißtraun auf ewig erlöschen oder auf ewig entzündet seyn? In welches Verhältniß wird er dann mit der Prinzeßinn treten? Welche Folgen wird Alphonsens Erscheinung bey der Umarmung haben? – Alles dieß sind Fragen, die man zu thun gezwungen ist, nachdem der Vorhang gefallen war, und deren keine sich aus dem Stück selbst auflöst. Alles dieß sind Zweifel, die der Dichter zu heben vergessen hat.[50]

For this particular critic even some of the best scenes early in the play were held together by nothing at all, 'höchstens durch eine Leidenschaft, die weder Anfang, Mitte noch Ende hat';[51] to his mind this drama was, in sum, 'ein mißrathenes Werk eines großen Genies.'[52] And present-day scholarship has not brought the answers to many of his very justifiable questions either. The fact is, the problematic nature of the final text seems to spring directly from its problematic genesis, which in turn has to do with the whole process of Goethe's literary production that we need to take into account in evaluating every work that he rewrote.

'[Goethe] kann nicht anders als sich selbst idealisieren und immer aus sich schreiben, so daß er sich zugleich selbst malet,' wrote Herder from Italy on the subject of *Tasso* on 14 March 1789; 'für mich ist das gut. Aber ich fürchte, wie das durch die fünf Akte gehn werde. Immer aber wird's ein geistvolles, interessantes Stück werden.'[53] In a letter to her husband about a week later Karoline Herder wrote that Goethe had confided to her the real meaning of the play as 'die Disproportion des Talents mit dem Leben,' and then went on to say the following:

---

50 *Neue Bibliothek der schönen Wissenschaften und der freyen Künste*; see Braun 2:90.
51 Ibid. 88
52 Ibid. 89
53 *Vertrauliche Briefe* 1:393

'Die gute Kalbin [Charlotte von Kalb] ... nimmt Goethens "Tasso" gar zu speziell auf Goethe, die Herzogin, den Herzog und die Steinin; ich habe sie aber ein wenig darüber berichtigt. Das will ja auch Goethe durchaus nicht so gedeutet haben.'[54] From what we have already seen of the extraordinarily close link between the life Goethe lived and what and how he wrote at this time, it seems entirely likely that Charlotte von Kalb was not far off the mark when she read the play as the poet's personal expression of his own experiences, yet his corrective interpretative comment has the air of a broad generalization designed to preserve that personal statement from penetration by others. Here, as elsewhere, we have an important insight into how the poet dealt with his own works once they were written: having invested a great deal of his own inner self in the writing and having thereby divested himself (in coded form that only he, Goethe, fully understood at all times) of matters that were currently preoccupying him, he did not want outsiders to penetrate his code, for this would be paramount to allowing them access to his innermost thoughts and feelings, which he increasingly learned to protect throughout his life, and which were in any case no longer exactly what they had been earlier once he had put them down in literary form, for the very act of writing often clarified and transformed these feelings for him into something else. Hence he could speak without dissimulation, for example, of the 'kind of general confession' that writing the first *Werther* represented for him, enabling him to feel he had earned the right to a new life (HA 9:283). I mean to show presently that the same could be said about Version Two, and that the seemingly specific statement in *Dichtung und Wahrheit* was more true of Goethe's state of mind in 1786 than in 1772, the period to which it ostensibly pertains. Whoever could not decode the secrets he had embedded in his work was not to be given any explanation other than that offered by the work itself; whoever came too close for his liking had to be persuaded that he or she was on the wrong track altogether, for, in the words of Tasso: 'Frei will ich sein im Denken und im Dichten; / Im Handeln schränkt die Welt genug uns ein' (HA 5:135).

In a remarkably sound book written a century ago, Kuno Fischer deals in detail with Goethe's writing of this play from first to last, attribut-

---

54 Ibid. 393f.

ing his difficulties with its completion in part to the fact that he had gained too great an inner distance from what he had originally written, and pointing out the dubious nature of the account Goethe himself gave of the rewriting in the *Italienische Reise*.[55] Fischer devotes considerable space to Goethe's chief sources for the drama (Manso, Seraffi) and reflects on how difficult it was bound to be to incorporate both of these sources successfully into a well-rounded whole. Antonio is not present in Manso's version of Tasso's life, and Fischer demonstrates from Goethe's finished text how confused the presentation is of Tasso's association with Antonio, whom the critic believes to have been introduced into the play only after Goethe went to Italy, after his reading of Seraffi. But Goethe never made use of any sources unless they had a particular appeal or acted as a catalyst for what he himself wanted to write, so if he did seize on particular sources here as elsewhere, it was again primarily because he saw in them something that suited his own current aims and needs. In attributing Goethe's difficulties with the play, therefore, to the incompatibility of various sources he chose to use, I think Fischer is wrongly evaluating his creative process. Despite this, however, the critic has still a great deal to offer in terms of a clear-sighted analysis of character that highlights many of the difficulties present in the final version of the drama, difficulties that continue to validate the questions raised in 1790 by the contemporary critic I have already cited. Fischer points, for example, to the culpable passivity of the Princess once the crisis has occurred with Antonio, and again when Tasso oversteps the boundaries of propriety in embracing her. He points also to the imperfect integration of the character of Leonore Sanvitale (Goethe's own invention) into the play, despite all her dramatic usefulness, and to many inconsistencies in the relationships between Tasso and Antonio, Antonio and Leonore. In addition he notes a certain similarity between the conciliatory ending of the drama, where Tasso is led back from the brink of madness, and the whole mood and message of *Iphigenie*.

It seems clear, if one reflects on the other works that Goethe substantially rewrote, that as the author underwent significant inner changes himself, so too did what he was writing. Those changes found their way into his works, and it was fundamental to how he wrote

---

55 Kuno Fischer, *Goethes 'Tasso,'* 1890, 29ff.

that they should – hence his comments on the need to relive old experiences in order to rewrite, his comments on rereading earlier works as an act of self-discovery, and his comments on the need to capture the substance of his own inner self through writing. Unfortunately no copy of the original *Tasso* has come down to us that would enable exact comparisons to be made with the final version. However, too much of the play as it exists in its final form reflects aspects of Goethe's changed attitudes of 1789 to the life he had led in Weimar up to 1786 and then on his return in 1788 for us to ignore them altogether – e.g., devotion to a high-minded 'princess' whose love, though real, is both passively expressed and subordinated to court propriety, a woman who encourages his verbal expressions of devotion to the point where he feels able to express that devotion also in physical terms, only to be rebuffed in no uncertain way; the glorification in court circles of restraint and cleverness over feeling; society's judgment of overt emotionalism and passion as akin to a criminal act – all of these were experiences or emotions Goethe himself had during the *Tasso* years (1780–9), when his inner life traversed an increasingly melancholy terrain that stretched from a rising pinnacle of joy (1780–1) to wind up finally in a chasm of bitterness, anger, hurt, and despair (1788–9). This movement from joy to despair appears to be reflected both in the difficulties he had with completing the play and in the final version itself, whose glorious language alone is not sufficient to bind together the conflicting information and emotions contained within it in any truly satisfactory way. If in its beginnings the play was an expression of Goethe's feelings for Frau von Stein, in its final form it was no less an expression of those feelings. The chief obstacle to completion arose from the irreconcilable gap that had opened up for the poet between the reality he was forced to experience and acknowledge and the ideal to which he had devoted his life for over a decade. Where the real and the ideal had once been one, they had been irrevocably and irremediably forced apart by 1789.

Not so in the case of *Iphigenie*, which was given its final form at the beginning of 1787. While this play was quite swiftly completed, *Tasso* was not, and I think the reason for this difference had a great deal more to do with Goethe's own inner state at the time he was working on the two dramas than with the sources on which he drew for each. Although shocked and hurt by Frau von Stein's little acts of vengefulness by early 1787, he continued to believe that they would be able to find a secure and lasting foundation for their life together on his return from Italy, in terms of the very kind of relationship she herself had repeatedly sought to extol. In *Iphigenie* he had celebrated his earlier achievement of a greater emotional equilibrium through her; this remained a fact of part of his past life and helped form his ongoing hope for the future at the point of the play's completion, even though truly serene phases had been little more than significant punctuation marks in the tormented prose poem of his first decade in Weimar. However, as time went on and he began to realize that Charlotte was far from being the ideal woman he had once believed her to be, his future hopes seemed less and less well-founded, particularly as the life he was leading in Italy offered him the opportunity to experience a sense of freedom and expansion that life in Weimar had denied him on all fronts. On his return he was forced to realize that there was to be no lasting cure for the real-life Orest at the hands of a courageous and exemplary 'sister' and high priestess of truth whose loving ministrations would continue to secure his precarious equilibrium and restore him for ever to a joyful tranquillity of mind and heart.

But this was not how he felt when he wrote the final version of *Iphigenie*, as I have said. He deemed the play ready for publication in the days immediately prior to his leaving Karlsbad in 1786, and became dissatisfied with its form only after reading Sophocles' *Electra*.[56] The play, like *Tasso*, had begun as an expression of his love and devotion towards Charlotte von Stein, and nothing had yet happened to make him see her in a totally different light, which meant that he could devote himself wholly to the task of perfecting the drama as a work of art. It was possible to give his full attention to polishing and rendering it into verse, as no change in content was necessary; here there was no division between Goethe, the man, and Goethe, the artist. And the other two works that he took with him to Italy that were altered very little for publication were similar, even though they were not completed until after his return to Weimar: *Lila* was published with little change in the sixth volume of Göschen's edition along with *Tasso*; *Jery und Bätely* was also published with little change in the

---

56 See letter to Herder, 1 September 1786, HA *Briefe* 2:8.

volume that followed.⁵⁷ What seems to have made the difference between Goethe's need to rewrite his material substantially or not was the degree of ongoing truth of any given work, as he saw (or, rather, felt) it, in terms of his own emotional situation at the time of final preparation or revision. Where the mood or message of the original no longer corresponded to what he believed or what he felt, it had to be substantially reworked; where it did correspond, no major reworking was necessary, at least not in terms of content.

While the rewritten *Werther* and the rewritten *Tasso* are very different works, they belong together in a particularly significant phase in Goethe's life, the one firmly rooted in a lengthy period of emotional confinement and total subjectivity in whose service he placed his literary talent, the other in a relatively brief period of freedom from which he would eventually develop a rather more complex attitude towards the task of literary creation, a more objective awareness of all forms of art and of the service he owed to literature for its own sake. But the dividing line between the two modes of writing is not as clear or as decisive as we might perhaps like to believe. When Goethe rewrote *Werther* in 1786 he was a tormented lover whose beloved, as the wife of another man, was inaccessible to him; this was the source of his greatest anguish, augmented by Charlotte's constant insistence on visible propriety – 'was sich ziemt.' Once he had left, she behaved in a variety of ways that were far from loving, and in this period he set about trying to rewrite *Tasso*, but without success. On his return to Weimar she behaved abominably to him, and so the difficulty in completing his drama was compounded. Once again he was back in a Werther-like framework, but this time he was determined that the old suffering on his part would not be renewed. With the advent of Christiane into his life in July 1788 there was no longer any real prospect of reconciling the old and the new. In June 1789 he exploded for

---

57 BA 4:681, 689. For more on the three versions of *Lila* see Gottfried Diener, *Goethes 'Lila,'* 1971. Goethe added the exchanges between Friedrich and Mariane/Almaide quoted on pp. 76f., introducing the past love relationship between himself and Frau von Stein in such a way as to portray himself as the ardent lover (Friedrich) who is willing to risk much for the sake of his love, and Charlotte (Almaide) as a woman for whom appearances must be preserved at all costs. This addition, however, represented no real change in the overall content of the play as a whole.

the first time with directness and great anger at Charlotte von Stein's daring to prescribe his life for him when she herself was no longer willing to show any evidence of fondness, let alone love, and the following month he completed the play that he had begun under such very different circumstances.

Tasso as 'ein gesteigerter *Werther*': this was Ampère's judgment on the drama, and one that Goethe eagerly endorsed.[58] The more closely one looks at the two works, the more clearly one sees correspondences between them that validate this judgment, but more so in terms of the second *Werther* than the first. Not only is Tasso an intensification of the second Werther, but the Princess is an intensified second Lotte and Antonio an intensified second Albert as well. Only a close examination of the changes Goethe made to his novel can furnish the grounds for such an assertion, however, and it is to these changes that I now want to turn my attention. As I said in my opening remarks, it seems that we may well have been rendered blind to the alterations to Version Two by the enormous impact made on readers everywhere by Version One. This impact, bolstered by various comments made by Goethe on *Tasso* and by our belief in the author's steady, harmonious development in the first Weimar period, seems also to have led us to overlook certain surprising similarities between the final *Werther* and the final *Tasso*. With the first of these two works Goethe arrived into Charlotte von Stein's life; with the second he departed from it for ever and began gradually to embark on a rather different course as a writer.

---

58 Eckermann 539 (3 May 1827)

3

The Changes in *Werther*

The many formal and stylistic changes Goethe made in the rewriting of *Werther* offer us little in the way of real insight into his development as a writer or into his mode of composition, for they are internally consistent and point in only one direction, namely, towards the poet's willingness for his work to be republished in what he had come to regard as standard German. By 1786, when these particular changes were made, he was twelve years older than he had been at the time of first composition, and eleven of those years had been spent in a small, homogeneous society where he had become gradually accustomed to hearing and expressing himself in a more standardized form of language, as his extensive correspondence up to 1786 progressively illustrates.[1] As time went on he came more and more to appreciate the inherent value and beauty of controlled expression and to see the positive advantages it could offer for his work – hence his dissatsifaction with the prose version of *Iphigenie*, for example, and his need to take it with him to Italy for transformation into verse. In contrast to Dieter Welz, who sees the formal and stylistic changes Goethe made to *Werther* as striking and significant evidence of his eagerness to comply with the overall ideology of the ruling class in Weimar and as evidence of his inner distance from the sufferings of Werther by the time of rewriting, I myself attach no particular significance to them,

---

1 That Goethe had unconsciously adopted a more even and stylistically elevated form of language is also clear from Herder's letter to him of July 1786, where he criticizes the speech of the characters in the rewritten *Götz* (particularly Weislingen) with the comment: 'einige zu feine Ausdrücke im Staatsstyl'; see Herder 8:182.

partly because of the poet's own gradual change in the way he used language, and partly because the details of how these changes in style and form came to be made to *Werther* tend to suggest a great measure of indifference to them on Goethe's part and thereby to underscore their relative lack of interest for the critical reader.[2]

The changes in substance are a different matter, of course, and must be very closely examined, for only such an examination can help us to appreciate the newly confessional nature of the second *Werther* and offer us a sound basis for reconsidering many of our assertions and assumptions about this work to date. These changes fall into two broad categories of new composition: (i) small additions/alterations (one or more sentences, or completely new notes inserted into the existing text), and (ii) large additions/alterations (the farmboy's story and substantially new passages in the Editor's Report), but I do not mean to deal with them either in terms of small and large or simply in accordance with the order in which they occur in the text.[3] Their chief significance, it seems to me, lies in the overall change in impression they give of the existing principal characters of Version One, and this overall change can best be appreciated by looking at each of the main characters in the context of the narrative as a whole. Often quite minor changes in terms of word-count have a major impact as far as altering the reader's impression of a given character is concerned, and for this reason it seems to me unwise to adhere to any system of scrutiny based primarily on the volume of words added or altered. However, having said that, I propose nevertheless to save my examination of the farmboy's story and of the altered narrative stance in the last part of the novel until somewhat later, and to begin by looking at

2 Welz himself unwittingly undermines the case he is making for the importance of the formal and stylistic changes to *Werther* by telling us that Goethe accepted without hesitation all the changes in accordance with Adelung's manual of style which had slipped into the novel through successive unauthorized printings (*Der Weimarer Werther* 14). What Goethe wrote to Göschen when he sent him the completed second version of *Werther* (2 September 1786) is relevant here, as it too underlines the disinterest he showed in attending to the formal changes himself. He left it to Göschen to see to it that Adelung was consistently adhered to throughout the new manuscript with regard to spelling and punctuation (WA 4,8:388).

3 A list of these substantive changes as they are to be found in sequence in the text is given in the Appendix. For details of changes in style see Martin Lauterbach, *Das Verhältnis der zweiten zur ersten Ausgabe von Werthers Leiden*, 1910, 4–85.

the three main players in the love triangle in ascending order of importance. My reasons for dealing with the changes in this way will become clear in due course as we look at the second version of the novel from the new perspective dictated by what we now know about the author's love of secrets, his process of writing/rewriting, and his emotional life prior to the final reworking of *Werther* in 1786. There appear to be quite a number of textual difficulties in the new version that have not yet been given sufficient critical attention, as we shall see.

Albert

Although Goethe wrote certain new passages that affected the portrait he gives us of Albert in Version Two, the deletions he made in the original portrait are by and large even more significant. Gone are the manifestations of petty jealousy and vindictive reflection, gone too are the traces of waning attentiveness towards Lotte in favour of matters of business on Albert's part.[4] We know that J.C. Kestner saw himself as the original Albert figure and objected strongly to the unfair portrayal of his character and personality in the novel, without realizing that Albert was in fact a composite picture of another husband and himself.[5] By specifically writing to Kestner of his intention to make Werther's unjust attitude to Albert rather clearer, Goethe seemed to acknowledge the rightness of Kestner's belief that he was indeed the sole model for Albert, but it was only a seeming acknowledgment, a seeming apology for a past injustice, and a seeming promise to make amends, for what he actually did in the rewriting was simply to obliterate the traces of any specific individual, making Albert now little more than a type. The primary interest of this character lies more clearly in Version Two in his representative function as the one insuperable obstacle for Werther by virtue of his very *being*, not as a man but as a husband. Albert is a less individual figure in the second

---

4 Cf. *Werther* 116–17L, 151L; see note 23, chapter 1.
5 The other husband was Peter Anton Brentano, who married Maximiliane LaRoche in January 1774. Many of the less generous qualities and characteristics written into the figure of Albert came from Goethe's experiences with Brentano rather than Kestner; cf. BA 9:626 and Hans-Heinrich Reuter 89.

version of the novel than in the first, his 'improved' behaviour merely a better foil for the changed portrayal of Lotte, as we shall see. Although Goethe did carry out his express intention to highlight Werther's inability to see his rival in a fair light, while ensuring that the reader saw him more objectively than before, the changes he made in what he added to the portrayal of Albert do not result in a new picture that necessarily evokes any great admiration in his readers. A certain type of reader, of course, would be likely to find the new Albert more acceptable, and Kestner belonged to that certain type.

It is important to note that the first addition to our information on Albert comes very late in the novel and from a prejudiced source, namely, Albert's friends, who are mentioned twice in the introductory paragraph of the Editor's Report – not villagers, not neighbours, not Lotte's friends, but Albert's. Interesting too is the fact that the inner distance from these friends adopted by the Editor, of whom I shall have more to say later, is made evident by the way in which he chooses to express himself. Werther, we are told, became an increasingly melancholy companion and increasingly unfair in his judgment of Albert. The new passage continues:

> *Wenigstens sagen dieß Alberts Freunde*; sie *behaupten*, daß Werther einen reinen, ruhigen Mann der nun eines langgewünschten Glückes theilhaftig geworden und sein Betragen sich dieses Glück auf die Zukunft zu erhalten, nicht habe beurtheilen können ... Albert, *sagen sie*, hatte sich in so kurzer Zeit nicht verändert, er war noch immer derselbige, den Werther so vom Anfang her kannte, so sehr schätzte und ehrte. Er liebte Lotten über alles, er war stolz auf sie und wünschte sie auch von jedermann als das herrlichste Geschöpf anerkannt zu wissen. *War es ihm daher zu verdenken, wenn er auch jeden Schein des Verdachtes abzuwenden wünschte*, wenn er in dem Augenblicke mit niemandem diesen köstlichen Besitz auch auf die unschuldigste Weise zu theilen, Lust hatte? *Sie gestehen ein*, daß Albert oft das Zimmer seiner Frau verlassen, wenn Werther bey ihr war, aber nicht aus Haß noch Abneigung gegen seinen Freund, sondern *nur weil er gefühlt habe, daß dieser von seiner Gegenwart gedrückt sey*.
> (117R, emphasis mine)

The italicized words and phrases in this passage all show either the deliberate distance the Editor places between himself and what these friends have maintained about Albert's motivation and behaviour (first three italics), or they clearly display a defensive, explanatory stance regarding his actions (last three italics). What is particularly interesting here is the way in which Albert's friends interpret his behaviour in avoiding Werther as evidence of his sensitivity and generosity of spirit towards the latter, for this interpretation is not borne out by the subsequent picture we are given of Albert's actions (more especially, his reactions) in new passages written for the second version of the work. All of these merely show Albert as a man who is solidly part of the bourgeois community in which he lives, a man who shares its values, and respects, even defers to, its judgment in matters pertaining to himself and, by extension, to his wife Lotte.

Reasonably enough, it seems, he supports the Amtmann in the view that justice must take its course in dealing with the farmboy (121R), but his private reaction to Werther's outburst of support for the supposed murderer[6] is not fear for his friend; rather, it is fear for himself – fear that Lotte and he may become the target of gossip if they continue to associate so frequently with Werther. The timing of his request to her to ensure that the latter comes to visit less often is important, as is the manner in which he expresses that request. We 'know' from Albert's friends that he is deeply in love with his wife ('Er liebte Lotten über alles,' 117R), and yet there is no evidence of this at a crucial juncture where both Lotte and the reader are led to expect some expression of his love. The relevant passage begins by telling us that on their way home from the house of Lotte's father she keeps looking around her 'als wenn sie Werthers Begleitung vermißte' (122R). Her behaviour is the spur for Albert to grasp the nettle which is the awkward and difficult subject of Werther, newly on his mind because of the outrageous defence of a murderer that he has just heard. This new passage goes on:

> Albert fing von ihm an zu reden, er tadelte ihn, indem er ihm Gerechtigkeit widerfahren ließ. Er berührte seine unglückliche Leidenschaft und wünschte, daß es möglich seyn möchte ihn zu entfernen. (122R)

Now comes the point at which he seems to be going to speak of his feelings for Lotte, perhaps of his longing to spend more time alone with her without having to share her with Werther:

---

6 The phrase 'supposed murderer' is deliberate; the reasons for my choice are made clear on pp. 195–201.

> Ich wünsch' es auch um unsertwillen, sagt'er ...

but as he continues it becomes clear that the overriding reason for his wish to have Werther visit his house less frequently stems only from a fear of what the neighbours will say:

> ... und ich bitte dich, fuhr er fort, siehe zu, seinem Betragen gegen dich eine andere Richtung zu geben, seine öftern Besuche zu vermindern. Die Leute werden aufmerksam, und ich weiß, daß man hier und da drüber gesprochen hat. (122R)

Lotte responds with no evidence of concern on her own part for what others will say or think, but with total silence, to which Albert in turn reacts by falling silent, and from that time forward the subject of Werther is taboo as far as he is concerned: '... seit der Zeit erwähnte er Werthers nicht mehr gegen sie und wenn sie seiner erwähnte, ließ er das Gespräch fallen oder lenkte es wo anders hin' (122R). Here we have the beginning of a failure to communicate newly introduced by Goethe, a failure of trust that establishes itself between Lotte and Albert and leads to a far greater failure, i.e., the failure to help Werther when he needs it most.

The silence that grows up between husband and wife around the subject of Werther is expressly singled out as a possible contributing factor in his death. This silence is characterized as anxious and awkward, even guilty, on Lotte's part, while on Albert's it has more the quality of an avoidance strategy.[7] But however it may be explained, the fact remains that the second version of the novel explicitly suggests that the breakdown in communication between Lotte and Albert may have had a role to play in Werther's fate. The new passage begins as follows:

> Wie schwer lag jetzt, was sie [Lotte] sich in dem Augenblick nicht deutlich machen konnte, die Stockung auf ihr, die sich unter ihnen festgesetzt hatte! So verständige so gute Menschen, fingen wegen gewisser heimlicher Verschiedenheiten unter einander zu schweigen an, jedes dachte seinem Recht und dem Unrechte des andern nach, und die Verhältnisse verwickelten und verhetzten sich dergestalt, daß es unmöglich ward den Knoten eben in dem kritischen Momente, von dem alles abhing, zu lösen. (150R)

---

7 Cf. *Werther* 122R, 149–51R.

The first sentence is written as if reported to the Editor by Lotte, but from the second sentence on the perspective seems to change to become his own: the very formulation 'so verständige so gute Menschen' betrays a distance and a collected clarity that the Lotte of the preceding sentence expressly does not possess, for example. How has the Editor come by this information? Is the view expressed here perhaps the reported joint view of a later Lotte and Albert, newly united in self-reproach and sorrow at their friend's suicide as they had not been for a long time before his death? It is difficult to answer this question with any certainty from within the early part of the given text, and it becomes more difficult as we read on: '... jedes dachte seinem Recht und dem Unrechte des andern nach, und die Verhältnisse verwickelten und verhetzten sich dergestalt, daß es unmöglich ward den Knoten eben in dem kritischen Momente, von dem alles abhing, zu lösen' (150R). What this suggests about Lotte and Albert is that each of them was resentful of the other, refusing to relinquish a sense of self-righteousness in order to break down the barriers of pride and coolness in their dealings with each other where Werther was concerned. The reader can of course understand and sympathize with such feelings, but does this cast a better light on the character of Albert? And what does it suggest about Lotte's sweet innocence and gentleness? This question has not yet been explored. And if we go back for a moment to part of the second sentence ('So verständige so gute Menschen *fingen wegen gewisser heimlicher Verschiedenheiten unter einander zu schweigen an ...*') there is a further difficulty: what can these 'certain secret differences' have been? The very formulation suggests that individually they were of no major significance, but taken together they have created an atmosphere between husband and wife which has rapidly worsened to the point of no return – the knot that cannot be unloosed. Yet each piece of suppressed information on Lotte's part up to this point has been vitally important: her real feelings for Werther (134L/Rff.), their passionate embrace (144–5L/R), her growing awareness that his talk of suicide is deadly earnest. Clearly, Lotte's silence is of a different calibre from Albert's, for what can his 'secret differences' have been? We know of his consistent coldness at evidence that his wish for a new distance between Lotte and Werther has not been fully met; we know too of his uncharacteristically forceful reaction to Werther's talk of suicide (150R). He seems to make and to have made no secret to his wife of how he feels about Werther's relationship with her, so his share of responsibility for the growing silence between Lotte and himself on this subject is not at all clear, particularly as the evidence of his jealousy has been removed in Version Two in favour of a newly heightened sense of social propriety on his part.

It seems to me that the most satisfactory explanation for this rather problematic passage may be the one offered by Gertrud Rieß, who suggests that it is evidence of Goethe's own preoccupations at the time of rewriting. Referring to the passage quoted on p. 126 ('Wie schwer lag jetzt ... lösen'), Rieß asserts: 'Hier überwuchert das Erlebnis die Dichtung. Und so wenig ist es durchkomponiert, daß es dem Kunstwerk nur mit der überraschenden Wendung angefügt ist'[8] – here she returns to the rest of the paragraph in the new text:

> Hätte eine glückliche Vertraulichkeit sie früher wieder einander näher gebracht, wäre Liebe und Nachsicht wechselsweise unter ihnen lebendig worden, und hätte ihre Herzen aufgeschlossen; vielleicht wäre unser Freund noch zu retten gewesen. (150R)

And Rieß is not alone in believing that this addition was closely related to Goethe's own personal situation in 1786; Adolf Schöll, the first publisher of the poet's letters to Charlotte von Stein (1848–51), was also of this opinion.[9] Silence had indeed become a major factor in the later years of his relationship with Frau von Stein, as we have seen, and Goethe, who was frequently taciturn himself, suffered greatly from the silences imposed on him by Charlotte when he hurt or offended her in some way. His introduction of the motif of silence specifically linked in a causative way to Werther's 'departure' thus seems to have definite confessional overtones.

The difficulties in logic and narrative consistency that arise from Lotte and Albert's newly introduced avoidance of the subject of Werther fade away altogether if we accept the idea that in the rewriting Goethe secretly gave vent to the sorrowful, but carefully concealed, reflections that were uppermost in his own mind at the time: the awareness that things had gone badly wrong between himself and Charlotte, that their failure to talk about their difficulties had been a

---

8 Gertrud Rieß, *Die beiden Fassungen von Goethes 'Die Leiden des jungen Werthers': Eine stilpsychologische Untersuchung*, 1924, 50
9 Schöll, *Goethes Briefe* 1:627

major factor in ensuring that these difficulties gained the upper hand, and that he had no option but to leave, now that a lack of mutual, loving concern had become part of their dealings with each other. Read in this way, the last sentence of the paragraph has a retrospectively wistful air about it in personal terms, despite being cast in the third person: 'Hätte eine glückliche Vertraulichkeit sie früher wieder einander näher gebracht, wäre Liebe und Nachsicht wechselsweise unter ihnen lebendig worden, und *hätte ihre Herzen aufgeschlossen; vielleicht wäre unser Freund zu retten gewesen*' (150R, emphasis mine).

In this section I have drawn attention to two details whose formulation should be looked at more closely: the first is the implicit reference to the *closed hearts* of Lotte and Albert reminiscent of Goethe's own experience. We know that he tended to interpret coldness or silence on the part of Frau von Stein as evidence that she had 'closed her heart to him,' and his one wish always was that she should open it to him again.[10] The second emphasis in the above passage refers to Werther's tragic end as something that might perhaps have been avoided if Lotte and Albert had been able to overcome their inability to talk to each other, but the words used inevitably evoke Werther's reaction to the plight of the doomed farmboy, contained in a newly written note also inserted in the Editor's Report before the passage I have quoted: 'Du bist nicht zu retten Unglücklicher! ich sehe wohl daß wir nicht zu retten sind' (121R). Now whereas Werther's identification with the farmboy is readily understandable, the total acceptance of this identification by any other character within the novel is not, and yet the re-use of almost the same words ('vielleicht wäre unser Freund zu retten gewesen') shows that such an identification has been made. But by whom? Not by Albert or Lotte, surely. By the conscientiously 'objective' Editor? I would suggest that in both of these italicized sentence parts it is the author who seems to dominate, even intrude into, a significant passage newly created for *Werther* Two.

Goethe as detectable intruder in his own rewritten text? More evidence will be needed for such a thought to become a credible assertion, but the incongruities of the new addition we have just been

---

10 For example, from July 1782: 'Das einzige Intresse meines Lebens ist daß du offen gegen mich seyn magst. Das Eingeschlossne halt ich nicht aus' (P918); 'Du hast mein Herz in Verwahrung und also brauchst du weiter nichts. Die Zeit wird ia wohl auch wieder kommen wo das deinige sich öffnet' (P919).

considering already give rise to this new question. Two points should be borne in mind here, both of which seem obvious echoes of Goethe's own experience: the very introduction itself of the motif of silence, and the specific way in which that motif is formulated. In terms of the rewritten novel qua novel, a ready explanation might seem to offer itself initially for the first of these, as the mere introduction of the silence motif could have been used as an alternative explanation for the tensions between Lotte and Albert once suspicion, jealousy, and vindictiveness on the part of the husband were expunged. However, while the text suggests that this silence was indeed responsible for the tensions, it gives us no supporting evidence to believe that Albert kept his feelings about Werther's relationship with his wife hidden from her. On the contrary: he stated his position and then refused to talk further on the subject, but in this refusal there was no concealment of the kind implied by the above passage. Albert spoke his mind once and for all and thereafter maintained total silence; he had nothing more to add. It is apparent from the text that Lotte is more guilty of silence on the difficult subject of Werther than Albert is, and yet the text tries to apportion equal blame to them both.

Why the inconsistency? Having seen how Goethe used his literary talent to create for himself a sphere of freedom in which he could openly express emotions that he felt obliged to conceal in his everyday life, I am inclined to believe that his need to unburden himself of feelings of unhappiness, regret, and resentment may in fact have been more dominant in his mind at the time of rewriting than any conscious respect for the integrity of his existing characters. If we accept this proposition, however, and think of him using his writing as a means to inner release and expansion here as so often elsewhere, then the fact that he placed the motif of silence in the relationship between Lotte and Albert rather than between Lotte and Werther raises another question: is it possible that he identified closely not only with Werther but also in part with Albert by the time it came to the rewriting? He certainly fulfilled the role of husband to Frau von Stein more attentively in most respects than her legal husband did for many years, providing her with his constant companionship until Josias von Stein's presence at the dinner table at home from late 1785 onward put an end to the near-fairytale 'marriage.' It seems no exaggeration to characterize their relationship in this way, for Goethe and Frau von Stein spent more time together in the course of their daily life in Weimar than the real husband and wife did; for many years they shared all their waking (and sleeping) thoughts with one another, both romantic and otherwise; they dealt with problems pertaining to her children and family together; they constantly sought advice from each other on all matters, even the most mundane. It is important to remember here too that Goethe knew very well for at least five years prior to 1786 that Charlotte loved him as she had never loved her legal husband, despite the attentiveness she displayed to von Stein for the sake of maintaining appearances.

Several pointers together lead me to believe that Goethe and she made a secret lifetime commitment to each other soon after 12 March 1781: first is the letter he wrote to her on that date, in which she underlined these words as being of great importance to her: 'Du weißt daß ich von dir unzertrennlich bin und daß weder hohes noch tiefes mich zu scheiden vermag. Ich wollte daß es irgend ein *Gelübde* oder Sakrament gäbe, das mich dir auch sichtlich und gesezlich zu eigen machte, wie werth sollte es mir seyn. Und mein Noviziat war doch lang genug um sich zu bedencken' (P596). Secondly, his letters to her around that time are full of exalted declarations of lifelong love, of how they are now truly inseparable, of how much joy her love brings him, etc.[11] Thirdly, the notion of himself as her husband is not one Goethe never thought of: it crops up explicitly, albeit with a tinge of irony, in a postscript to a letter he wrote to her on 8 July 1781, which he begins by inquiring with concern about her sore foot and the children's coughs; he then goes on: 'Wir sind wohl verheurathet, das heist: durch ein Band verbunden wovon der Zettel aus Liebe und Freude, der Eintrag zus Kreuz Kummer und Elend besteht. Adieu grüse Steinen. Hilf mir glauben und hoffen' (P688). Further massive evidence that such a commitment existed can be seen from the malevolent behaviour and writings of Frau von Stein for a good ten years after the poet's return from Italy.[12]

---

11 Cf. P596, P597, P606, P607, P609, P613, P624, P643, etc.
12 Perhaps the most convincing evidence that they in all likelihood made a lasting commitment to each other which Goethe then 'betrayed' is provided by Frau von Stein's attacks on him in her play *Dido* (1794). One of her chief assaults concerns how little an oath ('Gelübde') really means to him; she casts him in the role of the fat, opportunistic, and self-indulgent poet Ogon, and the following exchanges take

But if Goethe was capable of writing himself into the mind and character of Albert in part when he came to revise his tale of tragic love, then he had come a long way from the perspectival simplicity of his original, conscious identification with Werther, despite his use of Jerusalem's suicide to provide the ending to his story. It seems possible that the substance of much of the new material he wrote may have had very different origins from what we have come to believe and that the principles of composition underlying the second version of *Werther* may have been very complex indeed.

Given what we have said and seen so far, the fact that Goethe used the power of society's opinion in Version Two to bolster up Albert's position as husband seems readily understandable. Personal jealousy and resentment on Albert's part towards Werther were simply superfluous to his representative function as the obstacle *placed by society* in the way of any happy resolution of Werther's predicament – a predicament once again so much like Goethe's own by the time he came to rewrite his novel. Despite earlier long periods of relative bliss, by 1786 he was in a state of torment all over again, torment even worse than before because he and Lotte had had an almost perfect relationship in many respects, but that was now changed by the increased presence of her husband at home. Love was once again subordinated to duty, propriety, and the acknowledgment of legal rights. Yet Goethe could not resent the person of his third 'Albert,' Josias von Stein. In Kestner he had experienced certain positive aspects of the Albert figure many years before, in Brentano certain negative aspects, but by the time he

---

place between Elissa, Queen Dido's confidante who was once very close to the poet, and Ogon himself:

OGON: Höre mich einmal, Elissa, mit dem Vertrauen, das du mir vormals gönntest, und willige ein dich eine Weile unsrer Führung zu überlassen, und durch unsre Führung leite alsdann die Königin. Sie muß die Vermählte des Gätulischen Königs werden.

ELISSA: Sie muß? Hast du das Gelübde vergessen, das sie den Göttern that, als wir aus Tyrus flohen? [The oath was to remain true to the end of her days to the memory of her beloved husband.]

OGON: Gelübde thun wir uns selber, und können uns auch wieder selbst davon entbinden.

ELISSA: Wer sich nicht treu bleibt, bleibt's auch den Göttern nicht. (Act 3, Sc. 2)

See *Dido: Ein Trauerspiel in fünf Aufzügen*, ed. Heinrich Düntzer, 1867, 39–40. The play was circulated widely in Weimar, and everyone was well aware that its chief message was a savage attack on Goethe.

came to terms with the existence of the good-natured von Stein as someone to whom he should be kind and helpful for the sake of his beloved Charlotte,[13] he could no longer harbour any real personal resentment towards the individual who happened to be the husband figure. And so Albert was changed. Goethe still resented the fact that his beloved was unavailable because she 'belonged' to someone else, but the particular someone else was no longer very important and could therefore be more generously portrayed – more generously, at least, as far as specifically individual traits were concerned. In Version Two Albert became simply a better husband in society's terms, one who acknowledged society's power and endorsed its views in all things. It is hardly surprising that Kestner should have liked the second portrait better than the first.

Lotte

The most significant changes Goethe made in rewriting *Werther* are to be found in his portrayal of Lotte, for of the three major characters it is only she who undergoes any real transformation as an individual.[14] The first version of the novel allows us to believe that her 'response' to Werther's love might well be nothing more than projected wish-fulfilment on his part, but the second does not. Here sizeable passages have been altered or rewritten to give us more insight into Lotte's mind and heart, and the result is that we become aware that she has indeed had deep feelings for Werther from early on, that she takes pleasure in seeing him and feels a growing need for his company; we also learn of the way in which she actively involves him in her life, and of new tensions between Albert and herself because of him. But perhaps most important of all is what we see of her heightened conviction that Werther's talk of departing this world ought to be taken very seriously indeed.

13 See p. 46.
14 In recent years a few excellent articles have appeared that either deal with, or have a bearing on, the altered portrayal of the characters in the second version of *Werther*; see Erika Nolan, 'Goethes "Die Leiden des jungen Werther": Absicht und Methode,' 1984; Thomas Saine, 'The Portrayal of Lotte in the Two Versions of Goethe's *Werther*,' 1981; Benjamin Bennett, 'Goethe's *Werther*: Double Perspective and the Game of Life,' 1980.

Seen from an objective standpoint, the additions that cast more light on Lotte in the earlier part of the novel prior to the Editor's Report add up to a certain culpability in her relationship with Werther, a culpability that arises from her encouragement of his visits and attentions. Seen from Werther's emotional standpoint, however, they are altogether different. Some of these additions take the form of new notes, some are merely sentences inserted into notes that already exist. The first change occurs in the note dated 13 July 1771, where Werther expresses his conviction that his love for Lotte is returned. Both versions read:

> Ja ich fühle, und darin darf ich meinem Herzen trauen, daß sie – o darf ich, kann ich den Himmel in diesen Worten aussprechen? – daß sie mich liebt! (42L/42R)

In Version Two the following sentence is inserted at this point:

> Mich liebt! – Und wie werth ich mir selbst werde, wie ich – dir darf ich's wohl sagen, du hast Sinn für so etwas – wie ich mich selbst anbethe, seitdem sie mich liebt! (42R)

Obviously Werther's sense of self-worth is greatly heightened by his awareness that she returns his love, but is this idea of reciprocation nothing more than projected wish fulfilment, as many would have us believe? I think not. If he had used the causal 'da' instead of the temporal 'seitdem' here it would have been easier to answer this question in the affirmative. However, 'seitdem' suggests a point in time from which he has been sure of her love for him, so the way in which he expresses his certainty tends rather to suggest a specific event that gave rise to it. He *knows* Lotte loves him, knows it in a way that the first Werther did not. Again the link to the author seems apparent. This particular addition to the text has been regarded as puzzling in its triviality,[15] but one can see that it might well have been important for Goethe as an expression of his own inner truth, for exactly the same idea of a heightened sense of self-worth deriving from the sure knowledge that one is loved arises often in his letters to Frau von Stein, particularly in 1781 around the time of the emotional break-

---

15 See Bernhard Seuffert, 'Philologische Betrachtungen im Anschluß an Goethes "Werther," ' 1900, 14ff.

through in their relationship.[16] The other additions to the novel also underscore Lotte's interest in Werther, with only one possible exception, which will be examined shortly.

A new note dated 26 July is a note from Werther to his beloved:

> Ja, liebe Lotte, ich will alles besorgen und bestellen; geben Sie nur mehr Aufträge, nur recht oft. Um eins bitte ich Sie: Keinen Sand mehr auf die Zettelchen die Sie mir schreiben. Heute früh führte ich es schnell nach der Lippe und die Zähne knisterten mir. (46R)

The tone here is much more personal than anywhere else so far, and the fact that the form of address 'liebe Lotte' is brought forward from Werther's existing note of six months later (20 January 1772 [77L]) indicates that a footing of intimacy is established much earlier in the second version than in the first. What these few lines add to the existing story is important, not for what they tell us about Werther, but about Lotte, for her request that he do various errands for her shows that, far from exercising caution and keeping him at a distance, she is actively weaving him into the fabric of her life. Another small insertion into the existing letter of the same date tells of how he uses her requests as an excuse to see her: '... sie gibt mir einen Auftrag und ich finde schicklich, ihr selbst die Antwort zu bringen' (46R). Lotte is bound to realize that his visits are more frequent because of the little tasks she asks him to perform, so we can conclude that she is at least happy to see him. Again a detail of Goethe's actual relationship with Frau von Stein has been included here,[17] and the effect it creates within the novel is to make Werther's ardour seem less as if there is no trace of an answering echo from Lotte, less as if his pursuit of her takes little account of what she truly feels for him. She extends evidence of friendship and pleasure in his company at the very least, and makes no secret of the fact in her dealings with him.

16 For example, P592 (7 March), P596 (12 March), P602 (19 March), P613 (27 March). We find the idea recurring as late as 1784; cf. P1278 (4 July), P1287 (18 August).
17 For some examples of Goethe's references to tasks Charlotte has given him and/or the pleasure he has in carrying them out for her, see: P658 (May 1781), P686 (5 July 1781), P901 July 1782), P915 (15 July 1782), P1264 (27 May 1784). Gottfried Fittbogen claims that this addition in *Werther* is more reminiscent of Goethe's relationship with Frau von Stein than of that with either Charlotte Buff or Maximiliane LaRoche, but he fails to draw any closer link, seeing it rather as an unexplained inconsistency (Fittbogen 571).

Yet she seems to be a truly affectionate wife to Albert, for a note she writes to him over a year later underlines her impatience for his return. This too is newly written into the second version: 'Bester, Liebster, komme so bald du kannst, ich erwarte dich mit tausend Freuden' (96R). On reading her note, Werther immediately delights in imagining that she could have written it to him rather than to her husband:

> Ich las es und lächelte; sie fragte worüber? – Was die Einbildungskraft für ein göttliches Geschenk ist, rief ich aus, ich konnte mir einen Augenblick vorspiegeln, als wäre es an mich geschrieben. Sie brach ab, es schien ihr zu mißfallen, und ich schwieg. (96R)

This passage may have been meant to show Lotte's love for her husband, her sense of propriety, and Werther's instant readiness to project himself into the role of Albert, but it does not fit in with any of the other additions or alterations that have a bearing on Lotte's behaviour and attitude towards Werther; nowhere else is there any indication of her displeasure at his assumption of special status in her life. Indeed, her behaviour in the newly written passage that now follows has different overtones altogether. Whether the introduction of the above note also represents the intrusion of Goethe's own experience into his narrative is something that cannot be proved, although some critics have suggested that such is evidently the case.[18] Whatever the explanation, the note becomes more puzzling if we consider that the next new piece of writing, which offers the most significant insight into Lotte's behaviour in this part of the novel, follows very closely on its heels; only a few lines of the existing text separate the two passages.

This next and last of the Lotte additions before the Editor's Report is an anecdote inserted between the letters of 6 and 15 September 1772. It tells of Lotte's habit of feeding her canary from her own mouth and of Werther's real sense of torment at the 'kisses' exchanged in this way. The incident described goes back to 5 August 1776, when Charlotte von Stein made a brief journey to Ilmenau to visit Goethe, bringing her pet canary with her.[19] Eight years later he recalled her

---

18 Cf. Lauterbach 126; Rieß 42f.
19 Düntzer tells us of this visit (CvSt 1:60), also Schmidt (*Charakteristiken* 1:297) and Bode (*Stunden mit Goethe* 6:217f.), but only Schmidt and Bode make the connection

Ilmenau visit with her 'tame little bird,' as he put it; evidently it had made a strong impression on him.[20]

The new passage opens:

> Sie war einige Tage verreist, Alberten abzuhohlen. Heute trat ich in ihre Stube, sie kam mir entgegen und ich küßte ihre Hand mit tausend Freuden. (97R)

A small point should be made here about wording: Lotte's note to Albert had said '... ich erwarte dich mit tausend Freuden'; now Werther tells Wilhelm of seeing her again after several days' absence and of kissing her hand 'mit tausend Freuden.' Is this more evidence of the author in his text? Or does it show that Lotte and Werther think in exactly the same words? Or should one argue that the repetition must be Werther's deliberate echo of Lotte's sentiments towards Albert, some strange sort of carry-over of several days' duration from him thinking himself into Albert's shoes? I personally favour the first explanation, simply because Goethe often used the same phrases more than once in letters he wrote around the same time to different people.

Erika Nolan emphasizes the fact that this new anecdote has an added impact because of the fact that it is placed *after* Lotte's marriage to Albert,[21] while Thomas Saine points out that one could justifiably interpret it as evidence that Lotte is not only encouraging Werther, but tormenting him also.[22] Both critics agree that her behaviour here is far from being entirely sweet and blameless, and their view has considerable substance, for Lotte deliberately parades the way the bird feeds from her mouth as an act of kissing; she then reaches it over so that it may kiss Werther too. It is not Werther, but Lotte, who turns the bird's eagerness for food into a human gesture to do with love

---

between Frau von Stein's visit and the new addition in *Werther*. Goethe's letters to Frau von Stein at this time show his clear awareness that he is again in Werther's situation; cf. P81-4 (24 July to 8 August 1776).

20 See P1224 (23 February 1784). In 1812 Goethe secretly sent Frau von Stein a new canary to replace her old one that had been accidentally trampled on; she tried to train this bird to feed in the same way as its predecessors, but without success: 'Wenn ich ihn küssen will, wie meinen vorigen, beißt er mich in die Lippen' (letter to Knebel, cited in Bode, *Charlotte von Stein* 218f.).
21 Nolan 209
22 'The Portrayal of Lotte' 61

rather than hunger. Just nice, innocent fun? By this stage there can be no doubt in Lotte's mind of the intensity of Werther's feelings for her, and so what she is doing can neither be wholly innocent nor wholly fun. At the very least it shows an element of blameworthy insouciance in regard to Werther's feelings, at most it betrays her as an out-and-out coquette. I believe it impossible to read the anecdote accurately as an example of her 'makelloser Unbefangenheit'[23] or as an enhancement of her guilelessness.[24] Lotte, it should be remembered, has just been given proof of the direction in which Werther's imagination immediately takes him, given even the remotest of pretexts – i.e., into the closest possible emotional involvement with her, much closer than she seemingly either wishes or permits, even as a fantasy.

There is nothing surprising or unpredictable about Werther's reaction to her offer of a kiss by proxy (= her handing over the canary she has just 'kissed' with the words: 'Er soll Sie auch küssen'):

> Das Schnäbelchen machte den Weg von ihrem Munde zu dem meinigen, und die pickende Berührung war wie ein Hauch, eine Ahndung liebevollen Genusses. (97R)

Here we have even more vivid proof of Werther's powers of imagination than in his identification with Albert as the intended recipient of the note from Lotte. Can she be unaware of this? I think the author never even dreamed of such a question. The text continues:

> Sein Kuß sagte ich, ist nicht ganz ohne Begierde, er sucht Nahrung und kehrt unbefriedigt von der leeren Liebkosung zurück.

Whether Lotte chooses to overlook or genuinely does not hear the implied sensuality in this ambiguous remark we cannot tell for sure, but either way her subsequent behaviour is bound to twist the knife in Werther's heart, now that she has fired his all-too-fervent imagination with her words and actions:

> Er ißt mir auch aus dem Munde, sagte sie. Sie reichte ihm einige Brosamen mit ihren Lippen, aus denen die Freuden unschuldig theilnehmender Liebe in aller Wonne lächelten.

---

23 Lauterbach 111
24 Fittbogen 571

Poor Werther! It is inevitable that he should experience real torment at this scene he is obliged to witness, and his spontaneous reaction is to look away, reproaching Lotte inwardly as he does so:

> Ich kehrte das Gesicht weg. Sie sollte es nicht thun! sollte nicht meine Einbildungskraft mit diesen Bildern himmlischer Unschuld und Seligkeit reizen und mein Herz aus dem Schlafe, in den es manchmal die Gleichgültigkeit des Lebens wiegt, nicht wecken!

The reader feels sympathy with Werther at this point, but has difficulty in seeing the whole scene through his eyes as evidence of Lotte's 'himmlischer Unschuld und Seligkeit' – all the more so since she was given clear evidence only a very short time ago of how Werther used his imagination to project himself into the closest possible relationship with her, supposedly to the point of her displeasure. But if she was indeed displeased, why should she now fuel the flames of his passion and imagination? While the conflict in Lotte's behaviour has escaped Werther altogether, it cannot escape the reader, whose impression of her sweet innocence is damaged as a result. I doubt, however, that it was meant to do so. It seems more likely that this piece of new writing was meant in Goethe's mind to enhance the view we have of Lotte. That it does quite the opposite in all probability escaped him because, like Werther in the novel, he had found the incident with the canary delightful in 1776, as in 1784 when he thought back to it again.

And the way in which the episode is brought to a close can best be explained in exactly the same way. From the point of view of how we see Lotte in the novel the ending is very damaging indeed, but as Goethe's tribute to his beloved Charlotte it is altogether different. Werther retracts his inner reproach to Lotte, but the terms in which he does so implicitly indict her rather than exonerate her from blame in all eyes but his own:

> [Sie sollte es nicht thun! ...] – Und warum nicht? – Sie traut mir so! sie weiß wie ich sie liebe!   (97R)

Only Lotte's ignorance of Werther's love for her would render her actions blameless, but the whole passage ends on a strong note affirming her awareness that he loves her dearly. Precisely this awareness ought to mean that she takes care not to fan the flames of his tormented love, and yet here she seems to do just the opposite. Is she an instinctive temptress? What is this woman really like? The questions force themselves upon the reader in spite of Werther's overwhelming generosity of spirit.

A short passage written to follow the original letter of 20 December 1772 in the Editor's narrative opens as follows:

> Was in dieser Zeit in Lottens Seele vorging, wie ihre Gesinnungen gegen ihren Mann, gegen ihren unglücklichen Freund gewesen, *getrauen wir uns kaum mit Worten auszudrücken, ob wir uns gleich davon, nach der Kenntniß ihres Charakters, wohl einen stillen Begriff machen können* und eine schöne weibliche Seele sich in die ihrige denken und mit ihr empfinden kann. (128R, emphasis mine)

This beginning to the first of the major changes that deal directly with Lotte's own thoughts and feelings lets us know more of the type of person we are dealing with in her: she is 'eine schöne weibliche Seele' whose thoughts and emotions are readily accessible to the imagination of those of like mind and soul. The Editor is clearly impressed by what he has come to know of her, but more than that, there is a tone of extreme delicacy in his attempt to broach the subject of her innermost thoughts (italicized above). It seems to me that this passage may well be a better example of how Goethe meant to realize his intention to 'elevate' his novel in the rewriting than any of the changes he made to the figure of Albert, but this is a train of thought to be pursued at a later stage.

The new passage continues with Lotte's determination to establish a distance between herself and Werther. We surmise on first reading that this is because of her desire to comply with the wishes of her husband, for she herself had shown no evidence of sharing his wish that Werther's visits should become less frequent (122R), but the text does not say or even necessarily imply here that such is the case. In fact, it suggests that her resolve has more to do with self-sacrifice and a high-minded notion of worthiness as a wife than with mere obedience to Albert. However, determined though she may be to fall in with her husband's wishes out of a sense of duty, that determination is undermined by her longing to spare Werther the anguish she knows that any act of discouragement on her part will cause him (128R). But time is running out; the tensions arising from the silence between

Albert and herself on the subject of Werther are becoming more than she can bear, so that the only solution is for her to deal Werther the blow she so much dreads. Only by consciously wounding the one man can she prove herself worthy of the other, or so she believes. This is clearly implicit in the new text, and Lotte's genuine dilemma, which was not at all clear in these emotional terms in the first version of the story, adds depth to her character and wins our increased sympathy here, while heightening the dramatic tension of the whole tale. One detail in particular is most important in the light of the information we have also just been given for the first time in Version Two. The relevant part of the passage on Lotte (with the detail referred to italicized) follows on her hesitation to ask Werther to stay away:

> Doch ward sie in dieser Zeit mehr gedrängt Ernst zu machen; *es schwieg ihr Mann ganz über dies Verhältniß, wie sie auch immer darüber geschwiegen hatte* und um so mehr war ihr angelegen, ihm durch die That zu beweisen, wie ihre Gesinnungen der seinigen werth seyen. (128–9R, emphasis mine)

Only a short time before we were told that she referred to Werther more than once in conversations with her husband after he had asked her to take steps to ensure that Werther's visits became less frequent; each time she did so, however, Albert changed the topic of conversation (122R). Lotte, therefore, was evidently quite happy to bring up Werther's name, though not the subject of her relationship with him, happy to introduce him not once but several times into her conversations with her husband until Albert put a stop to it, having made clear to her where he stood on the subject of their friend's 'unfortunate passion' for her. Now she is under pressure; she must act to send Werther away. The formulation of the text implies that her sense of pressure arises from the fact that her husband has been refusing to talk about the relationship with Werther, *just as she herself has always kept quiet about it* – note the qualitative difference between the two acts of silence, here in English, but also contextually present in the original German despite the use of 'schweigen' in both cases. What does this difference mean? Albert, we know, has openly broached the subject of the relationship between Werther and Lotte at least once, but Lotte herself has never done so. Why not? It should have been easy for her to talk to her husband about Werther's obvious fondness for her, especially early on. Why should the subject have been taboo for Lotte even before it became taboo for Albert? The answer to our question is that she is in love with Werther, of course, but this only becomes clear by degrees, after we are given more insight by the Editor into her mind and heart, by which stage she has already carried out her resolve to ask Werther to stay away and has even suggested that he find someone else to love, someone worthy of him and not tied to another man as she is (130L/R).

Her subsequent state of mind is described as follows:

> Lotte war indeß in einen sonderbaren Zustand gerathen. Nach der letzten Unterredung mit Werthern hatte sie empfunden, wie schwer es ihr fallen werde sich von ihm zu trennen, was er leiden würde, wenn er sich von ihr entfernen sollte. (134R)

Again there is something strange about how this is expressed: she *is going to* find a separation very difficult, we are told ('wie schwer ... werde') – this is a fact, whereas Werther's suffering, we are also told, *would be* enormous if he *were to* go away from her ('was er leiden würde ... entfernen sollte'). By this point she has already asked Werther not to come back for several days and fully expects him to comply with her request,[25] which makes the speculative subjunctive here very odd indeed. It is as if she has accepted how much she will miss him without being convinced that he will indeed stay away, as if she has sorrowfully accommodated, for her own part, to the separation that now lies ahead, while at the same time envisaging this separation from Werther's perspective merely as a looming and painful possibility, not as a *fait accompli*. But why does she think of 'separation'? He is only to stay away for a few days, and yet both 'trennen' and 'sich entfernen' as used here seem to imply a more lengthy period of absence with overtones of finality. Here we have another problem, but again it is a problem that is readily disposed of if we think of the writer and his situation by mid-1786: he is contemplating the possibility of a long journey; he knows for a fact that Charlotte will find it very hard to do without him, knows too that, were he to go, he would suffer enormously. The problems of the sequence 'werde,' 'würde,'

---

25 Cf. 130-1L/R, 134R, 135-6R.

'wenn ... entfernen sollte' all disappear if we bring Goethe's emotional situation at the time of writing into play at this point and accept that he had not yet finally decided to do what he had been contemplating off and on for about ten years, but that he was considering it more seriously now than ever before – i.e., to flee from Weimar for a lengthy period. Again we seem to have here more evidence of Goethe's presence in the narrative of his rewritten *Werther*, for Lotte's dual perspective on the projected separation is difficult to explain otherwise.

It is in the next new passage on Lotte's state of mind that we discover how very dear Werther is to her and how dear he has been to her from the very beginning. Only with this revelation do we understand the reason why she has not ever dared to talk to Albert about the relationship. Both the changes and the additions to the text are important at this point. Albert is away for the night on a business trip, having learned that Werther will not be coming again until Christmas Eve; both versions contain this information, though in slightly different form.[26] Where the two texts begin to diverge significantly is in Lotte's attitude to her husband, which precedes the revelation of her feelings for Werther. For the purpose of comparison I shall cite both versions:

I Sie saß in ihrer Einsamkeit, ihr Herz ward weich, sie sah das Vergangene, fühlte all ihren Werth, und ihre Liebe zu ihrem Manne, der nun statt des versprochenen Glüks anfieng das Elend ihres Lebens zu machen. (134L)

II Sie saß nun allein, keins von ihren Geschwistern war um sie, sie überließ sich ihren Gedanken, die stille über ihren Verhältnissen herumschweiften. Sie sah sich nun mit dem Mann auf ewig verbunden, dessen Liebe und Treue sie kannte, dem sie von Herzen zu gethan war, dessen Ruhe, dessen Zuverlässigkeit recht vom Himmel dazu bestimmt zu seyn schien, daß eine wackere Frau das Glück ihres Lebens darauf gründen sollte, sie fühlte was er ihr und ihren Kindern auf immer seyn würde. (134R)

---

26 Version One makes more of the fact that Albert would not have gone without knowing that Werther will stay away; cf. 134L/R.

Each alteration weakens the impression we have of a young wife who is vulnerable to the distressing behaviour of her husband because of her love for him. There certainly seems to be rather more Stein than Buff in this Lotte. In II she lists Albert's good qualities ('Liebe,' 'Treue,' 'Ruhe,' 'Zuverlässigkeit') but in such a way as to suggest a lesser emotional involvement than in the first version of the text: note, for example, the clause 'dessen Liebe und Treue sie kannte' – the verb 'kannte' is almost devoid of emotional content in a way that 'schätzte' or some such other term would not have been; note too the objectivity of the portrayal of her husband's calmness and reliability, qualities so marvellous 'daß eine wackere Frau das Glück ihres Lebens darauf gründen sollte.' She seems to be attempting to be fair rather than expressing any depth of personal emotion, for the phrase 'eine wackere Frau' has an emotionally distancing effect that tends to suggest an objective, even ironic, awareness of Albert's 'suitability' as a husband in many respects – but for another woman, not herself. Even Werther is prepared to go this far in his appraisal of Albert in Version Two! The indications of how she loves her husband, present in the first version, have been taken out: 'Ihr Herz ward weich ...' becomes 'sie überließ sich ihren Gedanken ...'; uppermost in Lotte's mind now is the awareness that there is no escape from her marriage ('Sie sah sich nun auf ewig mit ihrem Mann verbunden ...'), which is followed by a fair-minded catalogue of her husband's many good qualities. There is also the replacement of the phrase 'ihre Liebe zu ihrem Manne' by 'dem sie von Herzen zu gethan war.' The new Lotte's feelings for Albert seem to be more objective, more wifely perhaps, but clearly less romantic than before. And as the new passage continues we begin to see exactly why, for the transition in her mind here from Albert to Werther emphasizes the importance of the latter for her and thereby heightens the reality of her emotional dilemma: '... sie fühlte was er [Albert] ihr und ihren Kindern auf immer seyn würde. Auf der andern Seite war ihr Werther so theuer geworden ...' (134R).

In the original text the transition in thought from one man to the other was quite different: 'Ihre Gedanken fielen auf Werthern. Sie schalt ihn, und konnte ihn nicht hassen' (134L). Whereas there she had felt sad because of her love for Albert ('ihr Herz ward weich'), and in that frame of mind her thoughts had turned to Werther, now she reviews both men in relation to herself, and her feelings for Werther seem more intense than those for her husband. Here is how the original passage continues:

I Ein geheimer Zug hatte ihr ihn [Werther] vom Anfange ihrer Bekanntschaft theuer gemacht, und nun, nach so viel Zeit, nach so manchen durchlebten Situationen, mußte sein Eindruk unauslöschlich in ihrem Herzen seyn. Ihr gepreßtes Herz machte sich endlich in Thränen Luft und gieng in eine stille Melancholie über, in der sie sich je länger je tiefer verlohr. (135L)

The new version reads as follows:

II ... gleich von dem ersten Augenblick ihrer Bekanntschaft an hatte sich die Übereinstimmung ihrer Gemüther so schön gezeigt, der lange dauernde Umgang mit ihm, so manche durchlebte Situationen hatten einen unauslöschlichen Eindruck auf ihr Herz gemacht. Alles, was sie interessantes fühlte und dachte, war sie gewohnt mit ihm zu theilen und seine Entfernung drohete in ihr ganzes Wesen eine Lücke zu reissen, die nicht wieder ausgefüllt werden konnte. O, hätte sie ihn in dem Augenblick zum Bruder umwandeln können! wie glücklich wäre sie gewesen! – Hätte sie ihn einer ihrer Freundinnen verheirathen dürfen, hätte sie hoffen können, auch sein Verhältniß gegen Albert ganz wieder herzustellen! (135R)

Every addition here in terms of Lotte's awareness of the emotional impact Werther has made on her during the time they have known each other coincides with an aspect of Goethe's relationship with Frau von Stein: 'die Übereinstimmung ihrer Gemüther,' 'der lange dauernde Umgang,' 'alles ... war sie gewohnt mit ihm zu theilen.'[27] Even the wish to have him as her brother, and the thought that he should perhaps marry someone else were ideas that Goethe had explored with Charlotte.[28] And yet he was very well aware that she loved him and

---

27 Cf., for example, Goethe's letters of 1776; also P447 (30 June 1780), P448 (3 July 1780), P843 (20 March 1782), P957 (25 August 1782), P1269 (9 June 1784), P1277 (28 June 1784), P1369 (10 March 1785), etc.
28 On the idea of a brother-sister relationship between them see P21 (24 February 1776), P43 (16 April 1776), *Die Geschwister* (October 1776), *Iphigenie* (begun February 1779). Regarding the notion that she would be happy for him were he to fall in love with and marry someone else, cf. P23 (4 March 1776), P754 (2 December 1781).

wanted to share him with no one else.[29] The new text goes on to make exactly this point:

> Sie hatte ihre Freundinnen der Reihe nach durchgedacht, und
> fand bey einer jeglichen etwas auszusetzen, fand keine der sie ihm
> gegönnt hätte.
>
> Über allen diesen Betrachtungen fühlte sie erst tief, ohne sich es
> deutlich zu machen, daß *ihr herzliches heimliches Verlangen sey, ihn für
> sich zu behalten* und sagte sich daneben daß sie ihn nicht behalten
> könne, behalten dürfe; ihr reines, schönes, sonst so leichtes und
> leicht sich helfendes Gemüth *empfand den Druck einer Schwermuth, dem
> die Aussicht zum Glück verschlossen ist. Ihr Herz war gepreßt und eine trübe
> Wolke lag uber ihrem Auge.* (135R, emphasis mine)

Her sense of sorrow in the original text, her girlish tears, result from her realization that she will have to turn her back on a friendship that has come to mean a great deal to her; in Version Two, however, the source of her sorrow is not the same: Albert is here no longer enough for her happiness. This Lotte needs Werther *as her own*; without him all prospect of happiness is closed off for her for ever. The brother solution is evidently no solution either. One is reminded of *Die Geschwister* of ten years before, though not of its happy outcome.

Such is the background to Werther's unexpected return in Version Two, and we can see how this return is a great deal more highly charged because of it. The new Lotte is more deeply involved both mentally and emotionally with Werther than her predecessor ever was. Her former 'Verwirrung' (135L) on realizing that he has come again, despite her request that he stay away, is now 'eine Art von leidenschaftlicher Verwirrung'; she is now torn between wanting the friends she sends for to come and wanting them to stay away (136R). In the original version Lotte was much more in control of her thoughts and actions in sending for these friends; there too she was defiant and proud of her own blamelessness vis-à-vis Werther and for this reason she did not summon the maid to keep her company. In Version One, when her friends reply that they are unable to come, her thoughts run

---

29 Cf. 'An Lida' (9 October 1781), quoted on p. 43.

as follows:

> Darüber ward sie einige Minuten nachdenkend, bis das Gefühl
> ihrer Unschuld sich mit einigem Stolze empörte. Sie bot Albertens
> Grillen Truz, und die Reinheit ihres Herzens gab ihr eine Festigkeit,
> daß sie nicht ... ihr Mädgen in die Stube rief, sondern ... sich
> gelassen zu Werther auf's Canapee sezte. (136L)

In the second version, however, things are very different. Here her pride, defiance, and sense of blamelessness have been taken out; she is caught in the throes of emotional turmoil and confusion:

> Sie wußte nicht recht, was sie sagte, eben so wenig was sie that, als
> sie nach einigen Freundinnen schickte ... Das Mädchen kam zurück
> und brachte die Nachricht, daß sich beide entschuldigen ließen.
>
> Sie wollte das Mädchen mit ihrer Arbeit in das Nebenzimmer sitzen
> lassen; dann besann sie sich wieder anders ... (136R)

Lotte is now consciously aware of the depth of her feelings for Werther and her defences against these feelings are not very strong. It is in this state of mind, then, that she asks him to read Ossian aloud to her. The passionate embrace that results no longer springs merely from an upsurge of overwhelming love on Werther's part; it is no longer simply his surprise assault on a Lotte too weakened by the emotional upheaval caused by their reading for her to be able to resist. The new depth of feeling she has for Werther means that although the description of their embrace remains the same as before, its emotional impact is greatly intensified. Can this have pleased the Kestners? I doubt if Goethe gave the matter any thought whatsoever while rewriting his novel.

The most important changes in the two remaining new passages concerning Lotte in the Editor's Report have to do with the wall of silence between Albert and herself, which we have already looked at, and with the clear evidence she has had for a long time of Werther's despairing intention to 'quit this world.'[30] In the opening few lines of what is a substantially rewritten passage, much of the wording is

---

30 See 149–51R. The ambiguity of the phrase 'diese Welt zu verlassen' is dealt with on pp. 206–9; see also note 83 below.

the same as that of the original version (149L), so I shall quote these lines from Version Two, simply emphasizing the new additions:

> Die liebe Frau hatte die letzte Nacht wenig geschlafen, *was sie gefürchtet hatte, war entschieden, auf eine Weise entschieden, die sie weder ahnden noch fürchten konnte*; ihr *sonst so rein und leicht fließendes* Blut war in einer fieberhaften Empörung, tausenderley Empfindungen zerrütteten *das schöne* [ihr] Herz. (149R)

Adjectives expressing Lotte's purity and inner beauty have again been added to the original, but the other addition is more important: the 'separation' she had so dreaded has been decided in a way she could not foretell. Werther has made up his mind to go.[31]

After the new passage already discussed, in which Lotte and Albert's silence is made partly responsible for Werther's final act of despair (150R), a clear emphasis is placed on the fact that he has always been quite open about his longing for escape, and this very openness seems implicitly to increase the blame that attaches to husband and wife for their subsequent lack of caution in dealing with his request for the pistols. However, once again they are by no means equally to blame. The final paragraph of the last new section that deals chiefly with Lotte's state of mind begins as follows:

> Noch ein sonderbarer Umstand kam dazu. Werther hatte, wie wir aus seinen Briefen wissen, nie ein Geheimniß daraus gemacht, daß er sich, diese Welt zu verlassen, sehnte. (150R)

Albert's reaction to this idea, in earlier discussion with Lotte, had been one of irritation, dismissal, even derision, as she now recalls:

> ... er hatte sich sogar darüber einigen Scherz erlaubt, und seinen Unglauben Lotten mitgetheilt. Dieß beruhigte sie zwar von Einer Seite wenn ihre Gedanken ihr das traurige Bild vorführten, von der andern aber fühlte sie sich auch dadurch gehindert ihrem Manne die Besorgnisse mitzutheilen, die sie in dem Augenblick quälten. (150R)

---

31 This insertion would suggest that by the time of its writing Goethe had at last made a definite decision to leave Weimar, which would mean that the passage was written at the earliest in June–July and at the latest between 16 and 22 August 1786.

Clearly, she draws no comfort from her husband's reaction, in fact, her inhibitions towards him are heightened to the point of making her deny her best instincts. She is afraid to make her continuing fear for Werther known to Albert, but yet her awareness of Werther's state of mind is clearer than ever it was, for just a moment earlier, when she was going over in her own mind how negatively her husband might react, were he to learn of the kiss, she had decided that Werther must from now on bear the responsibility alone for his own fate, despite her feelings for him:

> ... immer kehrten ihre Gedanken wieder zu Werthern, der für sie verlohren war, den sie nicht lassen konnte, den sie leider! sich selbst überlassen mußte, und dem, wenn er sie verlohren hatte nichts mehr übrig blieb. (149–50R)

However regretful the Editor's reflections on the damaging silence that exists between husband and wife may be at this point, the weight of responsibility for that silence falls more clearly on Lotte than on Albert, despite the attempt in the text to make them share the burden equally.[32] Lotte has always kept quiet about her relationship with Werther, and now that he has kissed her, now that she has responded to his kisses, she is less likely than ever to broach the subject with her husband, aware though she is that Werther's ominous talk of putting an end to things must be taken very seriously. Fear for herself is quite simply more important than fear for Werther. When Albert returns in an ill humour from his unsuccessful business trip and becomes even more displeased on hearing that Werther has been to see Lotte during his absence after all, it is clear that she will now never tell him about the kiss (151R). As Thomas Saine points out, the price Lotte pays in order to re-establish her relationship with her husband is her deliverance of Werther to a fate that she well knows may be tragic.[33] Be-

---

32 Cf. 149R: 'Sie hatten so lange gegen einander geschwiegen, und sollte sie [Lotte] die erste seyn, die das Stillschweigen bräche und eben zur unrechten Zeit ihrem Gatten eine so unerwartete Entdeckung machte?' The answer to this question is surely yes, as only she has been guilty of any concealment, and therefore only she has anything more to say on the subject of Werther. However, it is not the implied answer offered by the text, with its unclear narrative perspective at this point, already discussed in connection with the continuation of the silence motif.
33 Saine, 'The Portrayal of Lotte' 76f.

cause of her increased awareness of Werther's mental and emotional state, the arrival of his servant to ask for Albert's pistols, although expressed in the same terms in both versions (151–2L/R), makes a different impact in the second. Lotte's action in handing over the weapons has newly heightened implicit overtones of culpable self-preservation.

On the basis of the canary incident both Saine and Bennett see in the second Lotte a woman who enjoys playing with fire just as long as she feels that she herself is running no real risk, *as long as she is in control of the situation*,[34] and I think both critics are right, but not in terms of this one episode alone. Lotte preserves a certain lack of friction between herself and Albert by her silence on Werther; she controls the danger that Werther represents for her by washing her hands of his fate. While her predicament may call forth the reader's sympathy to some degree, the fact remains that her prime concern at each juncture where action is called for seems to be to safeguard her own position. The earlier Lotte, who was gentler, more innocent, more justifiably self-righteous, more in love with her husband and less obviously involved with Werther, had a stronger emotional commitment to her marriage than her successor, and so her anxious and timid behaviour towards her husband elicited greater sympathy and understanding in the reader. Her emotional priorities were clear and she did not betray them. This is much less true of the Lotte of Version Two.

Was Goethe wholly aware of the composite impact the changes he introduced into the portrayal of his heroine would make? I doubt it. I do not think that in rewriting *Werther* he consciously meant to portray the new Lotte of these passages as more of a controlling and egotistical woman than her earlier counterpart, for we have already seen that many small details of the Lotte additions all tend to suggest a more noble and exalted view of her than before.[35] It seems much more likely that both a highly positive bias created by love's blindness, and at the same time certain suppressed resentments and disappointments found their way into Goethe's text as he rewrote it. In 1776 he wrote *Der Falke*, in which the central female character, Giovanna, was

---

34 Ibid. 61f.; Bennett 65ff.
35 Lotte has become in Version Two 'eine schöne weibliche Seele' (cf. 128R); she now has 'ein schönes Herz,' 'so rein und leicht fließendes Blut,' for example (149R).

to be a deliberate mixture of Lili Schönemann and Charlotte von Stein; in 1786 he rewrote *Werther* and could not avoid recreating Lotte from his real-life experiences of the previous ten years, for he loved Frau von Stein more deeply than he had ever loved any other woman. As we have seen, every thought was for her, every line he wrote he claimed was above all meant for her; by the time he came to revise *Werther* she had long been for him the only real dialogue partner he felt he either had or wanted. As he himself wrote to her on the day that he finished 'this most difficult task': 'Ich dencke immer an dich bey allem was ich mache' (P1597). Had she been less in his thoughts, undoubtedly the rewritten novel would have turned out to be very different.

Werther

Of the three major characters in the novel, Werther is the one whose portrayal undergoes the least obvious alteration in terms of real substance, in spite of the fact that Goethe wrote more new material pertaining to him than to either Lotte or Albert. But although the hero remains substantially as before in terms of his emotional volatility and his inability to compromise the dictates of his heart, the changes made in his portrayal are nevertheless highly significant, as they all combine to intensify the hopelessness of his emotional predicament. Strangely, however, this intensification has tended to be overlooked in favour of the relative 'sameness' of the central character in both versions, a perceived 'sameness' that seems to have fostered the perpetuation of a widespread and tenacious misconception about Werther's relationship with Lotte: the notion that his interest in her stems largely, or even primarily, from the fact that she is bound to someone else. This is a view held by scholars who see in Werther a man obsessed by his own love, regardless of its object,[36] but I must confess that I find it difficult to explain, particularly in light of the changes made to Lotte and Albert in the revised version of the novel. In the original it was perhaps possible to see Werther's tendency to idealize his beloved as

---

36 Cf. Gerhard Kurz, 'Werther als Künstler,' in *Invaliden des Apoll: Motive und Mythen des Dichterleids*, ed. Herbert Anton, 1982, 101; Müller-Salget 540; see also note following.

being helped, rather than hindered, by her relationship with Albert, but in the second version this is not the case. And yet the idea refuses to go away. Erika Nolan in an otherwise excellent article on *Werther*, for example, points out that on the evening Werther meets Lotte he is given to understand no less than three times that she already has a serious suitor; Nolan then goes on to draw the conclusion that had Lotte been unattached, Werther's interest in her would have faded swiftly.[37] Contesting Thomas Mann's belief that Werther's most fundamental urge is to escape from all human and earthly limitations into the boundlessness of the Beyond, Nolan suggests instead that exactly the opposite is the case.[38] But what unites these two Goethe scholars, and many more besides, despite all the differences in their reasoning, is the firm belief that Werther's passion for Lotte is kept alive and even intensified by his knowing that she can never be his – an extraordinary view, given the evidence of the text. Admittedly Lotte suggests to Werther at one point that it must be her unavailability that attracts him so strongly to her (130L/R), but he is very angry at this suggestion, not, I think, because she has penetrated his most deeply guarded secret, but because her thoughts and the way in which she expresses them demonstrate exactly what Werther has always hated most: a Philistine view of love as something best subjected to the constraints of reason and reasonableness.[39] Lotte, his one true soul-mate and beloved, has never been so remote from him mentally and emotionally as at this point, and this remoteness has an even greater impact (without any change of wording) in Version Two, simply because she has more actively encouraged his attentions than her forerunner ever did, which makes her proposed solutions to his predicament ring even more hollow than before. Whereas the first version of the novel admits of the possibility that Werther may well have loved Lotte despite (or

---

37 Nolan 199
38 Ibid. Nolan cites Thomas Mann's 'Goethes Werther,' in *Goethe im XX. Jahrhundert*, ed. Hans Mayer, 1967, 5.
39 The passage referred to brings to mind Werther's original letter of 26 May 1771, where he poured scorn on the Philistine's reasonableness and wilful moderation in affairs of the heart as appropriate only for a dry official incapable of love (13–14L/R). Cf. Werther's response to Lotte's various pieces of 'reasonable' advice (which sound very much like echoes of Albert): ' "Das könnte man," sagte er mit einem kalten Lachen, "drucken lassen, und allen Hofmeistern empfehlen" ' (130L/R).

even because of) a lack of encouragement or response on her part, the alterations and additions made to the second version lend greater weight to the idea of their mutual love, whatever the insuperable obstacles to its lasting fulfilment may be. Since the changes made to the figures of Albert and Lotte have a considerable impact on our impression of Werther in Version Two, let me briefly sum up our findings so far in terms of these changes.

Albert becomes gentler, less vindictive, less jealous, less resentful, and less preoccupied with his business affairs to the detriment of his relationship with his wife; he becomes a better husband to Lotte, but also a 'better' member of bourgeois society, more mindful of its good opinion and therefore a better upholder of its standards. None of these changes casts any necessarily negative light on Werther or makes it seem that Lotte has made the better choice by choosing Albert over him, particularly in view of the feelings she has for both men.

In the second version Lotte is more appreciative and more objectively aware of her husband's many fine qualities, but her involvement now seems to have more to do with her head than with her heart. While her relationship with Albert has become less intense in emotional terms, her relationship with Werther is quite the opposite: her feelings for him right from the start have been such as to make her avoid talking about him in any depth with her husband, and gradually the silence that grows up between them on the subject of Werther undermines the happy and open relationship they once had. Lotte's fears are augmented, for *she now has something to hide*, unlike in Version One, where she was proud of her own blamelessness and defiant of the strictures that Albert thought it necessary to impose on her. As for the prospect of losing Werther – she realizes just how much he means to her and dreads his leaving, aware that his departure is going to create a yawning gap in her life that can never again be filled.

Taken together, these changes must alter our perception of Werther as an obsessed and obsessive lover whose psychological make-up is such that he is doomed to perish from the start, whatever happens. Instead it is clear that he has been given considerable indications that Lotte takes pleasure in his company, that she regards him as a special friend of whom she can ask various favours, and that she is quite uninhibited in his presence when Albert is not around. All of these make Werther a man who has reason to hope, both before and after the marriage, that perhaps some way may be found to help him continue to endure the recurrent pain of this love triangle for the sake of the bliss he experiences in it. However, as time goes on and Lotte attempts to reverse what she has actively encouraged – i.e., Werther's very frequent visits – so that her deteriorating relationship with Albert may be improved, it becomes progressively impossible for Werther to continue his hope. It may have been a fragile and unrealistic hope from the very beginning, based as it was on the assumption that the bond of marriage would not ultimately prove stronger than everything else, but it was a hope that continued to keep Werther from taking his final decision. Once all such hope was lost, there could be no reason for further delay.[40]

Leaving aside the highly important farmboy story for the moment, the lesser changes Goethe made with a focus on Werther begin with an undated note inserted between the existing letters of 8 and 10 August 1771:

> Mein Tagebuch, das ich seit einiger Zeit vernachlässiget, fiel mir heut wieder in die Hände, und ich bin erstaunt wie ich so wissentlich in das alles Schritt vor Schritt hinein gegangen bin! Wie ich über meinen Zustand immer so klar gesehen und doch gehandelt habe wie ein Kind, jetzt noch so klar sehe, und es noch keinen Anschein zur Besserung hat. (50R)

What this new note does is to show Werther's full awareness of the situation in which he finds himself, as well as the helplessness he feels in terms of attempting to improve it. The note is placed immediately after a letter to Wilhelm in which he registers his need to escape ('wenn ich nur wüßte wohin? ich ginge wohl' 49L/R), and before another in which he emphasizes the heart as the source of all happiness ('Ach so gewiß ist's, daß unser Herz allein sein [des Menschen]

---

[40] A similar hope for the happy outcome of a triangular love relationship can be found in the first version of *Stella*, where the constellation is one man and two women: in the end, the wife (parallel to Albert in *Werther*) agrees to share her husband (parallel to Lotte) with the 'genius of love,' Stella (parallel to Werther). Goethe revised this drama shortly before he revised *Werther* for republication, but it was not until 1805 that he altered its ending to reflect a loss of all hope for happiness in the love triangle. The violence of the altered solution in *Stella* (double suicide) seems to me to be matched by some of the changes introduced through the farmboy story into *Werther*. This is dealt with in more detail below.

Glück macht' 50L/R). The addition therefore provides a good transition from one existing letter to the other: Werther's head struggles to dominate his heart but cannot do so with any promise of a happy outcome. Here he has more objective clarity regarding his true situation than he had in the earlier version, but it does not help him resolve his inner conflict – indeed, the conflict is actually intensified by his new clarity; his rational self asserts its existence and its helplessness here at one and the same time. Try as he will, he cannot bring himself to break away. Yet we can now see, as we could not do before, why it should be so difficult for him: Lotte's behaviour has convinced him that she loves him (42R), and so leaving is even more problematic than it was in Version One.

But why should one isolated reference to a diary be written into the second version, a diary of which no other trace was ever found? Is this too an indication of the author in his text? Bernhard Seuffert is convinced that it is, and that the introduction of the diary reference is not the result of any artistic reflection but of an exaggerated involvement on Goethe's part that led him to write the reality of his own activity into the novel at the time of rewriting.[41] Goethe's habit of reviewing his past life again and again tends to support this view, but the chief interest of the new passage lies in the contribution it makes to our understanding of Werther, whose capacity for decisive action it reveals as even less in the second version of the novel than in the first. His insight into the real truth of his situation is heightened, which makes his anguish even more intense and more paralysing than it was in the original.

There are seven other small insertions of direct relevance to Werther from this point up to the beginning of the Editor's Report. Of these, two highlight his love for Lotte as the only meaningful reason for his existence, while the other five either add a greater objectivity than before to his judgments or show his increased clarity towards himself and his situation.[42] No major change is made to the portrayal of Werther by virtue of any one of these additions, but taken together they

---

41 Seuffert, 'Philologische Betrachtungen' 5. For a discussion of the entire novel as a 'Tagebuch-Roman' rather than a 'Brief-Roman' see Gerhard Storz, 'Die Leiden des jungen Werthers,' in *Goethe-Vigilien*, 1953; Gerhard Kurz (101) finds too that Werther's letters have the quality of diary entries.
42 The relevant passages are 77R, 78–9R, 88–9R, 90R, 102R, 106R, 107R.

lend him a more secure footing in reality, for his indictment of the destructive artificiality of court circles gains in validity and thereby both validates and enhances the need he feels for Lotte as the apotheosis of the natural and the good.

'Ich muß Ihnen schreiben, Liebe Lotte, hier in der Stube einer geringen Bauernherberge ...' – it is with these words that Werther's first letter to Lotte began in the original version of the novel, and the whole letter is retained in the second (77L/R), but to it is added a new passage of some nine lines that more clearly spell out the reason for his current torment among the alien hearts and minds of the aristocracy: to be separated from one's beloved is to endure nothing but anguish and a sense of deep futility:

> Des Abends nehme ich mir vor, den Sonnenaufgang zu genießen und komme nicht aus dem Bette; am Tage hoffe ich mich des Mondscheins zu erfreuen und bleib in meiner Stube. Ich weiß nicht recht, warum ich aufstehe, warum ich schlafen gehe. Der Sauerteig, der mein Leben in Bewegung setzte, fehlt; der Reiz, der mich des Morgens aus dem Schlafe weckte, ist weg. (77R)

Separation from his beloved as the source of paralysis and hopelessness – this is what is added to the existing letter by virtue of these lines, and the same is true of another small addition, a note written on 17 October: 'Ich habe so viel und die Empfindung an ihr verschlingt alles, ich habe so viel und ohne sie wird mir alles zu nichts' (102R). Both additions are very much in tune with the letter of 10 August in which the heart was proclaimed the only possible source of happiness, but in their extremity of tone they show Werther's inner state while separated from Lotte as one of utter devastation. Do they illustrate his increasingly precarious hold on mental equilibrium and help to prepare the way for the final act of leavetaking? I think they do, but they also show an extraordinary similarity to the feelings the author expressed throughout his long relationship with Charlotte von Stein, experiences necessarily revitalized in his mind when rewriting his original text. Reliving past experiences, as we saw, was how he set about the task of reworking all his old material. Just a few examples from his letters to Frau von Stein over a period of more than nine years will help to demonstrate why I make such a claim specifically in regard to *Werther*:

Es ist und bleibt Gegenwart alles! – Was hilft mich's dass Sie in der Welt sind, dass Sie an mich dencken. Sie fehlen mir an allen Ecken, ich schleiche meinen Tag herum und es ist mir eben weh bey der Sache. (P75, 2 July 1776)

Liebe Lotte komm zurück! Ich weis bald nicht mehr warum ich aufstehe. (P957, 27 August 1782)

Ich kann mich keinen Augenblick von dir entfernen ... ich bin eingeschränkter als iemals ... Mit Sehnsucht verlang ich wieder bey dir zu seyn, denn ich habe nichts eignes mehr. Manchmal wünsch ich es mögte anders seyn manchmal wünsch ich meinen Gedanken eine andre Richtung zu geben. Es ist und bleibt unmöglich. (P1114, 16 June 1783)

Es wird mir so ein unüberwindlich Bedürfniß dich zu sehen daß mir wieder einmal für meinen Kopf bange wird. Ich weis nicht was aus mir werden soll. (P1275, 24 June 1784)

Nun wird es bald Zeit liebe Lotte daß ich wieder in deine Nähe komme denn mein Wesen hält nicht mehr zusammen, ich fühle recht deutlich daß ich nicht ohne dich bestehen kann. (P1277, 28 June 1784)

Was ich thue verschwindet mir und was ich schreibe scheint mir nichts. O komm wieder damit ich wieder mein Daseyn fühle. (P1441, 17 September 1785)

Wollte Gott du bestimmtest deine Rückkunft denn ohne dich ist doch kein Leben. (P1446, 3 October 1785)

A similar link exists between Goethe's experience of life at the Weimar court and the new passages he wrote concerning the abhorrent values of high society as seen through Werther's eyes. Before going to Weimar he had shared in the beliefs that characterized the *Geniezeit* as a whole, among them a belief in the superiority of the peasant over his aristocratic lord, but he had not himself had the kind of first-hand experience of life among the aristocracy that would have enabled him to write about it with personal authority. Jerusalem's tragic fate was known to him, of course, and offered significant substance for a negative view of the behaviour and values of high society,

158 Werther's Goethe

but personal experience came only with his life in Weimar, and whatever may have been said by scholars to support the idea that Goethe had an almost reverential respect for the aristocracy,[43] it is clear from his letters that this was not so – at least not for his first ten years in Weimar. During this period we find a recurring wave of regret, impatience, and dislike for the behaviour of these people that is not dissimilar to what he had written into Werther's experiences in 1774. Although he very much wanted to be 'worthy' of Charlotte von Stein, and from 1781 onward tried for her sake to do nothing that would arouse society's disapproval,[44] deep down he retained a greater liking for the common folk than for their supposed superiors, so it is not surprising that he should introduce a new peasant hero into his work in 1786 and build further on the negative picture of the aristocracy already present in the first version of *Werther*.[45]

A new letter is added to the novel, dated 8 February 1772, in which the destructive nature of the aristocrats in whose company Werther finds himself is emphasized to the point where his extreme dislike of them seems to find greater vindication than before:

> Wir haben seit acht Tagen das abscheulichste Wetter und mir ist es wohlthätig. Denn solang ich hier bin ist mir noch kein schöner Tag am Himmel erschienen, den mir nicht jemand verdorben oder verleidet hätte ... (78R)

Whereas this might be nothing more than a reflection of Werther's self-pity and discomfiture among members of high society, the passage goes on to deal with his lament, not on how he himself is treated, but on how the aristocrats treat each other:

43 Cf. Welz 34ff. Perhaps Goethe's wish to do nothing that might compromise or embarrass Frau von Stein has helped to give rise to this mistaken view; cf. notes 44 and 45.
44 See P733 (29 October 1781) and P965 (9 September 1782); evidently Goethe was a widely respected member of the Weimar court community by 1783 – cf. *Vertrauliche Briefe* 1:291, 294.
45 On Goethe's dislike of many aspects of court life see P57 (24 May 1776), P62 (1 June 1776), P148 (30 March 1777) and note (P1,2:571), P308 (6 March 1779), P362 (1/3 January 1780), P594 (10 March 1781), P1268 (7 June 1784), etc.; also CvSt to Knebel, 20 April 1785 (P1,2:541) – cf. *Werther* 74–6L/R. See also P1597 (23 August 1786), where Goethe anticipates his departure as an act of liberation and looks forward to casting off the bonds of social stratification.

> Es ist nichts worum sie einander nicht bringen. Gesundheit, guter
> Nahme, Freudigkeit, Erhohlung! Und meist aus Albernheit, Unbegriff
> und Enge *und wenn man sie anhört mit der besten Meinung.* Manchmal
> möcht' ich sie auf den Knieen bitten, nicht so rasend in ihre eigne Einge-
> weide zu wüthen.   (79R, emphasis mine)

This letter follows on the one I have already referred to, in which the setting of the peasant inn brings Lotte to mind, and what it does is to endorse by implication Werther's love for her naturalness as evidence of his right-mindedness; to be repelled by these artificial and destructive people is to come out on the side of the natural and the good. Even giving them the benefit of the doubt, he says, (italicized clause) there is no getting away from their narrowness and stupidity. By inserting this note in support of Werther's earlier criticisms, Goethe makes him seem more, not less, justified in his negativity towards court society, and by adding the earlier lines in which Werther expresses the futility of being among such people and separated from Lotte he lessens our impression of the hero as a social misfit, strengthening his image as a man whose values are more sound than those of the higher social ranks around him.

To Werther's new self-awareness as a rational being unable to command the rule of reason to prevail over his emotions is added a deeper self-irony than exists in Version One:

> Ich kann nicht bethen: Laß mir sie! und doch kommt sie mir oft als
> die Meine vor; Ich kann nicht bethen: Gib mir sie! denn sie ist eines
> andern. Ich witzle mich mit meinen Schmerzen herum; wenn ich
> mirs nachließe es gäbe eine ganze Litaney von Antithesen.   (106R)

The self-irony here is clearly negative. On the one hand there is an increased sense of hopelessness in Werther due to the clarity he has about his relationship with Lotte, while on the other there is a seemingly wry, even masochistic, quality to his reflections on that relationship and his own attempts to deal with it. With these words he seems to be striking out at himself, rather than establishing any sense of distance from his difficulties that might enhance his ability to cope with them. This is a characteristic both of many letters from Goethe to Frau von Stein and also of the story of the farmboy that will be examined presently.

The last of the minor additions I have referred to, while creating a bridge to the existing story of the unfortunate mad lover looking for flowers in winter (108–11L/R), also illustrates a new, if unwilling, awareness in Werther that his sufferings are not unique but already recorded in the annals of literature:

> Manchmal sag' ich mir: Dein Schicksal ist einzig; preise die übrigen glücklich – so ist noch keiner gequält worden; dann lese ich einen Dichter der Vorzeit, und es ist mir als säh' ich in mein eignes Herz. Ich habe so viel auszustehen! Ach sind denn Menschen vor mir schon so elend gewesen? (107R)

This too makes things worse rather than better for him, for as long as he could believe his situation to be unique, there could still be some hope for a positive outcome, but if his sufferings belong in a category of recurring human experience whose outcome is trauma and tragedy, then such hope must be severely diminished. There is an unpleasant, self-pitying quality to these lines that might seem to bolster the scholarly view that Goethe distances himself from Werther in the second version, but this is only one possible reading, the reading of someone who cannot empathize with the hero. Nothing obliges us to it except perhaps an unwillingness to attribute to Goethe rather than to Werther the mixture of self-pity and fascination with himself as a literary subject that these lines reveal.[46] Precisely this unwillingness is something we shall have to explore in more depth at a later stage, for I think a similar unwillingness occurs in the modern reader at other points in the novel and helps to explain many of the discrepancies between what the text itself says and how it has been interpreted over the years.

Of all the changes Goethe made to *Werther*, the most substantial and most important is the addition of the three-part story of the farmboy. Complete in itself, it offers more insight into the author's own revised understanding of Werther's emotional and psychological development than the rest of the changes put together. But it should not be seen in

---

46 Goethe in fact often projected himself into various situations depicted in literary works and evidently enjoyed doing so. See Karl Maurer, 'Die verschleierten Konfessionen: Zur Entstehungsgeschichte von Goethes Werther,' 1963, 430f.

isolation, for it supports the other changes and is also supported by them, an added parallel story to the existing account of the central character's suffering in love. The tale of the farmboy underlines Werther's love of naturalness and spontaneity, his instant and total identification with the happy, then despairing and finally tragic lover; it underlines too the primacy for him of love over everything else. All of this we know and it needs no amplification here. What I wish to do is to suggest that the text also contains a hidden level of meaning that has never yet been explored. It is to this that I want to give my attention in the first instance, for it is possible to read the whole farmboy story as Goethe's cleverly concealed summary of his own emotional life from the time he first thought of rewriting *Werther* in 1782 to mid-1786 when he decided to leave for Italy. The poet's love of secrets, his passion for self-revelation and self-concealment through his writing, his almost total silence on his first decade in Weimar and his relationship with Charlotte von Stein, together with the fact that the only major piece of work he revised substantially for publication during these years was *Werther* – all of these make the possibility of such a personal reading one that ought not to be dismissed out of hand.

It is clear from Goethe's letters, diaries, and autobiographical writings that he always had a more sympathetic attitude in many respects towards the peasantry than towards the nobility,[47] and the groundwork for the new tale of the young farmhand is already prepared in the text of Version One when Werther's sense of ease in the company of humble, uneducated people is first established in his letter of 15 May ('Die geringen Leute des Ortes kennen mich schon und lieben mich' [7L/R]). This sense of ease is then further emphasized through

---

47 The word 'Bauer' occurs frequently in these writings, which reflect his very positive view of the peasantry; see *Das Goethe Wörterbuch*, 1978ff., 2,1:cols.100–5. An example of the poet's pleasure and delight in the company of common folk is contained in a letter to Frau von Stein from his Harz journey in late 1777: 'Wie sehr ich wieder auf diesem dunckeln Zug Liebe zu der Classe von Menschen gekriegt habe! die man die niedre nennt! die aber gewiss für Gott die höchste ist. Da sind doch alle Tugenden beysammen, Beschränckheit, Genügsamkeit, Grader Sinn, Treue, Freude über das leidlichste Gute, Harmlosigkeit, Dulden – Dulden – Ausharren in un – ich will mich nicht in Ausrufen verlieren' (P202). Notice the similarity between his sentiments here and throughout the farmboy story, in particular the second part (95R). Significant for the rewriting of his novel is the fact that he was in a similar state of mind when he wrote to Charlotte shortly before leaving for Italy; cf. P1597.

his meeting with the young mother and her two children, recorded in the letter of 27 May, where he explicitly acknowledges the calming effect that simple, good people have on him when he is at his most tormented (15L/R). Immediately following on the end of this letter comes the new one of 30 May, in which the first part of the farmboy's story is presented. Thus, by the time we learn of the farmboy we are prepared to accept him as someone whom Werther can readily relate to and appreciate. And it is no coincidence that it should be a farmboy whom Goethe chooses here as his hero, for in 1776, only a few months after his first arrival in Weimar, he is known to have dressed up in such a guise at Kochberg, Charlotte von Stein's country estate, in order to present before the assembled company a joking outline to Duke Karl August of how he should exercise the authority of his position as ruler.[48]

Not only the person of the farmboy himself, but also the preamble to the first part of his newly added story offers an evident link with Charlotte von Stein as reader. As we know, she had strongly objected to only one passage in the first version of the novel – that passage in the letter of 26 May, in which Werther launched a direct attack on the dictates of bourgeois society as something hostile to all spontaneity and naturalness, lethal for true love and true art. Charlotte von Stein's objections do not surprise us, given the fact that she herself was an ardent supporter of society's ways and values, given too that she, more than many another, expended considerable energy in erecting around herself precisely those kinds of precautionary fences Goethe disliked, as a means by which to fend off all threats to her carefully ordered existence. When Goethe revised his novel for republication, the earliest substantive change he introduced into his existing text was the insertion of a new letter that both referred back to the passage his beloved Frau von Stein had found so objectionable and also told the blissful first part of the farmboy's tragic story.

---

48 A descendant of the von Stein family dates the event as 6 December 1775, Hans Wahl as 17–18 January 1776, Erich Trunz as 1778 – see Freiherr von Stein-Kochberg, 'Goethe in seinen Beziehungen zu Schloß Großkochberg und dessen Theater,' 1932, 45; Hans Wahl, 'Sebastian Simpel,' *Jahrbuch der Goethe-Gesellschaft*, 1949, 62ff.; Trunz, HA 1:513. A comment by Gleim to Bertuch by mid-February 1776 suggests that Wahl's dating may be the most accurate; cf. Biedermann/Herwig 1:187. For the text of the poem see HA 1:106.

The new letter (30 May) begins in a conciliatory tone with a weakened and clearly unexceptionable statement about art as a whole:

> Was ich dir neulich von der Mahlerei sagte, gilt gewiß auch von der Dichtkunst; es ist nur daß man das vortreffliche erkenne und es auszusprechen wage, und das ist freylich mit wenigem viel gesagt. (16R)

The implicit exhortations to allow oneself free rein in the matter of feeling, from which all great loves and all great art emanate, are now downplayed; instead we have merely a plea for the courage to acknowledge excellence wherever it is to be found. And yet almost at once comes a new, if implicit, reiteration by Werther of what he has already said in the 'objectionable' letter of 26 May on the supreme adequacy of nature as a model for the artist. The new letter goes on:

> Ich habe heut eine Scene gehabt, die, rein abgeschrieben die schönste Idylle von der Welt gäbe; doch was soll Dichtung, Scene und Idylle? muß es denn immer geboßelt seyn, wenn wir Theil an einer Naturerscheinung nehmen sollen?

Here Werther implicitly rejects all artificial mediation of any natural experience as an appropriate artistic expression of that experience. In so doing, he is once more attacking 'die gelassenen Herren auf beyden Seiten des Ufers' (14 L/R) who create a 'safe' kind of artificial beauty they can sigh over, while taking care that they never expose themselves to the full power of either nature or emotion, and so his initial conciliatoriness is immediately undermined, if not in actual words, then certainly by implication.

He continues in this same defensive yet mildly defiant tone, introducing the farmboy as the antithesis of those lofty expectations he may have engendered in his reader, and repeatedly stressing his inability to do justice to his subject or to moderate the tone of what he has to say. There is a new irony here vis-à-vis the 'du' to whom he is writing, and one unparalleled throughout either version of the novel, a heightened degree of gently self-assertive irony reminiscent of Goethe's own letters and notes to Charlotte von Stein:

> Wenn du auf diesen Eingang viel Hohes und Vornehmes erwartest, so bist du wieder übel betrogen; es ist nichts als ein Bauerbursch, der mich zu dieser lebhaften Theilnehmung hingerissen hat ... (16R)

We have already seen how Goethe rejoiced in playing games through his writing and how much weight he placed on Frau von Stein as his reader and helpmate for all that he wrote in the decade from 1776–86, and if one bears this in mind while reading the first of the new Werther-passages, one quickly gains the impression that it too may well be one of those multi-purpose literary productions of the kind both he and she so much enjoyed – at once a valid and valuable addition to the existing tale, but at the same time a hidden and intensely private avowal of exalted devotion for his (beloved) reader. The choice of a farmboy as hero, one should remember, was bound to strike a chord with those who belonged to Karl August's inner circle, and in particular with Charlotte von Stein.[49]

The retarding impulses before the beginning of the story itself end with Werther's defensively defiant awareness that his reader will once again find him inadequate and exaggerated as a storyteller, and with a gentle accentuation of the symbolic nature of the name 'Wahlheim' ('chosen home'), referred to only once before up to this point (12L/R) and not again until the letter of 21 June, after the first evening spent with Lotte, by which time it has become 'mein Wahlheim' (29L/R):

> – ich werde, wie gewöhnlich, schlecht erzählen, und du wirst mich, wie gewöhnlich, denk ich, übertrieben finden; es ist wieder Wahlheim, und immer Wahlheim das diese Seltenheiten hervorbringt. (16R)

Given that he has been in this place for only a short time, the emphases 'wieder Wahlheim und immer Wahlheim' betray the setting as a locus of the mind with which he is only too familiar: an emotional Utopia. And it is of precisely such a Utopia that he writes to a reader whose reactions he already knows well, one who evidently tends to a certain impatience or anxiety in reaction to his volatility and lack of

---

[49] It was precisely Goethe's promotion of 'peasant' behaviour that had so displeased and incensed Frau von Stein on his first arrival in Weimar; also, in his letters to her he often made reference to his love of common folk and his sense of ease in their company: see note 47; also P204 (9 December 1777), P1105 (28 May 1783), P1602 (3–4 September 1786, Petersen 2,1:274). Goethe dressed up as a farmboy not only in 1776, but also again in 1785 en route for Karlsbad; his letters to Frau von Stein of that year contain no reference to this episode, but he recalled it in his diary forty years later, on 2 May 1825 (WA 3,10:50).

moderation. Charlotte von Stein often reacted in this way towards Goethe in similar circumstances,[50] and another detail of their private little disputes is reflected in Werther's avoidance of the coffee-drinkers with which his tale here begins (16R).[51] If we take these small details together with Werther's swiftly established familiarity with the farmboy, the result appears to be the introduction on one level of a covertly intimate letter from Goethe to his beloved Charlotte. I shall try to make my reasons for this assertion clear as we go on.

In taking up the subject of love once again from where he left off on the 26 May, Werther relates the tale of the young farmhand in the following manner:

Er [der Bauernbursche] erzählte mir, daß er bey einer Wittwe in
Diensten sey und von ihr gar wohl gehalten werde. (17R)

Quite apart from the obvious identification to be made by Frau von Stein between Goethe and the farmboy from early 1776 onward, there is also a ready identification to be made between his mistress, the widow, and Charlotte herself, for in the two dramas Goethe wrote that same year she had already been cast as such. These were *Der Falke* (August 1776) and *Die Geschwister* (October 1776), both of which he used as a vehicle for the overt and covert expression of his own personal experiences, as we saw. Thus the two principals in the story of the young farmhand have evident links with the two most important people in the poet's life at the time when he replayed his Werther experience and ultimately rewrote his Werther novel: Charlotte von Stein and Goethe himself. During this time he wrote her many notes and letters similar in tone to much of *Werther*, and to help my reader gain some awareness of the more striking points of contact between the one body of writing and the other, I would ask him to read on with me from this point in the newly created text of the second version of the novel as if what follows were a clever, multi-faceted love-letter from Goethe to Frau von Stein as well as an important addition to Werther's experiences. The new letter of 30 May continues:

---

50 Cf. CvSt to Zimmermann, 6–8 March 1776 (*Vertrauliche Briefe* 1:166f.); also to Luise von Döring, 10 May 1776 (ibid. 180f.); see also Düntzer, *CvSt*, passim.
51 For example, P183 (31 August 1777), P1073 (25 March 1783), P1652 (1 June 1789)

> Er [der Bauernbursche] sprach so vieles von ihr [der Wittwe] und lobte sie dergestalt, daß ich bald merken konnte, er sey ihr mit Leib und Seele zugethan. (17R)

In a note from Goethe to Frau von Stein on 5 November 1783 he wrote: 'Fritz bringt einen guten Morgen und ich möchte garzugerne recht viel von meiner Geliebten hören, der ich so einzig gehöre und mit Leib und Seele zugethan bin' (P1162), and less than a month later, on 2 December 1783, almost the same formulation occurred: 'Da heute Conseil ist und ich es nie ohne die höchste Noth versäumt habe, entschliese ich mich hinein zu gehn. Es ist mir so ziemlich. Wenn ich wieder herauskomme hörst du wieder von mir. Ich bin dir mit Leib und Seele ergeben' (P1178).[52]

It should be called to mind before we go on that Frau von Stein was seven years older than Goethe, which made her thirty-nine years of age in 1781, the likely year of first composition of this passage in my opinion, and forty-one in 1783, which was in all likelihood when he thought of including the farmboy's story in a new version of *Werther*, '[um] ihn noch einige Stufen höher zu schrauben,' as he wrote to Kestner.[53] Never a beauty, she was then also well past her prime, at least by contemporary standards. The narrative continues:

> Sie sey nicht mehr jung, sagte er [der Bauernbursche], sie sey von ihrem ersten Mann übel gehalten worden, wolle nicht mehr heirathen

– Petersen, Bode, Schmidt, and Düntzer[54] all furnish us with information on Frau von Stein's personal life that bears out these remarks –

> und aus seiner Erzählung leuchtete so merklich hervor, wie schön, wie reizend sie für ihn sey, wie sehr er wünsche, daß sie ihn wählen möchte, um das Andenken der Fehler ihres ersten Mannes auszulöschen ...

---

52 Although this formulation occurs only twice in Goethe's letters to Frau von Stein, both times in 1783, when he was again working on *Werther*, the kind of quietly ecstatic devotion expressed here is to be found often in what he wrote to her in 1781; cf. note 57.
53 May 1783; see note 24, chapter 2.
54 Petersen 1:xii; Bode, *Charlotte von Stein* 46ff.; Erich Schmidt, 'Frau von Stein' 1:304. Düntzer cites a letter written by Frau von Stein to her son in 1794 which explicitly states that she had never been happy with her husband, who had died a few months earlier (*CvSt* 2:4; cf. 1:385).

Goethe's desire to marry Frau von Stein is expressed often and in many different forms throughout his correspondence with her; of these the most notable is contained in his letter of 12 March 1781, which we have looked at already and which, in its total commitment and exalted emotion has much in common with Werther's portrait of the farmboy as seen in this first part of the story.[55]

And now an even more playful coyness tinged with self-irony seems to come into the *Werther* text:

> ... daß ich Wort für Wort wiederhohlen müßte, um dir die reine Neigung, die Liebe und Treue dieses Menschen anschaulich zu machen. Ja, ich müßte die Gabe des größten Dichters besitzen, um dir zugleich den Ausdruck seiner Geberden, die Harmonie seiner Stimme, das heimliche Feuer seiner Blicke lebendig darstellen zu können.   (17R)

One should note here that exactly these physical qualities were those commonly attributed to Goethe by the men and women of Weimar alike.[56] Also, the times and ways in which Goethe wrote of his love for Charlotte von Stein in his correspondence with her are legion, but references to the beauty, purity, and truth of his devotion to her abound,[57] while his protestations of the inadequacy of words as a vehicle for the full expression of his love begin with the very first

---

55 Some other instances of Goethe's reiterated longing for marriage or long-term togetherness can be found variously in P305 (2 March 1779), P936 (4 August 1782), P1440 (11 September 1785), P1498 (late December 1785); also from Italy, 21 February 1787 (P1634).

56 See Biedermann/Herwig 1:174 (Zimmermann); 1:181f. (Julie von Berchtolsheim); 1:182 (Wieland); 1:239 (Falk); 1:251 (Julie von Hirtental), ibid. (J.F. Kranz); 1:386 (von Lose). In her play *Rino* (1776) Charlotte von Stein herself had gently mocked the general acclaim in Weimar for Goethe's fine dark eyes; in *Dido* (1794) she spitefully attacked his 'Schauspielergeberden' as being calculated for maximum effect on women; see Act 3, Sc. 3, and note 12 above.

57 From 1776 to 1783 Goethe repeatedly emphasized these qualities in his love for Frau von Stein, but such emphasis was noticeably more marked from 7–27 March 1781, which leads me to the conjecture that the first part of the farmboy story may well have been written as a tale in itself originally in 1781 (when she became his 'liebe Lotte'), and revised in 1783 for his planned republication of *Werther*. The style of the Bauernbursche story in its first part is reminiscent of Goethe's letters of 12 and 13 March 1781 (P596–7) and 9 September to 2 October 1783 (P1145–50); other avowals of purest and utmost devotion in his love for Charlotte can be found, for example, in P521, P575, P592, P602, P606, P607, P610, P613, P635, P638, P652, P656, P694, P718, P728, P733, P762, P844, P856, P871, P902, P957, P965, etc.

168   Werther's Goethe

letter we have from him to her (January 1776, P1) and continue for a very long time.[58] Notice how the text of the farmhand's story goes on at this point:

> Nein, es sprechen keine Worte die Zartheit aus, die in seinem ganzen Wesen und Ausdruck war; es ist alles nur plump, was ich wieder vorbringen könnte.

Following on these lines is a sentence which bears the hallmark of a gentle tease, for it touches on something very dear to Frau von Stein's heart – her concern with propriety and with society's good opinion of her at all times:

> Besonders rührte mich, wie er fürchtete, ich möchte über sein Verhältniß zu ihr ungleich denken und an ihrer guten Aufführung zweifeln.

But now 'Werther' becomes bolder, more intimate, in the re-telling of his tale, cancelling out all thoughts that 'the widow's' lack of youthfulness could in any way lessen her physical attractiveness for her lover, and this in a tone of exalted love calculated to reassure and delight Frau von Stein, who read every line, according to Goethe, as if it were written expressly for her:

> Wie reizend es war, wenn er von ihrer Gestalt, von ihrem Körper sprach, der ihn ohne jugendliche Reize gewaltsam an sich zog und fesselte, kann ich mir nur in meiner innersten Seele wiederhohlen. Ich habe in meinem Leben die dringende Begierde und das heiße sehnliche Verlangen nicht in dieser Reinheit gesehen, ja wohl kann ich sagen, in dieser Reinheit nie gedacht und geträumt. (17R)

Again we have emphatic reiteration of the purity of the lover's devotion to his lady, but this time it comes in a context of suppressed sensuality – suppressed, perhaps, but fully absorbed and deeply felt, capable of repetition by Werther only in his 'innermost soul,' as he says. Many of Goethe's letters and notes to Charlotte von Stein, going all the way back to 1776, contained sensual passages in which he

---

58 Cf. P42 (April 1776), P84 (8 August 1776), P313 (24 March 1779), P528 (24 December 1780), P596 (12 March 1781), P803 (February 1782), P1269 (12 June 1784), P1283 (3 August 1784), P1596 (20 July 1786).

expressed his yearning for physical nearness;[59] by his own admission he was 'immer der ganz sinnliche Mensch' (P107), and so expressions of this kind are by very much in character for the author himself. It is this undercurrent of sensuality, merely touched upon here in the first part of the tale of the farmhand, that erupts to cause the trauma of the young man's dismissal in the second part of his story, which comes much later in the revised version of the novel.

But to return for now to the text of the letter of 30 May: after the exalted reverie by Werther on the powerful attraction felt by the farmhand for his lady-mistress comes, I believe, a direct-indirect appeal from Goethe to Charlotte von Stein that is wholly disarming; the total identification of Werther with the farmboy is quite clear:

> Schelte mich nicht, wenn ich dir sage, daß bey der Erinnerung dieser Unschuld und Wahrheit mir die innerste Seele glüht und daß mich das Bild dieser Treue und Zärtlichkeit überall verfolgt, und daß ich, *wie selbst davon entzündet*, lechze und schmachte. (17–18R, emphasis mine)

The reason I claim for this passage the capacity to disarm, apart from Werther's passionate identification with the exalted state of mind of the lover, lies primarily with its opening plea, 'Schelte mich nicht,' for there is massive evidence from Goethe's letters to Frau von Stein that this is indeed how she very often reacted to him. Again it is not possible to present all, or even much, of this evidence here, but one or two examples should be enough to illustrate the point. On 10 January 1778 he responded to a 'checklist' from her of his failings or bad behaviour in this way: 'Die drei ersten Punckte ohne weitres zugestanden. Was den vierten betrifft ob gleich der Vordersaz falsch ist so sey doch auch Ihnen das unüberwindliche Gelüst mich zu schelten gewährt' (P212). One of their very numerous quarrels brewed up between them in July 1782, and we have already looked at the series of notes from him to her at that time.[60] Although everything was restored to a happier footing within a matter of days, the tension continued and Goethe's torment and vulnerability were plain up to early August. Never one to forget the hurt of any disruption in the harmony of their relation-

---

59 Cf. P105 (2 November 1776), P106 (3 November 1776), P725 (22 September 1781: 'Der Becher'), P843 (20 March 1782), P865 (2 May 1782), P1275 (24 June 1784), P1440 (11 September 1785), P1467 (15 November 1785), P1498 (late December 1785).
60 See pp. 49–52.

170 Werther's Goethe

ship, in September he sent Frau von Stein a lengthy poem whose opening quatrain he had written for her four years before, in June 1778, a poem that now ended with these words:

> Mein Schutzgeist eil es ihr zu sagen
> Durchstreiche schnell das ferne Land.
> Sie soll nicht schelten soll den Freund beklagen.
> Und bitte sie zu Lindrung meiner Plagen
> Um das geheimnißvolle Band. (P968)[61]

The disarming nature of a plea that she not scold him, in the context of an ostensibly covert avowal of love of the loftiest and most heartfelt kind through the farmboy story, seems clear enough, as does the equally disarming effect of the playful ending of this opening part of the young lover's tale, seen from our present perspective:

> Ich will nun suchen, auch sie ehstens zu sehn, oder vielmehr, wenn ich recht bedenke, ich wills vermeiden. Es ist besser, ich sehe sie durch die Augen ihres Liebhabers; vielleicht erscheint sie mir vor meinen eignen Augen nicht so, wie sie jetzt vor mir steht, und warum soll ich mir das schöne Bild verderben? (18R)

The first part of the farmboy story, then, is idyllic on both working levels, artistic and personal; there is no difference between Werther and the young lover in terms of devotion, piety, humility, ecstasy, and purest desire vis-à-vis his beloved – indeed, Werther's major point in retelling the story is to make his reader aware of the exalted sense of inner joy he experiences in the all-encompassing sweetness and quiet passion of the farmboy. This is for him true love, ideal love, the kind of love that he too would like for himself, hence his total identification with the other man. Werther's first meeting with the Bauernbursche is the prelude to his first meeting with Lotte and anticipates the joyful

---

[61] The original quatrain is contained in P252 (June 1778). Some other references to her annoyance and/or scolding are to be found in P43 (16 April 1776), Goethe's diary entries of 15 January (WA 3,1:31), P216 (1 February 1778), P227 (10/11 April 1778), P458 (9 August 1780), P485 (10 October 1780), P504 (24 November 1780), P528 (23/24 December 1780), P672 (6 June 1781), P701 (4 August 1781), P711 (29 August 1781), P1175 (26 November 1783), P1437 (3 September 1785), P1532 (18 February 1786).

springtime of his love. This part of the story, I feel sure, is also Goethe's account of the same phase in his own emotional life.

But however joyful the springtime, there was a melancholy autumn to follow in which all hopes of fulfilment in love were dashed. In Part Two of the farmboy's story the inevitable happens, prepared for already by a significant sentence in the earlier segment: 'Ich hab in meinem Leben die dringende Begierde und das heiße sehnliche Verlangen nicht in dieser Reinheit gesehen, ja wohl kann ich sagen, in dieser Reinheit nie gedacht und geträumt' (17R). As time goes on, the farmhand's love for his lady-mistress increasingly overwhelms his capacity for self-restraint in the expression of that love, and disaster ensues. He attempts to embrace her, she resists and her brother intervenes with such commotion to eject him from the household that all hope of continuing the love relationship is lost.

What is most interesting in this new piece of writing is the strange role of the widow, who, when implored by the farmboy to allow him some physical sign of love or affection, refuses to respond, and in so doing inflames his growing passion even more: '... da sie seinen Bitten kein Gehör gegeben, hab' er sich ihrer mit Gewalt bemächtigen wollen, er wisse nicht wie ihm geschehen sey' (94R). The fact is, she has already given him grounds for encouragement ('kleine Vertraulichkeiten,' 'Nähe' [94R]) – a most important point in defence of the physical advances the young man makes on his beloved, but one he is reluctant to admit to because of his sense of delicacy and love. The widow, it seems, is not altogether above reproach, despite the farmboy's attempts to elevate her beyond that level, and in this she shows certain similarities with the new Lotte of Version Two, for she too has encouraged the attentions of a young man rendered vulnerable through love to her wishes and whims; she too has on occasion been less than altogether 'proper' in society's terms in promoting moments of intimacy that at the very least demonstrate her pleasure in her lover's interest and continuing proximity.

The widow is not tied to another man as Lotte is, however, and so she can give free rein to her recurring coquettish impulses – which she has obviously done in the past, or else this particular farmboy, as presented by Werther, would not have dared even to ask for her favours, let alone tried to claim them. Taking her silence in the face of his entreaties as no real lack of encouragement, and given her past willingness to grant him at least a degree of physical intimacy, he makes his advances, only to discover that this time she had really meant no. 'Sie erwehrte sich sein' is all that we are told (95R). What form did his advances take, and how did she resist? We know nothing of either, nothing of whether he merely attempted to kiss her, or of how she reacted to his attempt. The formulation used to express the widow's unwillingness to yield to the farmboy at this point could cover everything from a gently dissuading movement of the hand or head to a series of screams capable of arousing the whole household. Whatever the details, her resistance may well have been such as to raise the alarm, for her brother comes on the scene: '... ihr Bruder kam dazu' – this is surely narrative at its tightest and most terse. The fact that the causal connection between the widow's resistance and her brother's appearance is omitted from the text leaves the possibility open that his arrival was nothing more than an unhappy coincidence.

But whatever the reason for his sudden appearance, this brother is eager to construe the situation to the detriment of the farmboy for the sake of his own children's inheritance; the result is that all hope of recovering a tenable position within the household is lost to the young man for ever. Is the widow relieved at having been rescued from his importunate advances? Again the text offers us no clear answer, but merely suggests that her wishes are of no importance to her brother, who has created such an uproar that she has no option but to consent to the dismissal: '... dieser [der Bruder] habe ihn gleich zum Hause hinaus gestoßen und einen solchen Lärm von der Sache gemacht, daß die Frau, *auch selbst wenn sie gewollt*, ihn nicht wieder hätte aufnehmen können' (95R, emphasis mine). In this, the farmboy's own account as told to Werther, all blame for the rupture attaches to the brother and by implication to society, but not to the widow herself.

Once the farmhand is dismissed, the widow wastes no time on regrets. Instead, she replaces one lover with another and straight away – at least according to village gossip – she breaks with her brother and is even said to be contemplating marriage with the farmboy's successor (95R). There seems to be a strange mixture of dynamism and passivity in play here in the widow's behaviour towards her brother and the two servants, which makes one wonder exactly what kind of picture one is meant to have of this woman. Was she not allegedly so traumatized by the memory of her first unhappy marriage that she had sworn never to marry again (17R)? How can she now be almost on the brink of matrimony to some hired hand she has only known for a very short time? Can it be that she had never loved the farmboy in the way she does his successor? This too is a problematic proposition, given the fact that she had encouraged the former's attentions, welcomed his physical proximity, and even allowed him what he haltingly confesses to as 'kleine Vertraulichkeiten' which he had understood as a validation of their mutual love:

> Da er eine Zeitlang geredet hatte, fing er an zu stocken, wie einer, der noch etwas zu sagen hat, und sich es nicht herauszusagen getraut; endlich gestand er mir auch mit Schüchternheit, *was sie ihm für kleine Vertraulichkeiten erlaubt, und welche Nähe sie ihm vergönnet*. Er brach zwey-dreimal ab und wiederhohlte die lebhaftesten Protestationen, daß er das nicht sage, um sie schlecht zu machen, wie er sich ausdrückte, daß er sie liebe und schätze wie vorher, *daß so etwas nicht über seinen Mund gekommen sey, und daß er es mir nur sage um mich zu überzeugen, daß er kein ganz verkehrter und unsinniger Mensch sey* ... (94R, emphasis mine)

The farmboy, in other words, tells Werther what special favours of intimacy he had already been granted earlier by the widow, in order to underline the defensibility of his own behaviour. Werther's discretion is even greater than that of the young peasant lad, however, for he conceals the details of these favours in retelling the story. We therefore have no means of knowing anything other than the farmboy's sense of hurt and confusion, and yet the widow is cast in a rather dubious light by implication, if not by straightforward revelation.

Up to this point a large part of the narrative has been given over to describing the young man's infatuation and progressive lack of control over his deepening passion for his beloved, and the terms of the description seem contrived to arouse the reader's sympathy rather than his outrage or censure:

> Er bekannte, ja er erzählte mit einer Art von Genuß und Glück der Wiedererinnerung, daß die Leidenschaft zu seiner Hausfrau sich in ihm tagtäglich vermehrt, daß er zuletzt nicht gewußt habe was er thue, wie er sich ausdrückte, wo er mit dem Kopf hin gesollt? Er habe weder essen

> noch trinken, noch schlafen können, es habe ihm an der Kehle gestockt, er habe gethan, was er nicht thun sollen, was ihm aufgetragen worden hab' er vergessen, er sey als wie von einem bösen Geist verfolgt gewesen, bis er eins Tags, als er sie in einer obern Kammer gewußt, ihr nachgegangen, ja vielmehr ihr nachgezogen worden sey; da sie seinen Bitten kein Gehör gegeben, hab' er sich ihrer mit Gewalt bemächtigen wollen, er wisse nicht wie ihm geschehen sey, und nehme Gott zum Zeugen, daß seine Absichten gegen sie immer redlich gewesen, und daß er nichts sehnlicher gewünscht, als daß sie ihn heirathen, daß sie mit ihm ihr Leben zubringen möchte. (92–4R)

The confessional nature of this piece of writing by Goethe seems clear; exactly why will become apparent in a moment. Encouraged by the widow's behaviour to believe that his love was reciprocated, the farmboy's yearning for physical intimacy increased to the point where he could no longer hold back. Why the unexpected rejection and subsequent passivity on the part of the widow in dealing with the situation? Was the farmhand's mistake in the action he took itself, or was it in daring to assume that he might give rein to his feelings as he, rather than she, saw fit? If we think of the widow's unclear reaction in fending him off, and the lingering possibility that she might not have wanted him to leave her service had it not been for her brother's intervention, then it seems quite possible that her rejection of his advances may have had more to do with her assertion of power over the young man than with anything else. This too could explain the speed with which another lover was found and the threshold of marriage reached with him. The real reason for the farmboy's rejection and ensuing crisis seems thus to be twofold: the widow's need for control, and the power of society to intrude with unhappy results on the lives of individuals. With all thought of future marriage rendered impossible because of her resolve never to marry again, the widow was in a position of supreme power emotionally, while her social standing also had the potential to act as a secondary level of protection if ever she wished to call on it. The text implies that she may not really have wished to do so; it also allows for the possibility that the young man may only have attempted to snatch a kiss from her. Her brother's success in driving the farmboy away, however, is based on society's capacity for outrage at behaviour it deems unseemly, for it is the uproar he causes, rather than any action on the widow's part, that precludes all possibility of the farmboy continuing in his role as servant. The portrayal of the brother is wholly unsympathetic, his motives blameworthy, and it seems to me that through his actions in this newly written passage society is more fiercely, if more obliquely, attacked than anywhere in the original novel. As we shall see when we come to consider the final section of the farmboy's tale, the view is implicitly presented through Werther that society cannot accept that passionate love should exist without punishment.

The tone in which the second part of the story is told and the way in which it is constructed contrive together to convey a clear sense to its intended reader of Werther's own extreme and seemingly doomed passion for Lotte. The text can be read here in two quite different ways, however. On the one hand, it is possible to see Werther's continuing endorsement of the farmhand's behaviour and his increasing identification with the latter's fate in strongly emotional terms as evidence of his growing inability to face reality and as a preparation, therefore, of the dangerous ground that will lead him to suicide. Read in this way, the second part of the story would become an important step in distancing the reader from the hero. On the other hand, it is equally possible to read it as evidence that the young farmboy has been most unfairly treated by the widow and through her by a society whose notions of propriety are simply used to serve its own interests. The first of these two readings has already been much explored, so it is the second to which I wish to give my attention, not as a replacement but as a co-existing possibility, for how one reads depends on one's attitude to Werther. If one views him and his eventual suicide in a negative light, then one is more inclined to the first of these readings, but if one adopts a position of sympathy for him and begins to see Lotte in the light I have suggested as possible only in the revised version of the novel, one can then see how both she and the widow are responsible for fanning the flames of passion in Werther and the farmboy respectively – which lends the behaviour of the two lovers rather a different slant. If each has good grounds to believe himself loved, then the betrayal of that love by the beloved woman can be more readily understood as the catalyst for anguish and even thoughts of violence.

Significantly, it is suppressed thoughts of violence on Werther's part towards Albert that provide the background to the introduction of this section of the unfortunate farmhand's tale. Where the story is placed is of considerable importance, for it follows on two letters from the original novel whose significance it highlights very clearly. The first is the letter of 21 August in which Werther's suppressed wish for Albert's death emerges for the first time, giving rise to terrifying flights of fancy in which he would have Lotte all to himself: 'Wenn ich mich so in Träumen verliere, kann ich mich des Gedankens nicht erwehren: wie wenn Albert stürbe? Du würdest! ja, sie würde – und dann laufe ich dem Hirngespinste nach, bis es mich an Abgründe führet, vor denen ich zurückbebe' (92L/R). This letter ends on an elegiac note expressing Werther's sense of self-alienation now that all his hope and vitality are destroyed and gone for ever, but it is immediately followed by one on 5 September which betrays his capacity for monomanic self-justification through love to the point where the thought that anyone else might love Lotte seems an offence against the natural order of things:

> Ich begreife manchmal nicht, wie sie ein anderer lieb haben *kann*, lieb haben *darf*, da ich sie so ganz allein, so innig, so voll liebe, nichts anders kenne, noch weiß, noch habe, als sie! (93L/R)

However, it is *not* only Werther for whom Lotte has a place in her life and heart, as her note to Albert, newly written to follow immediately after the second section of the farmboy's story, reminds us. Thus this second part of the tale, placed as it is between Werther's deepest wish and deepest fear, is used to emphasize the end of all hope for a happy outcome to his love. Small wonder that he chooses to fantazise himself into Albert's shoes rather than to confront the fact that the latter holds a place in Lotte's life for ever denied to him!

As I have said, both the structure and tone of Werther's account of what has happened to the farmboy are important. From their first meeting he had derived inspiration and hope, but not so from the second, and an air of decline and resignation dominates the whole framework of the tale now as a result. It opens with Werther in an elegiac mood, aware that his emotional springtime is past (93R), and it draws to a close with an assertion of inner calmness that has a chilling quality about it in view of what has gone before:

> ... lies die Geschichte mit Andacht, ich bitte dich. Ich bin heute still, indem ich das hinschreibe; du siehst an meiner Hand, daß ich nicht so strudle und sudle wie sonst: Lies mein Geliebter und denke dabey, daß es auch die Geschichte deines Freundes ist. Ja, so ist mirs gegangen, so wird mirs gehn, und ich bin nicht halb so brav, nicht halb so entschlossen, als der arme Unglückliche, mit dem ich mich zu vergleichen mich fast nicht getraue. (95–6R)

Notice the tone of fervent appeal to his intended reader. This is a major feature of the whole section, with almost as much weight being given by Werther to addressing his reader directly as to the actual retelling of the farmhand's unhappy story. The relationship with his reader is given greater prominence than ever before – in fact, it is so important that even Werther himself displays a rising irritation at his own emotional dependence on it:

> ... er [der Bauernbursche] erzählte mir seine Geschichte, die mich doppelt und dreyfach gerührt hat wie du leicht begreifen wirst, wenn ich dir sie wieder erzähle. Doch wozu das alles, warum behalt' ich nicht für mich, was mich ängstigt und kränkt? warum betrüb' ich noch dich? warum geb' ich dir immer Gelegenheit, mich zu bedauren und mich zu schelten. Seys denn, auch das mag zu meinem Schicksal gehören! (93R)

Observe how Werther attacks both himself and his intended reader simultaneously here: 'Why must I tell you all this?' he asks; 'Why do I keep giving you the opportunity to feel sorry for me and scold me?' He has mulled over the story of the farmboy's experiences this time instead of rushing to write about the encounter as he had done before,[62] and the summary of his reactions is that he feels a premonition of dread and anguish that will subsequently prove only too valid.

Werther has inquired about the farmboy in Wahlheim, only to be told that he has been dismissed and is now regarded as an outcast; he then meets him 'auf dem Wege nach einem andern Dorfe' (93R), i.e., not in Wahlheim itself, that Utopia of the mind and heart in which one meets with happy lovers, but in an emotional no-man's-land. And it is exactly here that Werther himself is located, metaphorically speak-

---

62 Cf. the introduction to the first part of the farmboy's story: 'Ich habe heut eine Scene gehabt' (16R) and the second: 'Gestern traf ich ihn' (93R).

ing, when he retells the tale. Just as he had been very much inside his own emotional Utopia when retelling the first part of the farmboy's story, so he is now quite clearly outside it, afraid that it can never be regained and unable to come to terms alone with what that represents. Not only does he devote approximately twice as much space to addressing his reader in this section of the story as the first, as if trying desperately to find understanding, but the tone of these addresses is also quite different: gone is his light-hearted irony, to be replaced by anguish in the fearful awareness that he will not readily find in this reader the acceptance and sympathy he so profoundly longs for.

'Ich korrigire am Werther und finde immer daß der Verfasser übel gethan hat sich nicht nach geendigter Schrifft zu erschiesen' (P1587): Goethe wrote these words to Frau von Stein on 25 June 1786 in a letter accepting her refusal to postpone her departure for Karlsbad despite all his pleas, and here we catch a glimpse of his capacity to strike out with suppressed anger and bitterness both at her and at himself at one and the same time, despite the touch of wry humour. With this one sentence he eradicates the positive value of their relationship of the past ten years and bitterly endorses Werther's own solution. By mid-1786, of course, he had been forced to accept a great deal in Charlotte's behaviour towards him that fell far short of his own ideal of mutual love, but he never did so without cost to himself. As his preoccupation with rewriting his earlier works continued to grow, and as he became progressively more absorbed in the old hurts, hopes, and fears of his own inner life, he withdrew into a shell of silence that even Frau von Stein found ominous. Not only did he keep his thoughts to himself at this time,[63] but he also secretly began to develop the plan for escape from Weimar that he had felt for a decade was the only possible solution to his unhappiness. Ironically, it was she who had strengthened his resolve sufficiently by that time for him to carry it through. 'Ja, liebe Lotte,' he had written in September 1782, '... ich bin dir so fest angebunden daß ich mein Leben zerreisen würde, wenn ich an eine Trennung dächte' (P964); and in April 1783: 'Ich darf nicht dran dencken daß ich mich von dir trenne. Ich meyne ich müsste dich mit nehmen' (P1084). 'Wüsstest du liebste Seele wie sehr du mir fehlst,'

---

63 See *Vertrauliche Briefe* 1:319: 'Wem wohl ist, der spricht! See also chapter 1, notes 93 and 94.

he wrote to her in Kochberg in September 1785, 'du würdest wenig Ruhe in deiner Einsamkeit haben, du würdest iede Stunde wünschen zu mir herüber zu fliegen und ein Leben mit mir zu theilen das mir ohne dich ganz und gar abgeschmackt und unerträglich wird' (P1440). What he had not yet grasped even by then – and it is something that Werther patently fails to grasp also, as we have just seen – was the fact that his love, however strong and pure, had no power to bring about the situation he so desired, in which he would have the unassailable first place in Lotte's life. This was a bitter realization for Goethe and one slow to dawn on him, but dawn it eventually did and with some force, for on 1 September 1786 he wrote:

> Ich habe bisher im Stillen gar mancherley getragen, und nichts so sehnlich gewünscht als daß unser Verhähltniß sich so herstellen möge, daß keine Gewalt ihm was anhaben könne. Sonst mag ich nicht in deiner Nähe wohnen und ich will lieber in der Einsamkeit der Welt bleiben, in die ich ietzt hinausgehe. (P1600)

Although Goethe's continuing hope to have Frau von Stein as his partner must have been shown up as illusory by her swift resumption of the role of dutiful and more attentive wife in late 1785, it was not until May 1786 that he stopped giving expression to this hope for the first time.[64] 'Goethe lebt in seinen Betrachtungen, aber er teilt sie nicht mit,' she wrote to Knebel that same month,[65] but had she known what these reflections were, she would scarcely have been well pleased, for here it was that he began to conceive the second and third parts of the farmboy story. These were evidently not exalted love letters in the manner of Part One, but an escape valve for dark emotions that could find no other ready outlet.

From Werther's overtures to his reader in the first section of the farmhand's tale we see this reader as a sceptic who may reject what he has to say as mere hyperbole, and who may well be inclined to rebuke him for an exaggerated readiness to cast himself in the role of a devoted lover caught in the throes of an exalted passion – a reader, in other words, who is exactly like Gertruth, the character whom Frau von

---

64 The last strong expressions of his longing for her to be with him before leaving for Italy can be found in P1564 and P1577 (April to May 1786).
65 *Vertrauliche Briefe* 1:319

Stein devised for herself in her early play *Rino*, first written in 1776 and reworked more than six years later.[66] Werther's protestations against the attitude of his reader in the opening section of the Bauernbursche story are ironic in part, but always gentle. Not so in Part Two. While his reader there is seen to be sceptical also and prone to think him exaggerated ('Was ich dir erzähle, ist nicht übertrieben, nichts verzärtelt, ja ich darf wohl sagen, schwach schwach hab' ich's erzählt' [95R]), this same reader is one who seems unlikely to accord him that total understanding he seeks, or such is his fear; alas, this reader seems likely to respond to what he has to say with pity and criticism: '... warum geb' ich dir immer Gelegenheit, mich zu bedauren und mich zu schelten. Seys denn, auch das mag zu meinem Schicksal gehören!' (93R). The bitterness of this last remark seems to be a strike by Werther against himself, connected with his anger at the need he has for his reader's empathetic response to what he has to tell. And yet this need is real. His repeated protestations of the integrity and high-mindedness of the farmboy,[67] together with his emphatic elevation of this young peasant to a level far above that of the comfortable bourgeois standing he himself outwardly shares with the person to whom he is writing, seem to betray his awareness of an emotional gulf between himself and this reader that he would give anything to overcome:

> Und hier, mein Bester fang' ich mein altes Lied wieder an, das ich ewig anstimmen werde: könnt' ich dir den Menschen vorstellen, wie er vor mir stand, wie er noch vor mir steht! *Könnt' ich dir alles recht sagen, damit du fühltest wie ich an seinem Schicksale Theil nehme, Theil nehmen muß!* Doch genug, da du auch mein Schicksal kennst, auch mich kennst, so weißt du nur zu wohl, was mich zu allen Unglücklichen, was mich besonders zu diesem Unglücklichen hinzieht ... Diese Liebe, diese Treue, diese Leidenschaft, is also keine dichterische Erfindung. Sie lebt, sie ist in ihrer größten Reinheit unter der Classe von Menschen, die wir ungebildet, die wir roh nen-

---

66 Schöll points out from minor changes to the text and the casting list that the final reworking of the play cannot have been completed before late December 1782; see *Goethes Briefe* 1:397, note 2.

67 See *Werther*, 93R: 'Könnt' ich dir, mein Freund, jedes seiner Worte vor Gericht stellen!' and 94R: '... er wisse nicht wie ihm geschehen sey, und nehme Gott zum Zeugen, daß seine Absichten gegen sie immer redlich gewesen ...'

nen. Wir gebildeten – zu nichts verbildeten, *lies die Geschichte mit Andacht, ich bitte dich.*

...

Lies mein Geliebter und denke dabey, daß es auch die Geschichte deines Freundes ist. (94-5R, emphasis mine)

In the first part of the story Werther's overwhelming urge was to present *himself* through the farmboy for the delight of his reader. In the second, however, there is a noticeable change that arises, to my mind, from the same need on Goethe's part to write at two levels simultaneously that we observed in the earlier segment. On both levels now the added emphasis on Werther's need for empathy and understanding underlines his growing isolation from all human beings and betrays his increasingly hopeless plight, but on the esoteric level it also seems to offer an anecdotal insight into the final stages of Goethe's relationship with Charlotte von Stein, the 'Geliebt[e]' of Werther's last entreaty in his retelling of the farmboy's story.[68]

While the poet was capable of great gentleness and generosity of spirit, almost to a fault,[69] there was another element in his makeup that found repeated expression in the course of his relationship with Frau von Stein. That element was a ready capacity for anger. In December 1774 he told Knebel, for example: 'Es ist der Zustand meiner Seele, daß, so wie ich etwas haben muß, auf das ich eine Zeitlang das Ideal des Vortrefflichen lege, so auch wieder etwas für das Ideal meines Zorns.'[70] There can be no doubt that in Charlotte von Stein Goethe discovered for the first time his ideal of the beloved counterpart, but as time went on and her behaviour towards him fell increasingly short of that ideal, he began to draw back into anger and hurt silence. As he said of himself in later years: 'Von Natur zu gelassener Betrachtung der Dinge aufgelegt, werde ich doch grimmig, sobald ich

---

68 Given the rather fulsome forms of address that arose from the friendship cult of the eighteenth century, the 'mein Geliebter' of the last sentence Werther addresses to his reader here need have no major significance. I would point out, however, that it does not occur at all in Version One and only at this point in Version Two. Goethe began using this form of address in letters to Charlotte von Stein in March 1781 and continued to do so until August 1785; he did not use it again until August 1786, after he had taken leave of her for the last time in Schneeberg.
69 For example, P420 (5 May 1780), P856 (10 April 1782), P1271 (14 June 1784), etc.
70 Knebel to Bertuch, 23 December 1774 (Biedermann/Herwig 1:128)

sehe, daß man dem Menschen das Unmögliche abfodert.'[71] Once he registered that the impossible was being asked of him as a way of life in the longer term, he resolved to get away.

Even as far back as 1776 he had from time to time displayed his dark side as a lover. Rage, despair, and the capacity to strike back at his beloved are all to be found in many of his letters to Charlotte, overwhelmed though they may be in number by outpourings of the most devoted love. But in striking out at her, he also lacerated himself,[72] and it is this quality above all that marks the writing of the two last segments of the farmhand's narrative on each of its two levels, but more markedly so on the personal, hidden one. In Goethe's letters to Frau von Stein there is recurring evidence of passive aggression with undertones of self-flagellation, going all the way back to 1776, as we saw in connection with his torment at her decision not to allow him to visit her at her country estate during her lengthy absence.

'Früh war Lenz da. Wegen Kochberg. Reine Trauer des Lebens' – so reads Goethe's diary entry on 10 September 1776 (WA 3,1:121); this was one period in his life that he never forgot, a period in which he wrote *Die Geschwister*, putting into Marianne's mouth his own sentiments which he wanted Frau von Stein to share: 'Unter allem konnt ich am wenigsten leiden, wenn sich ein Paar Leute lieb haben, und endlich kommt heraus, daß sie verwandt sind, oder Geschwister sind' (HA 4:367). In this case Goethe's writing offered him the chance of creating an instant happy end for ever after, but real life was not so easy to write. Only a few days after completing the play he was lamenting the lack of physical love he was having to endure and appealing to Charlotte to remedy it, and a week after that he reviewed his past year in Weimar with not altogether happy results: 'Ich mußte mein Tagbuch nachsehen um Ihre Zettelgen zu verstehen hie und da, und fand alles. Wieviel wieder lebendig wurde! Ach die acht Wochen

---

71 Conversation with Falk, 9 May 1808 (ibid. 2:313)
72 For example, P132 (7 March 1777), P161 (5 May 1777), P163 (7 May 1777), P191 (31 October 1777), P211 (9 January 1778), P212 (10 January 1778), P216 (1 February 1778), P227 (10/11 April 1778), P482 (18 September 1780), P485 (10 October 1780), P485 (11 October 1780), P672 (6 June 1781), P688 (8 July 1781), P920 (22 July 1782), etc.

[while she was away with Lenz in Kochberg] haben doch viel verschüttet in mir, und ich blieb immer der ganz sinnliche Mensch ...' (P107).

Upsets like this, we know, were neither exceptional nor confined to the early stages of Goethe's relationship with Frau von Stein. Unsure of her feelings for him altogether by March 1786, he began to spend more of his time writing, and soon he began to reassert the primacy of love over all else once again. His own personal tribulations, which derived almost solely, as he believed, from society's pressures and the whims of court life, had been bitterly augmented by his reflections on the infamous 'necklace scandal' of the French court,[73] and so his natural inclination to extol the peasantry was further vindicated and strengthened. Thus the three ingredients that make up in essence the last two parts of the farmhand's story were all significant elements of Goethe's consciousness by the time of writing in mid-1786: love was supreme; the upper classes were a renewed object of scorn; and he could not count on Charlotte for the constant loving support he sorely needed.

Whether or not Goethe was rebuffed by Frau von Stein at some point in exactly the same way as the farmboy by his lady is impossible to say with certainty. However, his letters to her do contain sufficient subtle intimations of her willingness to allow and bestow at least some of 'the little intimacies' of love to suggest that Werther's account of the unhappy farmhand's version of events was not far removed, at the very least, from his creator's own experiences.[74]

It is my view that there was a definite physical aspect, limited or not, to Goethe's relationship with Frau von Stein already by 1776, and that it was partly fear of this which made her prevent him from accompanying her to Kochberg in September of that year. Both *Der Falke*

---

73 'Schon im Jahr 1785 hatte die Halsbandgeschichte einen unaussprechlichen Eindruck auf mich gemacht. In dem unsittlichen Stadt-, Hof- und Staats-Abgrunde, der sich hier eröffnete, erschienen die greulichsten Folgen gespensterhaft, deren Erscheinung ich geraume Zeit nicht los werden konnte; wobei ich mich so seltsam benahm, daß Freunde ... mir später gestanden, daß ich ihnen damals wie wahnsinnig vorkam.' (*Tag- und Jahreshefte 1789*, WA 1,35:11).
74 In all fairness to the 'widow' perhaps a comment in a letter by Zimmermann to Lavater (3 November 1777) should not be overlooked: 'Die Liebkosungen von Goethe scheinen mir die Liebkosungen eines Tigers. Man faßt unter seinen Umarmungen immer an den Dolch in der Tasche ...' [!]; see *Vertrauliche Briefe* 1:221.

184   Werther's Goethe

and *Die Geschwister* lead me to this conclusion, supported by Goethe's lamentations in the poem 'An den Geist des Johannes Sekundus,' written for her just a few days after her return to Weimar. Traces of the continuing tension of September-October were still in evidence even by late November,[75] with the first hint of any happy resolution coming on Goethe's return from Wörlitz on 22 December: 'Wie ich Ihnen dancke fühlen Sie, sonst hätten Sie *das* nicht geben' (P116). What the gift was we do not know, but then references that might well indicate an intimacy in their relationship are never clear – as on 5 April 1782, for example: 'Deine Wörte kommen mir mit den Frühlingslüfften gar zu lieblich entgegen, und rufen mich zu dir hinüber ... Bewahre mir deine Liebe in der Stille und gieb mir auf einmal was die Entfernung mir versagt' (P853). A similarly oblique message comes in a letter three months later, almost immediately prior to the major row that began on 18 July, a row reminiscent in its emotional impact on Goethe of events six years before, in September-October 1776. On 16 July he wrote: 'Die Melone wollen wir zusammen verzehren, und uns zusammen noch einer süseren Kost freuen die Sommer und Winter das schmackhaffteste ist. Lebe wohl. Eh ich in's Conseil gehe komm ich einen Augenblick' (P916). His note on the 18th expresses his disquiet of the day before – evidently the aftermath of their evening together on the 16th: 'Gieb L.L. ein Zeichen des Lebens und der Liebe von dir. Gestern konnte mir den ganzen Tag nicht wohl werden' (P917), and by the following day a full-scale emotional crisis has erupted, as we saw.

What perhaps lends greatest credibility to the belief that Goethe's relationship with Frau von Stein was not wholly platonic are the changes made to the poem he wrote for her in August 1777: 'An den Mond.'[76] In these we come closest, I believe, to any admission on her part that some degree of physical intimacy existed between them. Whatever the exact chronological sequence of the three versions we now have of this poem may be – and there are good grounds for thinking that the final version of 1789 derived from one written by

---

75 See P110: 'Hier liebe Frau den Rest von allerley Bildnerey, die mein Herz unter ihrer Regierung vollbracht hat. Ich wollt dass das der letzte Transport wäre, und ich aufhören könnte Sie zu plagen durch meine unhimmlische Gegenwart.'
76 Petersen offers evidence for claiming that the poem was first written in 1777 (1,2:579f.), and challenges the original dating (1778) on grounds that seem convincing (576ff.).

Charlotte von Stein two years earlier[77] – the most important alteration was the introduction of the lines 'So verrauschte Scherz und Kuß, / Und die Treue so.' Both parties accepted this, so whether the lines originated with Goethe or Charlotte is unimportant. She wrote them out under the title 'An den Mond, nach meiner Manier' in 1787 while Goethe was away in Italy; he used them in his published poem of 1789. It seems clear that there *was* a degree of physical intimacy between them to which Goethe gave expression here and there, but expression so oblique that only he and his one special dialogue partner, Frau von Stein, could be sure of what he was truly saying. Appropriately enough, he created and maintained for others a veil of secrecy around his real relationship with her, a veil so clever and impenetrable that it has remained intact for over two centuries, helped on by the fervour of nineteenth-century scholarly reverence and love of myth-making where Goethe was concerned. Were it not for the fact that he so consistently wrote his life into his works, and not always in an aesthetically satisfying way, it would be altogether insignificant and a secret better left alone.

The farmboy's crisis, however, is also Goethe's crisis; it is a tale of woe, of love subjected to impossible constraints, a melancholy tale wrought by a social code that applauds Werther's Philistine and deplores the true lover. It is also the tale of a man betrayed by his beloved, and in this I think we see something of Goethe's capacity for aggression and self-laceration, for in describing the conduct of the widow he is giving bitter, though covert, vent to his own worst imaginings: the widow does nothing to prevent her young lover's eviction, and as soon as he is gone she finds herself an immediate replacement whom she may even marry. Like the Bauernbursche, Goethe too felt obliged to put a distance between himself and the scene of his torment; like him he was also evidently incapable of expressing anger at the behaviour of his beloved in forthright terms, betrayed though he felt himself to be. The farmboy needed Werther as

---

77 The original and the final versions can be found in BA 2:570 and BA 1:69f. respectively. Frau von Stein wrote another poem around the same time after Goethe's departure for Italy, in which she also gave vent to anguish and despair at the loneliness of her present existence without him. This poem, found among her posthumous papers, is cited by Alphons Nobel, in *Frau von Stein: Goethes Freundin und Feindin*, 1939, 109.

an outlet to lessen the emotional burden of what had happened to him, and Goethe seems to have needed both characters for much the same end.

The Editor's Report

At that point in both versions of the novel where the Editor takes over Werther's narrative for the sake of offering his readers as complete an account as possible of the hero's last days, an important shift seems to take place in the major fictive premise of the work, for until his voice is heard the reader has been caught up in the belief that he has been reading a collection of private letters originally intended only for one specific addressee of Werther's choosing. Yet this belief, like the figure of the Editor himself, is merely a fiction created and exploited by the author. Without this character who is external to the events of the narrative he presents, we would have no access to Werther's account of his love and suffering. Or so we are led to believe on opening the book, for the Editor's preface tells us so. Not only that, it also tells us how we will respond to the story we are about to read:

> Was ich von der Geschichte des armen Werthers nur habe auffinden können, habe ich mit Fleiß gesammlet und lege es euch hier vor, und weiß daß ihr mir's danken werdet. Ihr könnt seinem Geiste und seinem Charakter eure Bewunderung und Liebe, seinem Schicksale eure Thränen nicht versagen.
>
> Und du gute Seele, die du eben den Drang fühlst wie er, schöpfe Trost aus seinem Leiden, und laß das Büchlein deinen Freund seyn, wenn du aus Geschick oder eigener Schuld keinen nähern finden kannst. (2L/R)

He has worked hard, he says, to build up as complete a record of Werther's tale as possible, and his readership will be grateful to him for his efforts; he is convinced too that his broader public can only react to Werther with admiration, love, and pity, while to the individual in a position to identify with the hero the book will be a source of comfort and companionship. How extraordinary for the tale of a life that ends in suicide to be presented as a source of comfort for those who, like Werther, have suffered torment in love! Not once, but twice

Goethe produced this preface to his work without any alteration in the wording, the second time long after he had supposedly left the emotionalism of his earlier years far behind.

There can be no doubt of the Editor's positive assessment of Werther's story and that assessment prevails throughout both versions, in the second even more strongly than in the first. In this Editor Goethe has created a character who controls, without seeming to control, what we read, a character rather like a biographer who has come upon a human subject he himself finds fascinating and for whose story he has a very high regard. He tries to let his primary documents speak for themselves wherever possible, but where these are fragmentary or non-existent he steps in to provide as many bridges or explanations as he has been able to find through the use of all available sources. Several fictive levels, first established in Version One and carried on throughout Version Two, operate simultaneously here: the first-person voice of the author is given over to two other 'I' voices in the Editor and Werther, each of whom addresses his own selected audience, the Editor the broader readership of the published work ('you' = 'ihr'), Werther the individual recipient of the letters ('you' = 'du'). The Editor has no 'du,' Werther no 'ihr,' for their intentions are ostensibly different – Werther's to bare his soul only to his chosen friend, the Editor's to present a story that he is sure will have an emotional impact on many people. All of this is true of both versions, 1774 as well as 1787, but when the text undergoes change, the hidden author re-emerges as the real controlling force behind the text, for although the fiction is maintained that only the Editor controls the presentation of his material, he too undergoes a certain transformation in Version Two, which exposes his implicit claim to omnipotence within the text as the fiction it has always been.

Two letters leading into the Editor's Report towards the end of the novel have been taken out and reinserted later in Version Two, after the conclusion of the newly written farmboy story, and the result is that the reader's impression of Werther differs in the second version and the first at that point where the Editor takes up the narrative. The first of these two letters (8 December, 113–14L) reveals Werther's overwhelming preoccupation with suicide, no longer as a theory but as an act he is now more than willing to contemplate. This train of thought is set in motion by his sight of Wahlheim physically destroyed by flood, with his memories of places where he had spent happy hours with Lotte now violated as a result. In the course of his subsequent longing for death his sense of inner and outer confinement is emphasized several times in the original novel,[78] but these are all emotions and sensations that are delayed in the second version until Werther has been defeated in his attempts to rescue the farmboy from the clutches of the law, and the resulting impact on the text is to add an even greater urgency to Werther's search for a lasting solution to his anguish. Also delayed are the emotions and sensations of the second relocated letter (17 December, 114–15L), where Werther is forced to recognize for the first time the clash between his own fiction and truth, between his conscious and subconscious self, for while he claims that his feelings for Lotte spring from the purest, most sacred, brotherly love ('die heiligste, reinste, brüderlichste Liebe,' 114L), his dreams reveal a reality that cannot be suppressed, despite all conscious effort: sensual passion is what he feels, passion that can never find an outlet. His conclusion is sinister and chilling: 'Mir wärs besser ich gienge' (115L).

Werther's own narrative ends in the second version with a letter that immediately precedes these two in the original text (6 December, 112–13L/R). It consists of two paragraphs, the first giving vent to his total obsession with Lotte – 'Wie mich die Gestalt verfolgt! Wachend und träumend füllt sie meine ganze Seele! ...' – the second a bitter lament on the deadening chill of the cold light of day, metaphorically speaking, that destroys the heights and depths of man's deepest emotions and thwarts his yearning for totality and infinity:

> Was ist der Mensch, der gepriesene Halbgott! Ermangeln ihm nicht eben da die Kräfte, wo er sie am nöthigsten braucht? Und wenn er in Freude sich aufschwingt, oder im Leiden versinkt, wird er nicht in beyden eben da aufgehalten, eben da zu dem stumpfen, kalten Bewußtseyn wieder zurückgebracht, da er sich in der Fülle des Unendlichen zu verlieren sehnte? (113L/R)

Whereas in Version One Werther's own section of his story ends with

---

78 Werther describes his inner state as 'ein inneres unbekanntes Toben, das meine Brust zu zerreissen droht, das mir die Gurgel zupreßt' (113L), and refers to himself as 'de[r] Eingekerkert[e],' 'ein[ ] Gefangene[r]' (114L).

a grim and melancholy statement hinting at his intention to put an end to his life, Version Two comes to a close on this quite different note of broader reflection and yearning, passionate and heartfelt though its tone may be. Thus the conclusion of this part of the novel leaves the reader in a different frame of mind from the first. Why the change? I think it arose in part from Goethe's need to re-engage with the novel in terms of his own inner state at the time of rewriting, and in part from his awareness of reader response to it during the previous twelve years. By the point at which the Editor took over the narrative in the 1774 *Werther*, the ending was unknown to the reader, the tension therefore considerably higher. Twelve years later, however, such tension was no longer possible because of the sensational impact of the work, above all because of its dramatic ending, and Goethe was well aware that this was the case. He never contemplated altering his account of Werther's suicide, even though it was more borrowed than original; what he did instead was to alter the role of the Editor in such a way as to be able to use him to fill in many important details concerning the chief players in the love triangle, details important to Goethe for a variety of reasons. The fact that Werther's eventual suicide could be assumed known to the reader of Version Two and assumed likely to predispose him either to rejection or emulation of the hero was only one of the reasons for making certain changes in the final section, which became half as long again as it was in the original.

The persona the Editor seeks to establish for himself at the beginning of his Report in Version Two is more clearly than before that of a cool, detached scholar who pursues his researches methodically and presents his evidence with care. His opening lament at the incompleteness of the primary documentation in Werther's own words, and his mention of the lengths he has gone to in order to gather all the pertinent information on Werther's final days link up with his long-forgotten preface to re-establish him as industrious and committed to the task at hand. He is also now noticeably clear-sighted, for he is aware of differences of opinion among those from whom he has gleaned information, even though there is consensus for the most part on the basic facts (116R). According to him, his task is to present his material conscientiously and with meticulous attention to detail, for the subject he is dealing with is no low or ordinary man:

> Was bleibt uns übrig, als dasjenige was wir mit wiederhohlter Mühe erfahren können, gewissenhaft zu erzählen; die von dem Abscheidenden hinterlaßnen Briefe einzuschalten und das kleinste aufgefundene Blättchen nicht gering zu achten; zumal da es so schwer ist, die eigensten wahren Triebfedern auch nur einer einzelnen Handlung zu entdecken, wenn sie unter Menschen vorgeht, die nicht gemeiner Art sind. (116R)

All of this is very reassuring. In Version One the Editor makes only a brief comment on how he has added eye-witness accounts to Werther's letters for the sake of greater completeness (116L), but in the new version he goes to some lengths to present himself as someone who takes his task seriously and who has enough of a distance from his subject to enable him to be dispassionate in the presentation of his material.

Whereas the equivalent passage in Version One had focused on the severely deteriorating relationship between Albert and Lotte and the atmosphere of resentful distrust that had grown up between them because of Albert's jealous and suspicious behaviour (116–17L), in the second version the primary focus is on Werther:

> Unmuth und Unlust hatten in Werthers Seele immer tiefer Wurzel geschlagen, sich fester unter einander verschlungen und sein ganzes Wesen nach und nach eingenommen. Die Harmonie seines Geistes war völlig zerstört, eine innerliche Hitze und Heftigkeit, die alle Kräfte seiner Natur durcheinander arbeitete, brachte die widrigsten Wirkungen hervor und ließ ihm zuletzt nur eine Ermattung übrig, aus der er noch ängstlicher empor strebte als er mit allen Übeln bisher gekämpft hatte. Die Beängstigung seines Herzens zehrte die übrigen Kräfte seines Geistes, seine Lebhaftigkeit, seinen Scharfsinn auf, er ward ein trauriger Gesellschafter, immer unglücklicher und immer ungerechter, je unglücklicher er ward. Wenigstens sagen dieß Alberts Freunde ... (116–17R)

In this passage the Editor establishes himself as sympathetic towards his subject and yet at the same time fair-minded: he presents Werther's loss of inner harmony, his asocial behaviour, his deepening melancholy and his growing unfairness in his attitude to Albert. The fact that he is merely reporting back what he has heard from those who have been approached for information is highlighted also, and so his objectivity is made clear. Or so it seems. In the remainder of the opening passage that objectivity is underscored several times, as we have seen,[79] and it is with the stance of the Editor thus defined and secured that we begin to read the prelude to the third and final part of the farmboy's story.

But a closer look at what we are now called on to read reveals that we were wrong to feel reassured by the greater promise of narrative objectivity, for no sooner is this established than it is abandoned again in favour of a creative reconstruction of the narrative by the Editor through the mind and heart of Werther. A few brief facts are given to explain why he sets out for the Amtmann's house (117R), but once the bare framework is established, the narrative perspective changes:

> Das klare Wetter konnte wenig auf sein trübes Gemüth wirken, ein dumpfer Druck lag auf seiner Seele, die traurigen Bilder hatten sich bey ihm festgesetzt und sein Gemüth kannte keine Bewegung als von einem schmerzlichen Gedanken zum andern ... (117–18R)

Nobody but Werther could reconstruct his inner state with any authority, yet this authority is implicitly claimed by the Editor. What happens here and from this point onward, however, thanks to the clever but covert narrative perspective, is that Werther's alleged quality as a human being of no mean calibre ('nicht gemeiner Art') is subtly underlined in a way that would scarcely have been possible without the Editor's promise that what follows is the result of lengthy researches and meticulous reporting. The implicit promise of dispassionate objectivity in his account, in other words, is a lure by which the reader is induced to accept much of Werther's version of events in a manner that he might well not have done otherwise, given his awareness of the eventual outcome of the story. Notice the emotive language in the lines above ('a dull weight on his soul,' 'the melancholy images,' 'from one painful thought to the other') and consider how the new passage now continues:

> Wie er mit sich in ewigem Unfrieden lebte, schien ihm auch der Zustand andrer nur bedenklicher und verworrener, er glaubte das schöne Verhältniß zwischen Albert und seiner Gattinn gestört zu haben, er machte sich Vorwürfe darüber, in die sich ein heimlicher Unwille gegen den Gatten mischte. (118R)

---

[79] See pp. 124f.

Because of its terse style and 'reliable' narrative stance this passage elicits from the reader already aware of the ending of the novel a greater sympathy for Werther than any of his own notes or letters could have done at this juncture. Everything rings true here, despite the fact that, if looked at more closely and objectively, it all turns out to be nothing more than a figment of the Editor's creative imagination. But such a close and objective look is clearly not what this Editor expects from the readers to whom he has addressed himself at the outset. Significantly, everything here also subtly contributes to a rebuilding of Werther's credibility and worth if we accept his premise that love is all, as the Editor of the preface believes we will: we are told that his own inner turmoil is responsible for his growing inability to sort out what is going on in the minds and hearts of other people; he is aware of having come between Albert and his wife – note how Lotte is referred to on this one and only occasion – and he reproaches himself for having disturbed their good relationship, but not without a secret feeling of resentment towards the husband. Is such resentment unnatural or difficult to understand? Isn't it a surprise to us, yet to Werther's credit, that he is newly capable of self-reproach? He cannot sustain this line of thought for long, however. The text continues:

> Seine Gedanken fielen auch unterwegs auf diesen Gegenstand. *Ja, ja sagte er zu sich selbst, mit heimlichem Zähnknirschen: das ist der vertraute, freundliche, zärtliche an allem theilnehmende Umgang, die ruhig daurende Treue!* Sattigkeit ists und Gleichgültigkeit!   (118R, emphasis mine)

Here the narrative voice is not that of any Editor, but quite simply of Werther, the lover, as he turns over in his mind the various qualities which are valued by society as those of a good husband, qualities which Albert undoubtedly has but which Werther utterly rejects as appropriate manifestations of love. And his rejection becomes more impassioned as his thoughts move on to the specifics of Albert's behaviour:

> Zieht ihn nicht jedes elende Geschäft mehr an als die theure, köstliche Frau? Weiß er sein Glück zu schätzen? Weiß er sie zu achten wie sie es verdient?

Albert is the very model of the Philistine lover in Werther's eyes, the only type of lover society finds acceptable, and one already heatedly attacked in the early stages of the original novel. There Werther had railed against those tenets of society that necessarily reduce love to an activity with which to while away one's leisure hours, tenets that dictate that the lover transform his urge to squander all his resources on his beloved into carefully calculated and predictably regulated punctuation marks of generosity in the larger story of his life. As the Philistine, that responsible bearer of public office, had said in his imagined advice to the young lover:

> Theilet eure Stunden ein, die einen zur Arbeit und die Erholungsstunden widmet eurem Mädchen. Berechnet euer Vermögen und was euch von eurer Nothdurft übrig bleibt, davon verwehr' ich euch nicht ihr ein Geschenk, nur nicht zu oft, zu machen, etwa zu ihrem Geburts- und Nahmenstage. (13–14L/R)

Werther had rejected this advice once before, and he more passionately rejects its seemingly heightened embodiment in Albert now, whose lack of attentiveness towards Lotte, lack of gratitude that she should be his wife, and lack of proper appreciation of her person all clearly render him unworthy in Werther's eyes of his role as her husband. But unworthy or not, there is no denying the fact that he *is* Lotte's husband, and Werther's anger and despair at this awareness make him round on Albert mentally with accusations of dishonouring the bond of their friendship by his resentful attitude:

> Er hat sie, nun gut er hat sie – Ich weiß das, wie ich auch was anders weiß, ich glaube an den Gedanken gewöhnt zu seyn, er wird mich noch rasend machen, er wird mich noch umbringen – Und hat denn die Freundschaft zu mir Stich gehalten? Sieht er nicht in meiner Anhänglichkeit an Lotten schon einen Eingriff in seine Rechte, in meiner Aufmerksamkeit für sie einen stillen Vorwurf? Ich weiß es wohl; ich fühl' es, er sieht mich ungern, er wünscht meine Entfernung, meine Gegenwart ist ihm beschwerlich. (118R)

Notice the crescendo of helpless resentment thoughout the passages I have cited: as the fact of Albert's *proprietorship* of Lotte grows in Werther's mind, he moves from self-reproach for coming between husband and wife to contempt for Albert as an embodiment of the stock husbandly virtues, on to thoughts of his unworthiness as Lotte's partner, and from there to the belief that he is a false friend. Unable to be fair to his rival, Werther tries to make of him a justifiable enemy, and it is this state of heightened animosity towards Albert that provides the emotional background to his discovery that the farmboy's rival has been murdered. Or so the Editor would have us believe, for the account is his. Fabricating Werther's own thoughts wherever he deems it necessary for his rendering of the 'complete' story, he neatly places the final part of the farmhand's tale between two passages that have to do with Werther's attitude of mind towards Albert. The 'prologue' to the tale consists of those parts of the text we have just looked at, where the reader is obliged to recognize Werther's unfairness to his rival; the 'epilogue' takes the form of a brief note, allegedly in Werther's own hand, in which he acknowledges this lack of fairness and the impossibility of his adopting any other attitude to Albert, however hard he may try:

> Was hilft es, daß ich mirs sage und wieder sage, er ist brav und gut, aber es zerreißt mir mein inneres Eingeweide; ich kann nicht gerecht seyn. (122R)

These words are a reiteration of Werther's alleged train of thought on the way to join Lotte at her father's house ('das ist der vertraute, freundliche, zärtliche an allem theilnehmende Umgang, die ruhig daurende Treue! ...' 118R), but with a difference: he now honestly faces up to his rival's real worth and his own inability to come to terms with it. Far from adding to our suspicion of his insanity or to our critical distance from the unbalanced mind that his reactions to the farmhand might have seemed to betray, this one small note restores a considerable degree of the willing reader's sympathy to Werther, whose clarity of mind, yet helpless love for Lotte, it so obviously underlines.

But why introduce the conclusion of the farmboy's tale through the eyes and mind of a biased and unbalanced Werther, only to bring the whole episode to an end by restoring him to a level of mental equilibrium that must surely be deemed above reproach? In this piece of clever editorial craftsmanship there seems to lie a valuable pointer to how we are meant to read the last part of the Bauernbursche tale – not as the manifestation of progressive madness through unrequited love, but as the dramatic climax of Werther's melancholy transition from joy to despair, where he gives vent for a short time, and a short time only, to an uncontrollable fury at the fact that, despite the purity, honesty, and power of his love, it can do nothing to alter his emotional situation. The word 'Wahlheim' once more features prominently here; Werther's emotional Utopia is finally destroyed: 'Er eilte nach Wahlheim zu, jede Erinnerung ward ihm lebendig ... [er] entsetzt' sich vor dem sonst so geliebten Platze ... Liebe und Treue, die schönsten menschlichen Empfindungen hatten sich in Gewalt und Mord verwandelt' (119R).

However, in assuming the guilt of the farmboy, Werther seems to leap to conclusions that may not be fully justified. They are certainly not fully substantiated. All that he needs in order to be convinced that the farmboy has indeed murdered his rival is to learn the *identity* of the dead man. Werther is more sure than anyone else of the farmboy's guilt; his response is instantaneous:

> Der Thäter war noch unbekannt, man hatte den Erschlagenen des Morgens vor der Hausthür gefunden, man hatte Muthmaßungen: der Entleibte war Knecht einer Wittwe, die vorher einen andern im Dienste gehabt, der mit Unfrieden aus dem Hause gekommen war.
>
> Da Werther dieses hörte, fuhr er mit Heftigkeit auf. Ists möglich, rief er aus, ich muß hinüber, ich kann nicht einen Augenblick ruhn. Er eilte nach Wahlheim zu, jede Erinnerung ward ihm lebendig und er zweifelte nicht einen Augenblick daß jener Mensch die That begangen, den er so manchmal gesprochen, der ihm so werth geworden war. (119R)

What has been inexplicably overlooked by readers and critics for over two hundred years is that no part of the text unequivocally supports the idea that the farmhand is indeed guilty of any crime. All that the latter says when he is confronted by Werther after his arrest is this: 'Keiner wird sie haben, sie wird keinen haben' (120R). The murder victim is not the widow, however, but her new lover, so both of these assertions are very strange indeed. How can the farmboy be so certain that his beloved will never belong to anyone else or anyone else to her? Only if he knows, or is totally convinced, that her brother is the murderer would his claims make sense. The brother was clearly committed to ensuring that the widow's estate was secured for his own children and unwilling to brook the thought of any threat to that plan; it was for this reason that he had put an end to the farmboy's relationship with his sister, and it was presumably for the same reason that he then had a major row with her over the next man she took into her life. Does the farmboy see the murder as evidence that his ex-mistress will be under her brother's control for ever? As I have said, only this would make full sense of his assertions. Nothing in the text gives us explicit grounds for believing that the brother is guilty, however. Must we therefore assume that the farmboy is indulging in wishful thinking, or that he is caught in the grip of an insane belief that he has eliminated all rivals for ever by killing his successor? The manner and tone of his answer to Werther's challenge 'Was hast du begangen, Unglücklicher!' would make this a very curious form of insanity in the wake of such an act of violence:

> Dieser [der Bauernbursche] sah ihn still an, schwieg und versetzte endlich ganz gelassen: 'Keiner wird sie haben, sie wird keinen haben.'
> (120R)

Are we to believe that what he says here to Werther amounts to an admission of guilt? Perhaps we are, but the ambiguous formulation of his response both in this one sentence and in his seeming resolve earlier not to be around for the marriage of his rival to his beloved widow ('er sey fest entschlossen das nicht zu erleben' [95R]) gives no proof of any guilt. In actual fact, the more closely we look, the more inconclusive the grounds for believing the farmboy guilty of murder turn out to be. The text in the second part of the tale, where his resolve to dispose of himself or his rival is supposedly expressed, is so wholly ambiguous that it may not refer to the farmboy at all, but to the widow's brother. The relevant words just quoted (95R) are undoubtedly a declaration of total hostility to the notion of marriage between the widow and her new hired hand, but the authorship of that declaration is quite unclear. For the sake of contextual clarity we should perhaps take another look at that particular passage. Werther, having just established his emotional solidarity with the farmboy in the strongest possible terms, continues in this way:

> Da ich das Blatt wieder durchlese seh' ich, daß ich das Ende der Geschichte zu erzählen vergessen habe, das sich aber leicht hinzu denken läßt. Sie erwehrte sich sein; ihr Bruder kam dazu, der ihn schon lange gehaßt ..., weil er fürchtet, durch eine neue Heirath der Schwester werde seinen Kindern die Erbschaft entgehn, die ihnen jetzt, da sie kinderlos ist, schöne Hoffnungen gibt; dieser habe ihn gleich zum Hause hinaus

gestoßen und habe einen solchen Lärm von der Sache gemacht, daß die Frau, auch selbst wenn sie gewollt, ihn nicht wieder hätte aufnehmen können. *Jetzt habe sie einen andern Knecht genommen, auch über den, sage man, sei sie mit dem Bruder zerfallen und man behaupte für gewiß, sie werde ihn heirathen, aber er sey fest entschlossen, das nicht zu erleben.* (95R, emphasis mine)

Notice the total absence of focus on the farmboy throughout these lines as Werther hastily relates the end of the sorry tale of the dismissal. Why, then, have we always read the concluding words of this passage ('er sey fest entschlossen ...') as if they were a clear declaration of suicidal or murderous intent on the part of the Bauernbursche rather than on the part of the brother? I think the answer lies in the subtle ambiguity of the writing at this point, combined with our failure as readers to pay sufficient attention to such subtlety throughout the entire farmboy story.

The one remaining reference to his reaction to his situation as alleged murderer comes as a postscript to the whole tale when Werther learns that he may be called upon to testify against him: '... besonders kam er [Werther] fast außer sich, als er hörte, daß man ihn vielleicht gar zum Zeugen gegen den Menschen, der sich nun aufs Läugnen legte, auffordern könnte' (123R). The phrase 'who was now taking to denial' is formulated in such a way as to suggest the farmhand's guilt, but this is merely the view of the community, reported back to Werther and through him to the reader. Perhaps his plea of innocence is justified? The text does not furnish adequate grounds to refute this possibility, and yet in every reading up to now the farmboy's guilt has been taken for granted. What appears to have happened is that a vacancy in the text has been uniformly filled in by readers without their registering its existence. Even a most attentive reader such as Georg Lukács wrongly fills in the logical lacuna of the farmboy's response to Werther's rhetorical question, 'What have you done, you unfortunate man!' Of the ambiguous statement spoken by the supposed murderer Lukács makes a clear confession of guilt. He writes: 'Mit bewundernswerter Kunst stellt Goethe in wenigen Zügen, in einigen kurzen Szenen das tragische Geschick des verliebten jungen Knechts dar, dessen Mord an seiner Geliebten und seinem Rivalen das tragische Gegenstück zu Werthers Selbstmord bildet.'[80] This is quite simply a misreading, for only the young rival has been killed, not the widow ('Der Entleibte war Knecht einer Wittwe ...' [119R]), and we cannot be sure who committed the crime.

But why have we been so eager to leap to the assumption that the farmboy is guilty of the murder? Is this evidence of a collective instinct to indict Werther, the lover who puts an end to his own life? He himself is in no doubt of the young farmhand's guilt, and it is the power of *his* conviction rather than any real textual evidence to support an objective indictment that sweeps the reader along. What are we to make of Werther's immediate and unshakable belief that the farmboy did indeed commit murder? It is a belief that seems to have more to do with Werther's own psyche than with any real circumstance concerning the farmboy, whom he has always looked upon as an *alter ego*. Is the explanation for Werther's instant assumption of the farmboy's guilt and his subsequent defence of the young man that he himself senses the power of suppressed violence towards his own rival in love to such a degree that he can understand and condone the crime of which the farmboy stands accused? Is it for this reason that he defends this man whose 'decisiveness and right behaviour' in the face of adversity in love he had once before felt he might not be able to match (96R)? Because of the ambiguity of the text it seems quite possible that what Werther responds to in his defence of the farmboy is nothing other than the subconscious but violent animosity he feels towards Albert as the husband of Lotte. We must remember the suppressed violence in his own reaction to the thought: 'What if Albert were to die ...?' Such a thought had led him to 'abysses of the mind from which he had shrunk back in horror' – not once, but many times (92L/R). And it is a thought expressed again in his last letter to Lotte, even though he has decided that he must be the one to die:

> Ja, Lotte! warum sollte ich es verschweigen? eins von uns dreien muß hinweg und das will ich seyn! O meine Beste! in diesem zerrissenen Herzen ist es wüthend herumgeschlichen, oft – deinen Mann zu ermorden! – dich! – mich! (132L/R)

But if the farmboy cannot be considered clearly guilty, then what

---

80 Georg Lukács, 'Die Leiden des jungen Werther,' in *Deutsche Literatur in zwei Jahrhunderten*, 1964, 61

does this signify for the last part of his tale and its insertion into the novel as a whole? Does Werther's reaction to the murder simply demonstrate, as many critics believe, that Goethe's aim was to distance the reader from the mind and actions of his central character and to transform his eventual suicide from an idealized act with an unfortunate, exemplary quality for many unhappy lovers into the lamentable act of a man who has lost touch with all reason and sanity? The answer must surely be no, not simply that, for not only Werther is immediately convinced of the farmboy's guilt, but society too is swift to assume him a murderer, even though real proof of his guilt is missing. If there is any possibility that he may in fact be innocent, then society's ready willingness to believe him guilty ought also to be reconsidered.

The conflict between Werther and society is nowhere more powerfully, if paradoxically, highlighted than through the tale of the Bauernbursche – powerfully, because of the implications of society's assuming the guilt of a peasant who may be innocent, and paradoxically, because of Werther's own instant conviction that the farmhand is indeed guilty. Society sees Werther as a potential witness for the prosecution, while he himself knows that he could only speak from a position of shared emotional solidarity and identity in the young man's defence, so the longstanding conflict between Werther and society in terms of love is brought into focus here in more extreme form than ever before. Quite some time earlier, in his first comments on society (26 May 1771), he had focused on the capacity of rules to protect against poor taste and asocial behaviour, but the price to be paid for such protection was too high: 'Folgt der Mensch, so gibt's einen brauchbaren jungen Menschen und ich will selbst jedem Fürsten rathen, ihn in ein Collegium zu setzen; nur mit seiner Liebe ist's am Ende, und wenn er ein Künstler ist, mit seiner Kunst' (14L/R). Society, and particularly that privileged portion of it that is closest to the lawmakers at the top, functions primarily on the premise of self-interest, in Werther's view. According to him, those who are in control and who have taken possession of the river banks, the prime locations, on which to make artificial incursions into nature by creating their 'Gartenhäuschen,' 'Tulpenbeete,' 'Krautfelder,' which must be shielded from the possible onslaught of the raging waters, do so at the cost of others. By erecting their dams and canals to protect their property and their organized, controlled enjoyment of nature, they rob others of the power and majesty of the swollen waters, claims Werther, impoverishing the lives of those around them for the sake of their own peace of mind. The whole metaphor is centrally concerned with society's need to control and subjugate everything that proceeds from genius or passion: privilege likes to associate safely with genius (for example, by erecting little houses for the enjoyment of art from close at hand), but it has a horror of true genius, which is powerful and a threat to the ordered existence of those professing most loudly to have a genuine interest in it:

> O meine Freunde! warum der Strom des Genies so selten ausbricht, so selten in hohen Fluten hereinbraus't und eure staunende Seele erschüttert? – Lieben Freunde da wohnen die gelassenen Herren auf beyden Seiten des Ufers, denen ihre Gartenhäuschen, Tulpenbeete und Krautfelder zu Grunde gehen würden, die daher in Zeiten mit Dämmen und Ableiten der künftig drohenden Gefahr abzuwehren wissen. (14L/R)

What the whole passage demonstrates is that great love and great art are a threat to society and as such to be regulated out of existence, trivialized, and reduced to something safe and predictable. What the farmboy's tale adds is an insight into society's response to those whose capacity for love oversteps the boundaries of acceptability and safety. Werther assumes the guilt of the farmboy because of his own contempt for such boundaries, whereas society does so for exactly the opposite reason. Proof of his guilt is of interest to neither the one nor the other. Nor, seemingly, to the author. According to his newly written text, it seems that as far as society is concerned, someone capable of overstepping its threshold of propriety – as the farmboy had done to warrant eviction by the widow's brother – is automatically capable of overstepping the ultimate threshold of respect for the life of another human being. Daring to love without appropriate restraint is already 'evidence' of madness or criminality in the eyes of society, in other words. This is surely the implication of the farmhand's unproven guilt: his supposed violence is there to show the extremes to which an immoderate capacity for love might conceivably be pushed by impossible pressures and circumstances. That this love should be wrongly understood by those who know nothing of (or feel threatened by) its power is an important aspect of the story. Violence becomes for Werther the readily understandable outcome of victimized helplessness.

Thus his defence of this supposed murderer is both a battle against Albert and against the society that stands behind him. But it is a battle that Werther cannot win. Society, as represented by the Amtmann, will not even listen:

> Er ließ ... unsern Freund nicht ausreden, widersprach ihm eifrig und tadelte ihn, daß er einen Meuchelmörder in Schutz nehme! er zeigte ihm daß auf diese Weise jedes Gesetz aufgehoben, alle Sicherheit des Staats zu Grund gerichtet werde.

Here the chief representative of law and order enunciates and upholds the principles on which all civilized society is based, but he then goes on to give quite different reasons for not helping the farmboy, and these reasons clearly reflect rather less well on the speaker as timid bureaucrat:

> ... auch, setzte er hinzu, daß er in einer solchen Sache nichts thun könne, ohne sich die größte Verantwortung aufzuladen, es müsse alles in der Ordnung, in dem vorgeschriebenen Gang gehen. (121R)

Werther's appeal for a disregard for the rules ('durch die Finger sehn') makes Albert weigh in on the side of the Amtmann, and Werther is defeated. With the fate of the farmboy his own fate is sealed.

Is Werther a dangerous man? His reactions to the lover he believes guilty of murder suggest that he may well be, but although these are mere reconstructions by the Editor, there is no trace of censure in how he presents them: 'Er [Werther] fühlte ihn so unglücklich, er fand ihn als Verbrecher selbst so schuldlos, er setzte sich so tief in seine Lage, daß er gewiß glaubte auch andere davon zu überzeugen' (120R). Evidently Werther feels capable of justifying a *crime passionnel*. While he himself might not be capable of committing such a crime, given the right frame of mind – and the Editor sees to it that we know the unfair and irrational frame of mind he was in before learning of the murder – he can support and identify with someone else he believes to have done so. What does this do for the existing novel? It certainly validates Werther's flight into death, even renders it necessary, for it is surely better for him to do violence to himself as the solution to his predicament than to give way to violence against another. The last stage of the farmboy's story may give us a frightening insight into

Werther's psyche, but I do not think that we are meant from this point on to regard him as unhinged and to distance ourselves from him. Whether we as readers actually do so is another matter, but the text seems to offer certain safeguards against our reacting in this way, safeguards that seem to be repeatedly overlooked because we think we know the Werther story and its background so well.

I think it important to register, for example, just how careful the Editor is to let us know, in terms that ought to reassure us, that Werther's crisis of violent emotion is quite swiftly resolved – this seems to me to be the reason for placing it between the two contrasting manifestations of how he reacts to his own adversary in Albert, the first largely irrational, the second largely rational. 'Du bist nicht zu retten Unglücklicher,' is Werther's summary of defeat in defence of the farmboy, 'ich sehe wohl daß wir nicht zu retten sind' (121R); and from this point on he is increasingly restored to rational thought. The new text continues:

> Was Albert zuletzt über die Sache des Gefangenen in Gegenwart des Amtmanns gesprochen, war Werthern höchst zuwider gewesen: er glaubte einige Empfindlichkeit gegen sich darin bemerkt zu haben, und wenn gleich bey mehrerem Nachdenken seinem Scharfsinn nicht entging, daß beyde Männer recht haben möchten, so war es ihm doch als ob er seinem innersten Daseyn entsagen müßte, wenn er es gestehen, wenn er es zugeben sollte. (121–2R)

Here the invisible Editor presents us with his own view of Werther's inner reflections: first there is a flickering of the old unfairness towards Albert, but this gradually makes way for a more rational reaction to the whole discussion of the murder, even though he cannot bring himself to admit that his opponents are right. An overt editorial comment follows immediately, introducing the note in which Werther expresses his awareness that he cannot be fair towards Albert, but the whole passage is strangely uneven, for while the lines just cited are again clearly a piece of imaginative writing on the part of the Editor, he makes use of their 'authenticity' to organize the sequence of his documents in a manner that is to Werther's credit:

> Ein Blättchen, *das sich darauf bezieht*, das vielleicht sein ganzes Verhältniß zu Albert ausdrückt, finden wir unter seinen Papieren ...

'Was hilft es, daß ich mirs sage und wieder sage, er ist brav und gut, aber es zerreißt mir mein inneres Eingeweide; ich kann nicht gerecht seyn.' (122R, emphasis mine)

There is no compelling, objective reason for the Editor to insert the note at this point, for the claim that it pertains to the previous lines – his own creation – does not in itself prove anything. There are links in wording, of course, but these links are necessarily inconclusive. Only Werther (or Goethe) could say with unassailable authority that the note about his attitude to Albert relates to his admission that Albert and the Amtmann may be right in their attitude to the murderer.

So why has the Editor chosen to place the note here, precisely at that point where it is likely to have the effect of restoring a great deal of his reader's lost sympathy to Werther? Is he perhaps blind to what he is doing? So caught up in a positive bias towards Werther that he cannot help but present him in a sympathetic light without realizing that this is the case? Or is the Editor, despite all his initial posturing as an outsider, chiefly a covert mouthpiece for the author, whose sense of identity with Werther and the farmboy was an established reality of his own experience? It seems to me that Goethe may have made a small but significant emotional leap here because of that sense of identity. The favourable bias on the part of the Editor towards Werther seems to indicate that he is very much concerned to explain the latter's behaviour in acceptable terms. Acceptable to whom? Chiefly, I believe, to Goethe himself.

Consider again for a moment the author's situation in 1786: his emotional predicament was a heightened version of the one he had already experienced and presented in his original novel, and in rewriting *Werther* he was once more editing his own story, this time in a double sense, for on the one hand he was working on a ready-made text shaped by the experiences he had had in Wetzlar some fourteen years before, while on the other he had relived those experiences in a more acute form since 1776. He had long ago 'edited' the first story, and now faced the task of editing it again, inevitably taking into account the second, as yet unrecorded, story of his emotional life in Weimar, another Werther-experience. Looked at in this way, does it not make complete sense that the 'Editor' of Version Two should slip in and out of Werther's mind in bringing the new material of this second experience to paper and in a manner that presents the hero in a sympathetic light?

But if this Editor has a profound sympathy for Werther, what impact may that sympathy have had on his narrative so far? Perhaps we are meant to believe that the farmboy did indeed commit the murder; perhaps society is meant to seem wholly justified in condemning him to pay for his action; but if so, then the writing is flawed, for we are denied the textual evidence that would validate such assertions. All that we are given is a text that offers remarkably little detail of the farmboy himself, so little, in fact, and formulated in such an ambiguous way that his guilt must remain in some doubt to the attentive reader. Yet at the same time the text focuses in great detail on Werther's emotional response to the supposed deed. Was this deliberate? The open question of the farmboy's guilt highlights the major problem in the Editor's Report, namely, the evident failure of the 'Editor' to escape long enough or far enough from Werther's inner perspective to satisfy the demands of objective story-telling, even within the framework of relative objectivity that he himself has established.

If we think of the whole story of the farmhand as Goethe's own hidden story, however, then the ambiguity surrounding the details of the murder makes a lot more sense, for what is chiefly highlighted in its tragic conclusion is the inner tension that culminates in a frightening, though suppressed, sense of violence in Werther, rather than the actual use of violence by the farmboy. Such extreme tension is a new ingredient in the novel, a new reality for Werther, through whom I believe Goethe tells his own unhappy story for the second time. He had been given someone else's ending to the tale of torment he himself had lived out in Wetzlar and which he wrote almost two years later in 1774, revived as it was in his mind by his Frankfurt experiences. In that ending he recognized a quality of greatness that his own real-life ending to the story had lacked, so he drew heavily on Kestner's account of Jerusalem's suicide as a suitable conclusion to the account of his own sufferings. Whereas he himself had simply taken flight from the pain of his hopeless love in 1772, Jerusalem had taken his life – an altogether more glorious and impressive ending than Goethe's own, and the allegedly immediate catalyst for writing his novel, even though this was not the case.[81] When rewriting it in 1786 he had a much greater fund of personal experience to draw on, a whole second Werther-story with its own heightened reality and validity.

Given the intensely personal stimuli that lay behind and found their way into a great deal of his writing at the time, it seems likely that the last part of the Bauernbursche tale represents Goethe's account of the end of that second story. Not that he ever contemplated murdering the somewhat hapless but good-natured Josias von Stein, Charlotte's husband, of course. No, but the farmboy he had been at Kochberg in early 1776, whose love for his 'widow' knew no bounds, had become a passionately devoted lover who not only enjoyed great peaks of happiness for almost a decade because of his beloved, but also endured at her hands recurring rejection and a great many emotional wounds throughout that same period. These he could tolerate, or so it seemed, until the point came where society's power asserted itself and her legal husband was installed as a significant part of her daily life by his ongoing presence at home. After that point Goethe's emotional situation was unbearable and so the very difficult decision to leave Weimar was made. The last part of the farmboy story was almost certainly written at this time, when rupture and death cannot have been far from the poet's thoughts, given his attitude to separation from the woman he loved.[82] It seems altogether likely that Goethe found in writing the last part of the Bauernbursche tale a safety valve for unthinkable thoughts and unspeakable, though real, emotions in the manner of his own Tasso: 'Und wenn der Mensch in seiner Qual verstummt, / Gab mir ein Gott zu sagen, wie ich leide' (HA 5:166).

Werther harms no one but himself, but he can understand how another might, especially a simple peasant who has no capacity for artifice or sublimation. Similarly Goethe – which is why the validation

---

81 Cf. HA 9:585ff. Goethe in fact learned of Jerusalem's death through Kestner in November 1772 but did not begin to write *Werther* until thirteen months later.
82 Cf. Seuffert WA 1,19:327ff. The equation of separation and death runs through Goethe's thought from the mid-1760s to the mid-1820s; cf. (to Behrisch) 'Tod ist Trennung / Dreifacher Tod / Trennung ohne Hoffnung / Wiederzusehen' (HA 1:24); (to Frau von Stein) 'An's Scheiden mag ich gar nicht dencken. Ich bin dir so fest angebunden daß ich mein Leben zereisen würde, wenn ich an eine Trennung dächte' (P964); (Werther) 'Wie klingt es rührend, wenn der Dichter singt, / Den Tod zu meiden, den das Scheiden bringt! / Verstrickt in solchen Qualen, halbverschuldet, / Gab ihm ein Gott zu sagen, was er duldet' (HA 1:381).

of the final suicide through this tale of murder is so important. He *must* get away. That much has become clear. But 'getting away,' 'going,' 'departing this world' are themselves ambiguous formulations that suggest both suicide and flight, and precisely this ambiguity is explicitly underlined in a new note written by the Editor for Version Two. Indeed, it is the only reason for the note's inclusion, which follows on a passage retained from the original where Werther again writes of renewed thoughts of suicide ('der Entschluß, diese / die Welt zu verlassen' 123L/127R). The new lines are these:

> Endlich ward er mit dem traurigen Gedanken immer mehr verwandt und befreundet und sein Vorsatz fest und unwiderruflich, wovon folgender zweydeutige Brief, den er an seinen Freund schrieb, ein Zeugniß abgibt. (127R)

The ambiguity anticipated here lies in the words 'mir wäre besser, ich ginge' present in both versions of the letter following (128L/R), but whereas there was indeed an ambiguity regarding their meaning in Version One, that ambiguity had been nullified by the widespread awareness from 1774 onward of Werther's eventual suicide. Why underscore now an ambiguity previously left unremarked, an ambiguity that has been weakened almost out of all existence and whose original impact can never be regained? Again I think we have a small example here of how Goethe wrote not only for a chosen public but at the same time for himself, inserting, as he did so, current personal sentiments into his text as part of the act of writing, for he himself often used the term 'die Welt' in his letters to Frau von Stein to mean the Weimar court, high society. Let me give just one example from a letter written on 11 March 1781:

> Wie offt hab ich die Worte *Welt, grose Welt, Welt haben* u. s. w. hören müssen und habe mir nie was dabey dencken können, die meisten Menschen die sich diese Eigenschafften anmasten, verfinsterten mir den Begriff ... (P595)[83]

---

[83] The term 'die Welt' is used similarly in P57 (27 May 1776), P62 (1 June 1776), P241 (19 May 1778), P420 (5 May 1780), P1150 (2 October 1783). See also Goethe's letters to Karl August, 5 July 1781 (HA Briefe 1:366); 25 January 1788 (ibid. 2:78ff.). He made use of the term in a similar way in parts of *Die Wahlverwandtschaften*: see Gerwin Marahrens, 'Der "Welt"-Begriff in Goethes *Wahlverwandtschaften*,' in *Sinn und Symbol*, 1987.

Werther's following letter, whose ambiguity is expressly pointed out by the Editor, conceals from his friend, Wilhelm, his intention to 'leave the world,' ('die Welt zu verlassen,' 127R). The text of the existing letter dated 20 December to which the reader's attention is now drawn is identical in both versions:

> Ja, du hast Recht: mir wäre besser, ich ginge. Der Vorschlag, den du zu einer Rückkehr zu euch thust, gefällt mir nicht ganz; wenigstens möchte ich noch gerne einen Umweg machen ... verziehe nur noch vierzehn Tage, und erwarte noch einen Brief von mir mit dem weiteren. Es ist nöthig daß nichts gepflückt werde, ehe es reif ist; Und vierzehn Tage auf oder ab thun viel. Meiner Mutter sollst du sagen: daß sie für ihren Sohn bethen soll und daß ich sie um Vergebung bitte, wegen alles Verdrusses, den ich ihr gemacht habe. Das war nun mein Schicksal, die zu betrüben denen ich Freude schuldig war. Lebwohl, mein Theuerster! Allen Segen des Himmels über dich! Lebwohl! (128L/R)

In his last days before setting off on his journey to Italy Goethe wrote the following to Frau von Stein, not having let her know of his secret destination or of his plan to stay away for a long time:

> Auf alle Fälle muß ich noch eine Woche bleiben, dann wird aber alles so sanfte endigen und die Früchte reif abfallen. (P1597)

> Nun geht es mit mir zu Ende meine Liebste, Sonntag d. 3ten S[eptember] denck ich von hier wegzugehn. (P1599)

It seems possible, even probable, that the ambiguity emphasized by the Editor in Werther's letter from Version One is no longer the original ambiguity, where a proposed journey was used to cloak the reality of Werther's plan to commit suicide, but rather, the reverse, i.e., that Werther's thoughts of suicide are used as a cloak for Goethe's forthcoming departure, a real journey that he means to keep secret. This is exactly the kind of personal detail that he often tucked away in his writing, a conscious reflection of the games he was prone to play with his readers. Now, as never before, he was firmly resolved to leave the world ('die Welt') as represented by the court. 'Werther hatte, wie wir aus seinen Briefen wissen, nie ein Geheimniß daraus gemacht, daß er sich, diese Welt zu verlassen, sehnte' (150R): while these new lines in the novel reflect the reality of the author's constantly recurring desire for flight for a whole decade before he finally left, it had become a firm resolve for the first time only by the late summer of 1786.

Immediately after Werther's farewell to Wilhelm comes the letter in which Lotte asks him not to return again until Christmas Eve. It begins, as we saw, with a newly written introduction in which the Editor's admiration and reverence for her becomes immediately apparent, and ushers in a subsequently revised picture of the heroine in the second version, a picture which, despite all reverence and admiration on the part of the Editor, is in fact much less innocent and girlish than that of the original. It is an altered portrayal that brings to mind the changes we saw wrought in the heroines of *Erwin und Elmire* and *Claudine von Villa Bella*. But if similarities exist here, there are also differences, for in both of these works the exploited or unappreciated male lover gives vent to his seemingly justifiable anger and frustration within the context of hope and an eventual happy ending. The two plays were not reworked until long after Goethe had already escaped the suffocation of life in Weimar, however, while the revision of *Werther* predated that escape and was therefore necessarily different. Though tragic in outcome, it bears no trace of the hero's resentment towards his beloved; in fact, the additional insights we are given by the Editor in Version Two into Lotte's mind and heart implicitly reveal as never before the validity of Werther's belief that she loves him and justify his having allowed the love he feels for her to grow and flourish on the wings of hope.

On the whole, the Editor of the second version does a great deal to render more credible Werther's sense of torment and ultimate decision to 'leave the world' that causes him such suffering and anguish. He does so, however, only for the sympathetic reader, the reader predisposed to react with warmth, admiration, and fellow-feeling for Werther. But this Editor can envisage no other kind of reader, as his preface to both versions of the novel makes clear. He himself evidently understands, admires, and sympathizes with Werther, and in the last editorial passage that centres on the hero, the picture we are given of Werther is significantly less small-minded and mean-spirited than in Version One. He no longer contemplates suicide as an act of revenge on a world that dares to wound and reject him (124L), but as an act of despair resulting from a wasted and painful existence that has robbed him of the possibility of ever becoming actively integrated into normal daily life. The futile monotony he perceives in his contact with Lotte further diminishes his strength so that he inevitably draws closer to 'a melancholy end' ('einem traurigen Ende' [124R]), not to that 'dreadful deed' ('der schröklichen That') of the original text (124L).

It is at this point that the two letters omitted from the end of the first section in the 1786 rewriting are reintroduced, and the effect they have is to increase the sense of bitter hopelessness Werther has experienced as a result of 'sharing' the farmboy's fate, as he understands it. They are prefaced now, however, by an editorial comment that does not fit together well with what the Editor himself has just told us in a passage newly written for Version Two. Both these letters display, according to the Editor, Werther's 'Verworrenheit, Leidenschaft, rastlose[s] Treiben und Streben,' as well as his 'Lebensmüde' (124R), and yet while they do deal with his passion for Lotte and his longing for an end to his misery, they contain no traces of his 'restless activity and striving'; indeed, the new information we have just been given explicitly emphasizes that Werther has reached a stage beyond all possibility of either:

> Alles was ihm Unangenehmes jemals in seinem wirksamen Leben begegnet war, der Verdruß bey der Gesandtschaft, alles was ihm sonst mißlungen war, was ihn je gekränkt hatte, ging in seiner Seele auf und nieder. *Er fand sich durch alles dieses wie zur Unthätigkeit berechtigt, er fand sich abgeschnitten von aller Aussicht, unfähig, irgend eine Handhabe zu ergreifen mit denen man die Geschäfte des gemeinen Lebens anfaßt ...*' (124R, emphasis mine)

Obviously there is no 'rastloses Treiben und Streben' here, just as there is none in the two relocated letters that follow, despite the Editor's claims. Is the faulty interpretation an editorial misreading? Hardly, as the Editor himself has composed the new passage. Once again I think the evident disjuncture of the two pieces of text, one old, one new, springs from Goethe's real need to express his current state of mind in what he was writing. For years he had been fully aware of how unsuited he was to the demands of his life at court, where he stayed only because of his beloved Lotte. Already in 1780 he had written to her:

> Unbegreifflich ist's, was Dinge die der geringste Mensch leicht begreifft, sich drein schickt, sie ausführt, dass ich wie durch eine ungeheure Klufft davon gesondert bin. Auch geht mein gröster Fleis auf das gemeine. Sie sehen ich erzähle immer vom *ich*. Von andern weis ich nichts, denn mir innwendig ist zu thun genug, von Dingen die einzeln vorkommen kann ich nichts sagen, nehmen Sie also hier und da ein Resultat aus dem Spiegel den Sie kennen. (P443)

'I always tell only about myself ...' A year or so later he had written: 'Ich dancke den Göttern, dass sie mir die Gabe gegeben in nachklingende Lieder das eng zu fassen, was in meiner Seele immer vorgeht' (P646), the same thought that is expressed in *Tasso*, completed in 1789.

In rewriting *Werther* Goethe was also rewriting his own story; there were certain differences in the experiences that went to make up that second story, differences that had to do in part with the new real-life Albert and Lotte, and these were used to replace or elaborate on the existing, but no longer current or true-to-life account of his unhappiness in love. Whatever the differences may have been in significant details of his new Werther-experience, however, there was very little difference in the nature of the writing process in which he was engaged. What he had to say in retrospect about the writing of Version One was even more clearly true of Version Two:

> Ich hatte mich äußerlich völlig isoliert ... und so legte ich auch innerlich alles beiseite, was nicht unmittelbar hierher gehörte. Dagegen faßte ich alles zusammen, was einigen Bezug auf meinen Vorsatz hatte, *und wiederholte mir mein nächstes Leben, von dessen Inhalt ich noch keinen dichterischen Gebrauch gemacht hatte.* Unter solchen Umständen, nach so langen und vielen geheimen Vorbereitungen, schrieb ich den 'Werther' ... *Ich fühlte mich, wie nach einer Generalbeichte, wieder froh und frei und zu einem neuen Leben berechtigt.* (HA 9:587f., emphasis mine)

In preparing to write *Werther*, as he says, he relived in his mind the events of his past of which he had not yet made any use for literary purposes; he also felt, on completing the novel, a sense of inner freedom similar to that conferred only by the absolution of a priest, a totally free conscience in other words, and the right to a new life. If this was true of his state of mind in 1774, it was even more so in 1786.[84] However, the

---

84 Although the connections I make between Goethe's experiences in Weimar and

experiences of Werther accompanied him to Italy, only to be purged and laid to rest by means of the sadness and anger he expressed in another work that he would complete on his return.

---

the revised *Werther* have not been made by others, the veracity of his account in *Dichtung und Wahrheit* of the genesis of the original version has been called into question by Wolfgang Kayser and Karl Maurer (see Kayser, 'Die Entstehung von Goethes "Werther,"' in *Kunst und Spiel*, 1967, 5–29; Maurer (428f.) points out surprising similarities between what Goethe writes on the genesis of *Werther* and Rousseau's account of the genesis of *La Nouvelle Héloise* in Book 9 of his *Confessions*).

4

Werther: The Case for a Rereading

The Final *Werther* in the Light of the Final *Tasso*

Tasso as 'ein gesteigerter *Werther*'? Only now that I have examined the changes in the novel can I return to my claim that this judgment on the play, so strongly endorsed by Goethe, had more validity in terms of the second version of the novel than the first. I do so because the text of the drama offers certain specific grounds for the belief that the same kind of personal links that I have attempted to highlight between Goethe and his rewritten *Werther* also had their part to play in the rewriting and completion of *Tasso*, a drama whose emotional background was altogether different in the beginning from what it became in the end. In the three years between the completion of the two works in their final form Goethe was to undergo a process of increasing disillusionment that left its mark on the drama he had begun in the throes of such joy and delight that writing it was in itself akin to an act of reverent worship. It was not with the first version of the novel that he wrote the Werther-problematic out of his system in 1774, nor with the second in 1786, but only with the completion of *Tasso* in 1789, and even then the personal anguish was far from being successfully overcome, as the text itself suggests.

From the following passage written later for the *Italienische Reise*, it would appear that by February 1787, just one month after the completion of *Iphigenie*, Goethe was already aware of difficulties in continuing on with his writing of *Tasso*: 'Tät ich nicht besser, "Iphigenia auf Delphi" zu schreiben, als mich mit den Grillen des Tasso herumzuschlagen? und doch habe ich auch dahinein schon zuviel von meinem

Eignen gelegt, als daß ich es fruchtlos aufgeben sollte' (HA 11:170). However, his actual letters to Charlotte at that time reflect no such difficulties. 'Nun kann ich auch fröhlicher an das Werck gehn,' he wrote on 1 February, for example, 'denn ich habe einen Brief von dir in welchem du mir sagst, daß du mich liebst ...' (P1630); and on the 19th: 'Tasso wird mit auf den Weg [to Sicily] genommen, allein von allen und ich hoffe er soll zu eurer Freude vollendet werden' (P1633). More important, however, than the clash between the mood of the letters he actually wrote in early 1787 and his later recollection of that period is his awareness, even in retrospect, of how impossible it was for him to give up work on the fragmentary drama altogether. This was certainly true at the time, for even then he registered in what was already written of the play a considerable investment of his own emotional self that could not simply be abandoned in favour of a new beginning. Yet however great his emotional investment in creating the original two acts of the play may have been, he invested a lot more in completing the remainder – too much, in fact, as he claimed in a letter to Schultz some forty years later in 1829: '... in meinen "Tasso" [hatte ich] des Herzenbluts vielleicht mehr, als billig ist, transfundiert.'[1] The degree of self-investment he had made in *Werther* was in his view very similar, for he called this work 'ein Geschöpf ... das ich gleich dem Pelikan mit dem Blut meines eigenen Herzens gefüttert habe.'[2]

It seems there is a hidden level of personal disclosure on Goethe's part in both *Tasso* and the rewritten *Werther* that supports the notion of the former as an intensification of the latter, and lends added weight to what has already been said here about the rewriting of the novel. Certain close thematic similarities in these two very different pieces of writing suggest that Goethe made use of each of them in significant measure as a means through which to express and attempt to overcome the emotionally difficult situation in which he found himself. As we saw, this practice was fundamental to a great deal of what he wrote or rewrote in the period up to 1789, constituting a large part of his stimulus to literary creativity as a source of personal freedom, self-assertion, consolation, and satisfaction. It also seems to have

---

1 To Ch. L.F. Schultz, 10 January 1829 (HA *Briefe* 4:312)
2 Eckermann 468. See also the reference to *Werther* as 'eine delikate und gefährliche Arbeit' (to Knebel, 21 November 1782; HA *Briefe* 1:415) and to *Tasso* as 'eine gefährliche Unternehmung' (to Karl August, 6 April 1789: WA 4,9:102).

been the source of certain flaws in his work at various points, however, for personal and artistic aims did not always blend harmoniously together. If *Werther* suffered in the rewriting from Goethe's lack of distance from what he wrote – and this seems to be the case in various places – then *Tasso* did so even more markedly.

Among Goethe's chief personal experiences between September 1786 and July 1789, when *Tasso* was finally completed, was a growing sense of hurt and disillusionment. *Iphigenie* had not been well received in Weimar in his absence, and he himself was not well received in person when he arrived back in June 1788. This was a most difficult period in his life that he never forgot, although he struggled hard to overcome it. What he wrote almost thirty years later about his experiences at that time shows that the trauma he had suffered on his return to Weimar was even then by no means a thing of the past:

> Aus Italien dem formreichen war ich in das gestaltlose Deutschland zurückgewiesen, heiteren Himmel mit einem düsteren zu vertauschen; die Freunde, statt mich zu trösten und wieder an sich zu ziehen, brachten mich zur Verzweiflung. Mein Entzücken über entfernteste, kaum bekannte Gegenstände, mein Leiden, meine Klagen über das Verlorene schien sie zu beleidigen, ich vermißte jede Teilnahme, niemand verstand meine Sprache ...
>
> Wie ich mich nun in diesen Regionen [reflections on art, nature, and society] hin und her bewegte, mein Erkennen auszubilden bemüht, unternahm ich sogleich schriftlich zu verfassen, was mir am klarsten vor dem Sinne stand, und so ward das Nachdenken geregelt, die Erfahrung geordnet, und der Augenblick festgehalten ... (HA 13:102)

The sense of isolation Goethe expresses here was at its height when he was at work on the completion of *Tasso*, and it is characteristic of the way in which he sought in later years to harmonize and universalize his past life that he should speak of the important role that writing played for him at this difficult time without making any reference to the play. What preoccupied him he sought to write down immediately, he says, and through doing so he was helped to regulate his reflections, order his experiences, and place on record the impressions or convictions of the moment. This was true of all his writing up to 1790, true of *Werther* before he left for Italy in the same way that it was true of *Tasso* on his return; exactly how true it was, however, was a secret that Goethe jealously guarded throughout his whole life, despite all his repeated insistence on the link between the life he led and the works he wrote.

The inconsistencies in *Tasso* have already been explained in convincing biographical terms by Walter Silz,[3] but the degree to which *Tasso* and *Werther* both deal on the level of Goethe's personal writing with similar problems has not been explored. We seem to have overlooked, for example, the fact that the tale of the Bauernbursche's expulsion from the household of his beloved mistress in the second *Werther* has a highly significant counterpart in *Tasso*. Why the oversight? Is it because of the 'impossible' difference in standing between the two characters, one a court poet, the other a peasant lad? Has it to do with our scholarly awareness of the sources Goethe drew on? Or is it because our idea of the poet's development in Italy tends to render substantial personal links between *Tasso* and *Werther* unlikely, causing us to disregard them? Whatever the answer, the link that binds Tasso, the farmboy, and his *alter ego*, Werther, together is much stronger than anything that separates them, namely, the strength of love and devotion the farmboy and the poet display to their cost for the widow and the Princess respectively. In both works, completed three years apart, a young lover makes a physical advance on his beloved, only to encounter a rejection that leads him into crisis and despair. The lover's reaction in the two works is very different, however: in the novel no negative comment is passed on the behaviour of his lady, whereas in the drama the negative comments are both clear and strong. Rejection by the beloved woman is no longer endured in almost mute anguish by the lover, as had been the case with the farmboy; instead, that rejection is seen as betrayal and calls forth in Tasso a mixture of disillusionment, resentment, anger, and despair.

More clearly than the widow, the Princess is responsible for the amorous overtures of her would-be lover. Tasso's first moment of euphoria comes in the wake of a very carefully formulated declaration by the Princess of her personal response to his work, and it is important to see that her implicit encouragement is the key to Tasso's change in the way he perceives his own role from that point: no longer

---

3 'Ambivalences in Goethe's *Tasso*,' *Germanic Review*, 1956

need he content himself with the role of mere 'Minnesänger' to an emotionally inaccessible noble lady who accepts all his poetic tributes as merely her due, for she lets him know, albeit in a covert and ambiguous way, that she hears these hidden tributes, understands them, and inwardly responds. Only on hearing this and realizing what her responsiveness seems to imply does Tasso begin to give voice openly for the first time to the joy of his love. He speaks first of his own work and of the hidden tribute to love that it contains:

TASSO: Was auch in meinem Liede wiederklingt,
  Ich bin nur *einer*, *einer* alles schuldig!
  Es schwebt kein geistig unbestimmtes Bild
  Vor meiner Stirne ...
  ...
  Und was hat mehr das Recht, Jahrhunderte
  Zu bleiben und im stillen fortzuwirken,
  Als das Geheimnis einer edlen Liebe,
  Dem holden Lied bescheiden anvertraut?
PRINZESSIN: Und soll ich dir noch einen Vorzug sagen,
  Den unvermerkt sich dieses Lied erschleicht?
  Es lockt uns nach und nach, wir hören zu,
  Was wir verstehn, das können wir nicht tadeln,
  Und so gewinnt uns dieses Lied zuletzt.
TASSO: Welch einen Himmel öffnest du vor mir,
  O Fürstin! Macht mich dieser Glanz nicht blind,
  So seh ich unverhofft ein ewig Glück
  Auf goldnen Strahlen herrlich niedersteigen.

The Princess, on hearing his excited outburst, breaks off the exchange with a warning that steers everything back into safer waters for her:

PRINZESSIN: Nicht weiter, Tasso! Viele Dinge sind's
  Die wir mit Heftigkeit ergreifen sollen:
  Doch andre können nur durch Mäßigung
  Und durch Entbehren unser eigen werden.
  So, sagt man, sei die Tugend, sei die Liebe,
  Die ihr verwandt ist. Das bedenke wohl! (HA 5:103)

And yet she cannot unsay what she has already said, nor can she halt the process of growing elation in Tasso that her words to him have brought into being. The fact is, her encouragement and subsequent retraction will have negative consequences for him for the rest of his life, and the whole drama is in large part a portrayal of those developing consequences.

The joy and sense of inner liberation that the Princess's understanding, appreciation, and personal response have brought to Tasso makes it impossible for him, despite her subsequent withdrawal, to preserve either distance or caution in his overtures to Antonio, that man of rules and reason whom Goethe introduced into the play explicitly as a 'prosaic contrast' to the leading character.[4] It is the failure on Tasso's part to be guided in his actions by rules and reason rather than feeling that leads to his confinement, to his being separated off from a society whose rules dictate the subjugation of emotion to notions of suitability and propriety in a manner reminiscent of Werther's Philistine. The young farmboy too was guilty of a failure to honour such rules, and he too was made to suffer for it. For Werther, the farmboy, and Tasso feeling is everything and cannot be contained by rules dictated by the head rather than the heart. However, their overt expression of feeling in their respective environments calls forth only censure and punishment from society. The 'criminal,' according to Tasso's perspective on his quarrel with Antonio, and indeed, according to the punishment meted out to him for it by the Duke, is one who presumes to allow the heart to dominate the head:

TASSO: Mir verstummt die Lippe,
  War's ein Verbrechen? Wenigstens es scheint,
  Ich bin als ein Verbrecher angesehn.
  Und, was mein Herz auch sagt, ich bin gefangen.   (HA 5:115)

Similar treatment was accorded to the farmboy, although his punishment was eviction rather than house-arrest as in Tasso's case, but his 'crime' was also more severe, for he had made physical overtures of love to his mistress to warrant his greater punishment. At this point in the play Tasso has been guilty only of an immoderate display of feeling that expressed itself first as an unwelcome and premature offer of friendship to Antonio and then as active fury that such a positive gesture should be coldly rejected. The farmboy's mistake in attempting

---

4 See Eckermann 546 (6 May 1827); the relevant passage is cited on p. 229.

to express his love for his lady in physical terms is a mistake that Tasso too will make, however, one that will bring disastrous results for him also in its wake, despite all his subsequent attempts at stoicism and purposeful resignation.

Certain similarities between Tasso and Werther (who identifies totally with the actions and fate of the farmboy) are matched by similarities between the Princess and the widow, the farmboy's lady mistress. Like the widow, the Princess is not altogether blameless, even before Tasso goes so far as to take her in his arms, and both women are strangely passive when a crisis occurs involving their young lover; both bow to the demands they perceive placed on them by a social code. On learning of the quarrel between Tasso and Antonio and of her brother's reaction to it, for example, the Princess withdraws to a safe position of non-involvement, although she knows of and deeply regrets Tasso's desire to leave the court. Are we not reminded here of the widow's behaviour towards the farmboy once her brother has come on the scene? According to Werther's report of the young man's own account: 'Dieser [der Bruder] habe ihn gleich zum Hause hinaus gestoßen und einen solchen Lärm von der Sache gemacht, daß die Frau, *auch selbst wenn sie gewollt*, ihn nicht wieder hätte aufnehmen können' (95R). Whatever regret the Princess may feel, like the widow, she is not prepared to do anything to interfere with the rules of her society. In one of many passages worthy of Werther, despite their classical verse form and different context, Tasso gives way to anguish and despair at her behaviour towards him:

> Ja alles flieht mich nun. Auch du! Auch du!
> Geliebte Fürstin, du entziehst dich mir!
> In diesen trüben Stunden hat sie mir
> Kein einzig Zeichen ihrer Gunst gesandt.
> Hab ich's um sie verdient? –   (ibid. 148f.)

Again it seems likely, from what we have already seen, that on one level these lines contain Goethe's own very personal feelings, this time feelings of desolation and anguish because of his rejection by Frau von Stein since his return from Italy. The same quality of self-laceration and self-pity that we saw in parts of the rewritten *Werther* echoes again here, and while on an artistic level one may read in the play a profound criticism of the Romantic poet obsessed with self, unresolved problems at this very level suggest the likelihood of insufficient distance between the author and his work, here as in other places. Consider how Tasso's monologue continues:

> Hab ich's um sie verdient? – du armes Herz,
> Dem so natürlich war, sie zu verehren! –
> Vernahm ich ihre Stimme, wie durchdrang
> Ein unaussprechliches Gefühl die Brust!
> Erblickt ich sie, da ward das helle Licht
> Des Tags mir trüb; unwiderstehlich zog
> Ihr Auge mich, ihr Mund mich an, mein Knie
> Erhielt sich kaum, und aller Kraft
> Des Geists bedurft ich, aufrecht mich zu halten,
> Vor ihre Füße nicht zu fallen; kaum
> Vermocht ich diesen Taumel zu zerstreuen.
> Hier halte fest mein Herz! Du klarer Sinn,
> Laß hier dich nicht umnebeln! Ja, auch *sie*!   (ibid.)

In this passage there are clear echoes of the struggle waged and lost by the farmboy against the need of his own sensual nature to find expression in physical love. Up to this point Tasso has managed, though barely, to hold himself in check, but it is as inevitable that he should fail in the end as it was inevitable that the farmboy should, for the beloved woman in both cases gives signs of encouragement that cause the man to lose the last remnants of control over his feelings.

Both Tasso and the farmboy are treated like criminals, yet neither is demonstrably guilty of any act that would warrant the name of 'crime,' the farmboy being merely the obvious culprit in the eyes of one society, as I have tried to show, Tasso in the eyes of another. If lack of restraint in response to Antonio's rejection in Act Two was enough to warrant Tasso's being treated like a minor criminal (house arrest), a similar lack of restraint in his expression of love for the Princess in Act Five, when he presumes to take her in his arms, leads to his being dealt with as a major criminal, at least for a time. It is here that the stories of the Bauernbursche and of Tasso coincide most closely, for the view of the lover as criminal in the eyes of society is reinforced when Tasso is arrested for having dared to embrace the Princess. 'Sie erwehrte sich sein; ihr Bruder kam dazu': such is the

Werther: The Case for a Rereading   221

text in the revised *Werther* at the point where the farmboy dares to press his attentions on the widow; it is also the action in *Tasso*, Act 5, Scene 4.

But what leads up to this action is most important. In a series of exchanges between Tasso and the Princess, she reveals even more clearly than before the very real place he holds in her affections, and as a result Tasso feels first encouraged to dedicate his life to her service as devoted caretaker of her garden and estate (ibid. 159f.), then further encouraged to work actively for reconciliation with her family and the court (ibid. 160f.), and from there he goes on to make a declaration of passionate love which results in his disastrous move to embrace her (ibid. 162). The explicit role of the Princess in all of this seems to me as suspect as the implicit role of the widow in response to the Bauernbursche, for she first tells Tasso how painful it is to her to see him withdraw from everyone (ibid. 159), then how inconsolable she is at the prospect of his departure: 'Ich finde keinen Rat in meinem Busen, / Und finde keinen Trost für dich – und uns ... / Ich muß dich lassen, und verlassen kann / Mein Herz dich nicht' (ibid. 160). With the Princess's mention of her own heart, her own emotional involvement, Tasso's pain and distrust give way to joy, and *feeling is restored to pride of place*; inevitably, however, this opens the floodgates of passionate devotion in a manner that causes the Princess great alarm:

TASSO: Ihr Götter, ist sie's doch
  Die mit dir spricht und deiner sich erbarmt!
  Und konntest du das edle Herz verkennen?
  ...
  Welch ein Gefühl!
  Ist es Verirrung was mich nach dir zieht?
  Ist's Raserei? Ist's ein erhöhter Sinn,
  Der erst die höchste reinste Wahrheit faßt?
  Ja, es ist das Gefühl, das mich allein
  Auf dieser Erde glücklich machen kann;
  Das mich allein so elend werden ließ,
  Wenn ich ihm widerstand und aus dem Herzen
  Es bannen wollte. Diese Leidenschaft
  Gedacht ich zu bekämpfen; stritt und stritt

> Mit meinem tiefsten Sein, zerstörte frech
> Mein eignes Selbst, dem du so ganz gehörst – [Emphasis mine]
> PRINZESSIN: Wenn ich dich, Tasso, länger hören soll,
> So mäßige die Glut die mich erschreckt.
> TASSO: Beschränkt der Rand des Bechers einen Wein,
> Der schäumend wallt und brausend überschwillt?
> Mit jedem Wort erhöhest du mein Glück,
> Mit jedem Worte glänzt dein Auge heller.
> Ich fühle mich im Innersten verändert,
> Ich fühle mich von aller Not entladen,
> Frei wie ein Gott, und alles dank ich dir!
> Unsägliche Gewalt, die mich beherrscht,
> Entfließet deinen Lippen; ja, du machst
> Mich ganz dir eigen. Nichts gehöret mehr
> Von meinem ganzen Ich mir künftig an.
> Es trübt mein Auge sich in Glück und Licht,
> Es schwankt mein Sinn. Mich hält der Fuß nicht mehr.
> Unwiderstehlich ziehst du mich zu dir,
> Und unaufhaltsam dringt mein Herz dir zu.
> Du hast mich ganz auf ewig dir gewonnen,
> So nimm denn auch mein ganzes Wesen hin!
> (*Er fällt ihr in die Arme und drückt sie fest an sich.*)
> PRINZESSIN (*ihn von sich stoßend und hinweg eilend*): Hinweg!
> LEONORE (*die sich schon eine Weile im Grunde sehen lassen, herbeieilend*): Was ist geschehen? Tasso! Tasso! (*Sie geht der Prinzessin nach.*)
> TASSO (*im Begriff ihnen zu folgen*): O Gott!
> ALFONS (*der sich schon eine Zeitlang mit Antonio genähert*): Er kommt von Sinnen, halt ihn fest. (*Ab*). (HA 5:160f.)

Tasso's anguish, like the farmboy's at a similar point, is quite extreme, but his immediate reaction is not simply one of wretchedness and self-reproach. Rather, he suspects all those around him of having plotted together to ensure his captivity in Ferrara and to prevent the development of his fame as an artist (ibid. 163f.). However, the chief architects of his wretchedness are for him Antonio and the Princess, neither of whom is now spared his wrath. What is most surprising in terms of dramatic action and structure is the proximity of his venomous reflections on the Princess in particular to the supposedly conciliatory ending of the play. Note the great bitterness with which he now refers to the woman for whom he had been willing just a short time before to sacrifice everything:

> Und du, Sirene! die du mich so zart,
> So himmlisch angelockt, ich sehe nun
> Dich auf einmal! O Gott, warum so spät!
>
> ...
>
> Wie lang verdeckte mir dein heilig Bild
> Die Buhlerin, die kleine Künste treibt.
> Die Maske fällt; Armiden seh ich nun
> Entblößt von allen Reizen – ja, du bist's!
> Von *dir* hat ahndungsvoll mein Lied gesungen![5]
>
> ...
>
> Euch alle kenn ich! Sei mir das genug!
> Und wenn das Elend alles mir geraubt,
> So preis ich's doch; die Wahrheit lehrt es mich.   (HA 5:164)

Can we not see here something of the bitterness and aggressive disappointment in regard to Frau von Stein that became even more apparent in Goethe's sequel to *The Magic Flute*, a change in his attitude to the beloved woman occasioned here by her behaviour towards him from 1786–9? Unlike the farmboy, who utters no word of reproach about the behaviour of the beloved woman who has caused his banishment, but swears that he loves her as before (94R), Tasso reacts to the consequences of his rejection with a torrent of criticism and abuse. He openly attributes his current wretchedness above all to the encouraging and teasing behaviour of the Princess, and in the strongest terms imaginable. Were these not qualities we perceived by implication in the second Lotte, despite Werther's own apparent blindness to them? Were they not qualities we also perceived behind the behaviour of the widow, even though the farmboy was similarly blind? Are Tasso's reactions here merely those of a man of emotional poetic temperament who is unhinged by rejection in love? Are his bitter accusations altogether unjustified? At best I think the text might permit the saving argument that the

---

5 In the eighteenth canto of Tasso's *Gerusalemme Liberata* Armida, having been spurned by Rinaldo, changes into a vengeful monster who spreads terror and alarm.

Princess was unaware of his vulnerability and unwittingly injudicious, therefore, in her words of encouragement to him, but yet much is made in the play of her extreme sensitivity towards people and situations, so why should she be less than sensitive towards Tasso? The idea that she loves the poet but not the man would surely only be evidence that she, no less than Tasso, is wholly self-absorbed. This is certainly suggested by the text, for like Lotte, who does not dare to risk Albert's wrath in spite of knowing that Werther is in a most precarious state of mental equilibrium that could well end in death, the Princess too is concerned above all with preserving what she already has; in her own words: 'Was ich besitze, mag ich gern bewahren / Der Wechsel unterhält, doch nutzt er kaum' (ibid. 124). These words say more than they seem to at first glance, more about the character and personality of the Princess than about her deep attachment to Tasso. Although she is referring here to her lack of interest in the prospect of new friends put forward by Leonore as consolation for the loss of Tasso, her behaviour towards his plight suggests that the preservation of all that she already has may indeed be more important for her than anything else.

Strangely, perhaps, the underlying message of the play, no less than in *Werther*, seems to be a thoroughgoing indictment of Philistinism, even though on the surface – and this is different from the earlier work – it seeks to endorse in the end the artistic and emotional straitjacket that court society feels bound to impose on everyone, including the man of genius. Hostility (Antonio), self-interest (Leonore), anger (Alfons), fear or alarm (Princess) are the responses of the leading figures at the court to what seems to them any manifest lack of moderation or control, and these are what cause Tasso's despair to the point of near-madness. The Princess, for example, cannot even delight in beauty or excellence, for they too have a frightening aspect, as she tells Leonore in Act 3 after the crisis has occurred between Tasso and Antonio:

PRINZESSIN: Zu fürchten ist das Schöne, das Fürtreffliche,
   Wie eine Flamme, die so herrlich nützt,
   Solange sie auf deinem Herde brennt,
   Solang sie dir von einer Fackel leuchtet,
   Wie hold! wer mag, wer kann sie da entbehren?
   Und frißt sie ungehütet um sich her,
   Wie elend kann sie machen! Laß mich nun.

> Ich bin geschwätzig und verbärge besser
> Auch selbst vor dir, wie schwach ich bin und krank. (ibid. 123)

Containment is the key to everything, it seems, just as it was the key to everything for the society represented by Werther's Philistine in both versions of the novel. Flower beds and garden houses to prettify the view from river banks carefully shored up against the dangerous swell of the rushing water – these were the delight of those opposed to genius, who feared all lack of moderation, and who were more comfortable with men carefully groomed for committee work than with artists or lovers. Isn't Ferrara depicted as rather similar? – a court whose prime heroes are Antonio and the Princess, the one who knows only the political face of Rome and not its glories, the other who loves and reveres art and delights in Tasso's love poetry, but only as long as it remains a flame that casts heat or light from a safe receptacle? This is how the two characters present themselves, so one assumes that this is how they should be read. Can Ferrara possibly be a fruitful environment for the man of real talent, let alone genius? Is this play not also on one level Goethe's own expression of despair at what the future seems to hold for him in Weimar, an attempt to face up to and make the best of the reality with which he sees himself confronted there? By the poet's own admission, his own life, his own experiences, and the people by whom he was surrounded in Weimar were all woven into the drama.[6]

A close examination of the whole attitude to art at this court reveals Tasso's 'madness' as far from strange, perhaps even as a higher form of sanity; it also suggests that the problematic ending of the play represents a rather sad accommodation on the part of the poet to a reality that is lamentably far from ideal. Werther failed to accommodate to the reality around him and chose instead to end his life; Tasso's ultimate success in accommodating to Ferrara promises to be a kind of death also, albeit a death with a brave face on it, in that life at this court seems to offer the real artist and lover little hope for fulfilment as either the one or the other.

Similarities exist in terms of mental and emotional makeup not only between Werther and Tasso, and between Lotte and the Princess, but also between Albert and Antonio, Goethe's 'prosaic contrast' to Tasso.

---

6 See p. 229.

Throughout the whole play, but particularly towards the end, when Tasso's torment is at its most extreme, Antonio's behaviour is reminiscent of the 'improved' Albert, and both men are clearly models of success, for while one has Lotte for his wife, the other enjoys the esteem of the whole court. Antonio is a man not given to the expression of powerful emotions under any circumstances; as we can see from his well-intentioned admonitions to Tasso towards the end of Act 5, manliness for him expresses itself as control, patience, and moderation (HA 5:164ff.). However, while Antonio's level-headedness may perhaps have much to recommend it, one cannot escape the rather uncomfortable sense that mere necessity is being turned into a virtue at the end of the play. Tasso cannot possibly change the court or its rules, so he must instead accommodate to them. And yet, although he turns his back in the end on his despair as a man in favour of hope and consolation as an artist, turning towards Antonio as friend and guide, the swift switch from one mode of feeling to another is highly unsatisfactory. Is not this Antonio the man of whom Tasso had said with considerable justification, on the basis of their first encounter:

> Wie lehrreich wäre mir sein Umgang, nützlich
> Sein Rat in tausend Fällen! Er besitzt,
> Ich mag wohl sagen, alles, was mir fehlt.
> Doch – haben alle Götter sich versammelt,
> Geschenke seiner Wiege darzubringen?
> Die Grazien sind leider ausgeblieben,
> Und wem die Gaben dieser Holden fehlen,
> Der kann zwar viel besitzen, vieles geben,
> Doch läßt sich nie an seinem Busen ruhn.[7]

By the end of the play Tasso is left with only one consolation, only one positive element in his life, and that is his artistic creativity which allows him an outlet for the expression of his sufferings. He has a new awareness of the reality and power of the rules of life at court, an awareness dearly bought by means of the process of shock, disappointment, and disillusionment that he has been forced to undergo, and it is partly this that makes him turn towards Antonio in the end. The

---

7 HA 5:99. Other reflections of Antonio's 'Philistinism' evocative of an intensified Albert can be found, for example, in lines 665ff. (p. 91), 1196–1407 (pp. 105ff.), 1487–1518 (pp. 113f.), 2104–60 (pp. 130f.), 2872–2974 (pp. 151ff.).

other reason is that he has been urged to do so, not by one person, but by all. Antonio is the hero, the non-dreamer, the adept politician, the articulate emissary, the highly competent man of affairs, the man who 'knows' the place that poetry should have in life, the ideal nature and function of the poet as well. He is presented as having all these qualities, but which of them could Tasso usefully acquire? Should he want to acquire any of them as they are presented in the play? Surely his turning towards Antonio in the end as the rock on which he will build his future, rather than suffer shipwreck as he had first supposed, can only be regarded as an act of helpless compromise, a melancholy end to the greatness that was Tasso, and an unsatisfactory ending to the play. It is an ending that seeks to avoid tragedy, but that avoidance in itself seems only to ensure tragedy of another kind. It is an ending too that seems to have been wrought more by an act of will on the part of the author than by any development that naturally evolves from within the drama itself, and therein lies its chief artistic flaw.

In the logical lacunae of *Tasso* there seem to be clear correspondences with the problems of the rewritten *Werther*, problems that lend weight to the possibility that Goethe's existential need to write at times either blocked or overwhelmed his judgment as an artist. We know that he was aware of this possibility when first writing his original *Tasso* in 1781; how aware he was of it in 1789 is a question we cannot answer with any certainty, but one to be explored at least tangentially when we come to consider briefly his views on writing, the response he sought from his readers, and how the modern reader actually responds to his work, specifically to *Werther*.

I realize that this reading of the play departs sharply from the widespread view that *Tasso* is a clear reflection of the greater classicism and maturity of the post-Italian Goethe, who no longer endorsed, let alone extolled, emotional excesses of the kind displayed by his hero. For some time now scholars have shied away from any biographical reading in favour of a purely aesthetic one, but in so doing they have often disregarded many of the difficulties presented by the text. The play is not seen as a personal lament or a sad coming to terms with unpalatable realities on the part of the author, despite the fact that this would help to explain, without glossing over, its many inconsistencies, and despite the fact that Goethe very forcefully acknowledged how much of himself he had invested in it. Instead, it is believed that, just as he was highly critical of Werther when he came to rewrite his novel, so too was he highly critical of Tasso's self-indulgence and successfully sought to place him securely on the path towards a new and better mode of life that would incorporate the greater wisdom and balance of Antonio. It is also generally held that Tasso's criticisms of the court are in themselves unsound, manifestations of his temporary pathological state as presented in the source materials, and that the Princess, like Iphigenie, represents Goethe's ideal of woman in his classical phase. But what exactly are our reasons for any of these assertions or beliefs? Doesn't the text itself oblige us to say that if such are indeed the insights Goethe meant us to gain from this particular work, then he fell far short of his own goal in presenting them to us as he did? His supreme control of form as reflected in the final version of the play undoubtedly reflects his greater classicism, his insights into life and the world a greater degree of experience and disillusionment than in the pre-Italian period, and yet this work is surely too problematic, too much of a 'gesteigerter "Werther"' in what it actually says for us to ignore the revelation of anguished subjectivity that it seems to contain. Unlike Erich Trunz, I find it difficult to see here 'das in Italien errungene klassische Kunst- und Dichtungsideal Goethes' which manifests itself not only in the form and structure of the work, but above all 'in der beinahe erbarmungslosen aber nie sympathielosen Objektivität, mit welcher alle Figuren des Dramas geschildert werden' (HA 5:511). It is precisely the *lack* of consistent objectivity with which the characters are treated that lies at the unalterably problematic heart of the work. Every character in this drama behaves strangely or inconsistently at one point or another, and what I have tried to do in brief is to offer a possible reason why this should be so. Here too Goethe's own emotional preoccupations at the time of writing seem to have found their fullest outward, though hidden, expression in various places throughout the work.

What I have suggested is obviously limited and in no way does justice to *Tasso* as a whole. I cannot here go into an examination of the other issues raised – for example, the role the work of art plays in the life of the artist, the role of the artist in society as seen from the different perspectives of the artist and the society, the process of artistic creativity, etc., – but these too were personal preoccupations of the playwright at the time of writing, so in not dealing with them I am not avoiding parts of the drama that might be difficult to accommodate within the framework of what I have already said. What interests me most at present is simply the similarity of certain events in *Tasso* and *Werther* and the depiction of the central character in each work in response to those events. Both works seem to reflect quite clearly their author's state of mind at the time of final writing, and what I have attempted to highlight is the fact that this awareness ought perhaps to give us pause for thought in relation to many of our established critical judgments. Invited by Eckermann to speak of the central idea of *Tasso* in 1827, Goethe responded in the following way:

> 'Idee?' sagte Goethe, '– daß ich nicht wüßte! – Ich hatte das *Leben* Tassos, ich hatte mein eigenes Leben und indem ich zwei so wunderliche Figuren mit ihren Eigenheiten zusammenwarf, entstand in mir das Bild des Tasso, dem ich, als prosaischen Kontrast, den Antonio entgegenstellte, wozu es mir auch nicht an Vorbildern fehlte. Die weiteren Hof-, Lebens- und Liebesverhältnisse waren übrigens in Weimar wie in Ferrara, und ich kann mit Recht von meiner Darstellung sagen: *sie ist Bein von meinem Bein und Fleisch von meinem Fleisch.*'[8] (Emphasis in the original)

Tasso, like Werther, is at odds with life and the world because his beloved is inaccessible to him and because he cannot endorse, let alone act out, the approved norms of behaviour of the society in which he finds himself. Like the farmboy, Werther's acknowledged hero and *alter ego*, he is encouraged to believe that his love is reciprocated, only to discover that he can go so far and no further. To go further, however impeccable the emotional motivation, is to cross over into the realm of what is regarded as 'criminal' behaviour in the environment of this court. The Princess, rather like the mistress of the Bauernbursche, appears to take secret pleasure in the awareness that she is loved, but on her own terms; she encourages the expression of that love in controlled ways that she can approve, but shrinks back in fear and alarm from the threat that any lack of moderation seems to her to represent. This fear is so strong that she denies to Tasso every vestige of support at the time of his first crisis, when a word from her would

---

8 Eckermann 546 (6 May 1827)

mean so much to him. But then we are dealing here with a woman whose penchant for still suffering and martyrdom prevents her from making any move to intercede on behalf of her friends, as she herself tells Leonore in a speech that is not without unpleasant undertones of self-regard (HA 5:120f.). She also shares certain traits that we saw newly introduced into the character of Lotte in the second version of *Werther*: each woman anticipates an irreparable sense of loss through the departure of the young man who loves her and whom she in turn loves, whatever obstacles there may be to any possible realization of that love; each woman also, by her passive reaction to the crisis situation of the hero, contributes to a worsening of that crisis; each woman too seems ultimately to place self-preservation and notions of perceived propriety above all else. Unlike those new, spirited female characters Goethe wrote into the plays he revised in Italy in 1787–8, women for whom love is all (Klärchen in *Egmont*, Rosa in *Erwin*, Lucinde in *Claudine*), the second Lotte, the widow, and the Princess are all seemingly unable to resist the demands placed on them by society, unable to undertake any positive steps to stand behind the man whose love they have encouraged in various ways and whom they themselves seem to love. Like Lotte and the widow, the Princess seems concerned above all to protect her own position and is unwilling to use her influence on those closest to her to ensure that Tasso is spared any further misery. Sorrow she will bear, but active intervention is beyond her (ibid. 120f.). How much more exemplary was the vision we were given of Iphigenie! Had *she* been prey to the lure of suffering and resignation in the manner of the Princess, her own fate and that of all those around her would have been very different. But then *Iphigenie* existed in its entirety as a drama long before 1786, whereas *Tasso* consisted of only two acts prior to Italy, two acts which Goethe felt he could no longer use and which were rewritten after his life underwent a major change in direction, a change that was irrevocable by mid-1789.

In claiming that in *Tasso*, as in *Werther*, Goethe used his extraordinary literary talent to give vent in his own way to personal sufferings and reflections that could otherwise find no ready outlet, I am not casting any fundamental doubt on that talent; rather, the reverse, for it seems to me that his ability to use his talent in this way while at the same time creating literary works of lasting value is clear evidence of an even greater poetic genius than that which proceeds from purely cerebral impulses lent shape by force of will. It is as if he experienced and responded to life itself in artistic categories, creating works of art in their own right as he recorded and rerecorded his own experiences in response to an inner imperative. However, subjective and objective criteria for good writing were not always identical, and we would do well to bear this in mind in dealing with his texts. Goethe's immense literary achievements should not blind us to the importance of the immediacy of his feelings for what he wrote or rewrote in the period up to 1790, or lead us to separate out the life from the work on the grounds that only the latter should be given our attention. 'Goethe distanced himself from *Werther* in the rewritten version of his novel.' Did he? 'Goethe presented the characters in *Tasso* with total objectivity.' Did he? Both texts remain highly problematic. It seems to me that there are certain important distinctions to be made between our reading and his writing.

Goethe on Writing and Being Read

Ill served though we may have been by Goethe's early biographers and by critics who used his biography as a primitive key to what he wrote, the fact remains that he asserted again and again that his literary works were an expression of his emotional life, and consciously so. As he wrote to Auguste von Stolberg on 7 March 1775, for example: '[Meine Arbeiten] sind immer nur die aufbewahrten Freuden und Leiden meines Lebens';[9] and on receiving the first four volumes of the new edition of his collected works some twelve years later in 1787:

> Es ist mir wirklich sonderbar zumute, daß diese vier zarten Bändchen, die Resultate eines halben Lebens, mich in Rom aufsuchen. Ich kann wohl sagen: es ist kein Buchstabe drin, der nicht gelebt, empfunden, genossen, gelitten, gedacht wäre, und sie sprechen mich nun alle desto lebhafter an. Meine Sorge und Hoffnung ist, daß die vier folgenden nicht hinter diesen bleiben.   (HA 11:399)

---

9 HA *Briefe* 1:179

Even towards the end of his life Goethe believed that the writer of talent could not do otherwise than reveal himself in his writings. 'Die Gabe der Dichtkunst,' he wrote in 1829, 'hat das Eigne besonders darin, daß sie den Besitzer nötigt, sich selbst zu enthüllen.'[10] Yet however much he believed in the need for self-revelation, he sought in increasing measure to obscure the degree to which he revealed his thoughts and feelings of the moment, while rejoicing in the release and expansion that the act of writing itself represented. What he had written always remained of the utmost importance to him, not merely because of its literary value, but also because he viewed it as a continuing, living part of himself – which helps to explain the process of retrieval, rewriting, publication, and republication of so much that he produced. It seems significant, for example, that in 1806 during the chaos of the French assault on Weimar, he was most alarmed by the thought that any of his papers, whether personal documents, completed works, or even fragments, might be destroyed, and so he resolved to have everything published or republished immediately. What was written down was in his view 'Teil unseres Daseins,'[11] and as such had to be preserved at all costs.

It was in letter-writing that Goethe had first discovered as a very young man a real substitute for conversation with an absent dialogue partner as well as a means of communicating ideas that could not, for whatever reason, be expressed directly.[12] The act of writing was therefore experienced in itself as an act of expansion and liberation. No less so the act of reading, for in going over what he had just written he not only experienced a real sense of self-encounter, but he also had the sense of an encounter with a work of inherent literary value and the gratifying awareness, therefore, of his own talent.[13] Whatever he produced in writing seems to have remained part of him in a way that his drawing, for example, did not, and the divestment of the self that was expressed as self-investment in the act of writing was a most important form of expansion and contraction, 'Einatmen und Ausatmen,' that could not be separated out or kept apart. What he had once created thus

---

10 Ibid. 4:326
11 HA 13:54; see also Koranyi 159ff.
12 Käser 109, 119; Martin Swales, *Goethe: The Sorrows of Young Werther*, 1987, 46
13 Käser 121

tended to become a kind of palimpsest mediated and transformed by the new self that he had become since first writing the original.

From the evidence we have looked at, it seems that for Goethe, to write was to create a personal dialogue with life that took on many different forms. And here it is obviously important to register the true complexity of his relationship with Charlotte von Stein, rather than to hold to the simplistic notion of her ennobling and calming influence on him, for she was the dialogue partner he had never had before and would never have again, the stimulus for many very different kinds of writing, the major focus of his love, devotion, playfulness, anger, resentment, joy, delight, anxiety, etc. up to the end of their relationship in 1788. He wrote nothing new of major importance for a long time after that, yet the first decade in Weimar is regarded as the most artistically barren period of Goethe's life. It was a decade, however, in which he experimented with many new literary forms and wrote a great number of works, albeit of very uneven quality. Strange though it may seem, this whole period was of great importance for much that he would do later, a training ground for the linguistic virtuoso who could do anything he turned his hand to. The fact that the results were so mixed and that completion dates have been used to bolster up the notion of his lack of productivity up to 1786 cannot alter the reality of his record as a writer throughout the supposedly barren years prior to Italy. Never was he more prolific than at this time, but also never more exclusively focused on the one reader, the one listener, whom he always had in mind, and never was his concern for the absolute artistic value of what he wrote less dominant. Charlotte von Stein should read, should hear, what he had written, and be pleased with all his efforts. No other principle guided his work throughout the period in question, and on the whole it was a fruitful principle, however mixed the results of his literary efforts. Everything he had or did or even thought was for her; as he wrote to her in Kochberg in July 1780, for example:

> Der erste Act der Vögel ist nahe fertig, dazu hat Ihre Abwesenheit geholfen. Denn solang Sie da sind lass ich mir's in unbeschäfftigten Stunden so wohl seyn und erzähle Ihnen und pp was alles in dem Augenblick mir die bewegte Seele eingiebt dem mach ich Lufft, wenn sichs thun lässt, und wenn Sie nicht da sind hab ich niemand dem ich soviel sagen kan da muss es einen andren Ausweeg suchen. (P448)

And in early 1781 from Neunheiligen:

> ... alle meine Beobachtungen über Welt und mich richten sich nicht, wie Marck Antonius, an mein eignes, sondern an mein zweites selbst. *Durch diesen Dialog, da ich mich bey iedem dencke was Sie dazu sagen mögten, wird mir alles heller und werther.* (P595, emphasis mine)

From his letters to Charlotte during more than a full decade it is clear that he was engaging neither in flattery nor in exaggeration when he wrote to her in August 1786 from Karlsbad, having just put the finishing touches to *Werther*: 'ich dencke immer an dich bey allem was ich mache' (P1597).

Goethe used his literary talent as a means by which to order his own inner world, to place on record his thoughts and emotions, to break through the constraints of reality by creating an expanded and more pleasing picture of his own situation. To write was above all to carry on a dialogue with himself which guaranteed him not merely survival,[14] but also the opportunity for self-assertion over a wider public for whom he had little respect, interest, or concern – self-assertion rendered possible by his awareness of the control he had over his creative medium.[15] As he wrote to Frau von Stein in April 1781 in seeming anticipation both of *Tasso* and the 'Marienbader Elegie' of some thirty-five years later, he regarded the ability to write as a great gift in which he rejoiced for his own existential reasons: 'Ich dancke den Göttern, dass sie mir die Gabe gegeben, in nachklingende Lieder das eng zu fassen, was in meiner Seele immer vorgeht' (P646). Later that same year a minor work of his, now no longer extant, was performed in Weimar; it too contains the same unmistakable echoes of Tasso:

> Zum Glück lebt noch mein Zauberstab,
> Sonst läg ich wahrlich längst im Grab,
> Doch der thut mich noch stärker;

---

14 On the matter of writing as the chief means of survival for Goethe see Eissler 1:560f.; Wolfgang Kayser, 1967, 23ff. Cf. Goethe's reference to his early habit of fashioning his own thoughts in the form of a dialogue (HA 9:576). Having completed the *Farbenlehre* in 1810 after twenty years' work, he wrote to Sartorius: 'Ich werde dadurch einer großen Last, aber auch einer guten Unterhaltung los' (HA *Briefe* 3:121).

15 Kayser, 'Goethes Auffassung von der Bedeutung der Kunst,' in *Kunst und Spiel*, 80f.

Denn wenn ich noch so Unmuths bin,
Ergötz ich mich in Phantasien
Und leb in meinen Werken.[16]

Schiller was obviously right to see in Goethe the instinctive, intuitive artist, just as Goethe was right to characterize the gift of the poet as an inborn potential for the expression of universal truth as far as all human thoughts and emotions were concerned. 'Die Region der Liebe, des Hasses, der Hoffnung, der Verzweiflung und wie die Zustände und Leidenschaften der Seele heißen,' he said to Eckermann in 1824, 'ist dem Dichter angeboren, und ihre Darstellung gelingt ihm.'[17] Great writers are born, not made, he claims, and on them the birth of literature depends, for they have the innate and intuitive capacity to give voice to lasting truth that transcends their own immediate experience. Goethe himself was often astonished when he reread something he had written years before, for example, astonished because of its ongoing validity, not only for himself but in general, and this he attributed to an inborn sense of truth that enabled him to see life and to record it in a way that also had meaning and significance for others. In his own words: '... hätte ich nicht die Welt durch Antizipation bereits in mir getragen, ich wäre mit sehenden Augen blind geblieben und alle Erforschung und Erfahrung wäre nichts gewesen als ein ganz totes vergebliches Bemühen. Das Licht ist da und die Farben umgeben uns; allein trügen wir kein Licht und keine Farbe im eigenen Auge, so würden wir auch außer uns dergleichen nicht wahrnehmen.'[18]

The poet's own experience, coupled with a knowledge of his subject, is the source of all worthwhile literary creativity, Goethe says in this conversation with Eckermann, but what he lays claim to here is a certain kind of poetic self that is capable in response to life of creating from its own inner world works of art that prove valid for all human existence. However, – and this he does not say here but elsewhere, – while the record of that self may transcend its own boundaries, in finding artistic expression it is not lost to the individual writer. Rather, it remains for him a record of his own inner life at the

---

16 According to Adolf Schöll, this 'Zauberspiel' was written as a cover for what Goethe wanted to say about his severe dissatisfaction with court life in Weimar; see 'Ein verlorenes Zauberspiel von Goethe,' in *Goethe in Hauptzügen*, 504.
17 Eckermann 84 (26 February 1824)
18 Ibid. 84f.

time of writing,[19] and this record Goethe always sought to preserve and protect from others. Part of the joy he found in writing sprang from the freedom it offered him to reveal and conceal himself at one and the same time, and for this reason we would do well to treat with caution much of what he himself says about his works in retrospect, particularly where he seeks to explain them in terms of the epoch in which he lived. An examination of *Dichtung und Wahrheit* in relation to the early works discussed there, for example, shows that where he is personal and specific he is at his most reliable as a commentator, least so where he is concerned to universalize his own past. If we draw on this source we must be very careful to measure his judgments against the primary evidence of his texts, and if, in expressing our own judgments on what he wrote, we draw on received notions of the course that his development took, then we must exercise even more care.

Having invested so much of himself in what he wrote, it was perhaps only natural that Goethe should seek endorsement or approval from certain readers or listeners who meant much to him. Rejection by others who were unimportant to him was in itself unimportant,[20] but from his target audience or readership he sought involvement and a positive response. For them alone, he declared, each book was written,[21] and from them he expected a degree of textual penetration that was not impeded by the devices he used in order to conceal himself from others. On the subject of his newly written *Wahlverwandtschaften*, for example, he wrote to Zelter in 1809: 'Ich bin überzeugt, daß Sie der durchsichtige und undurchsichtige Schleier nicht verhindern wird bis auf die eigentlich intentionierte Gestalt hineinzusehen';[22] and on the same subject he wrote to Reinhard: 'Die Wahlverwandtschaften schickte ich eigentlich als ein Zirkular an meine Freunde, damit sie meiner wieder einmal an manchen Orten und Enden gedächten. Wenn

---

19 Cf. to Eckermann (29 October 1823): 'Setzen Sie unter jedes Gedicht immer das Datum, wann Sie es gemacht haben ... Es gilt dann ... zugleich als Tagebuch ihrer Zustände. Und das ist nichts Geringes. Ich habe es seit Jahren getan und sehe ein, was das heißen will' (Eckermann 54).

20 For more information on the kind of reader for whom Goethe wrote see Katharina Mommsen, 'Goethes Vorstellung von einer idealen Lesergemeinde,' *Seminar* 1974.

21 For example, 'Künftiger Divan' (HA 2:195), where Goethe expresses his conviction 'daß doch am Ende jedes Buch nur für Teilnehmer, für Freunde, für Liebhaber des Verfassers geschrieben sei.'

22 HA *Briefe* 3:107

die Menge dieses Werkchen nebenher liest, so kann es mir ganz recht sein. Ich weiß zu wem ich eigentlich gesprochen habe, und wo ich nicht mißverstanden werde.'[23]

How valid is this kind of claim for understanding? Are we to be blamed if we do not perhaps respond as Goethe might wish? What he says here shows clearly how consciously esoteric his writing had become by 1809, but this was no new departure in kind, merely one of degree, in his later years. It was an esotericism designed to be penetrated only by readers whom he regarded as those of like mind, people on whom he could count for a ready understanding and appreciation of what he had written, without any further explication by him. How he wished to be read was evidently a factor in how he wrote, but perhaps this very notion of the reader for whom he wrote represents a barrier for the modern literary critic. A significant statement on the kind of critic Goethe sought for himself is recorded by Eckermann as follows:

> Die höchst gelungene Übersetzung der dramatischen Werke Goethes von Stapfer hat in dem zu Paris erscheinenden 'Globe' des vorigen Jahres durch Herrn J.J. Ampère eine Beurteilung gefunden, die nicht weniger vortrefflich ist und die Goethen so angenehm berührte, daß er sehr oft darauf zurückkam und sich sehr oft mit großer Anerkennung darüber ausließ.
>
> 'Der Standpunkt des Herrn Ampère,' sagte er, 'ist ein sehr hoher. Wenn deutsche Rezensenten bei ähnlichen Anlässen gern von der Philosophie ausgehen und bei Betrachtung und Besprechung eines dichterischen Erzeugnisses auf eine Weise verfahren, daß dasjenige, was sie zu dessen Aufklärung beibringen, nur Philosophen ihrer eigenen Schule zugänglich, für andere Leute aber weit dunkeler ist als das Werk, das sie erläutern wollen, selber, so benimmt sich dagegen Herr Ampère durchaus praktisch und menschlich. – *Als einer, der das Metier aus dem Grunde kennt, zeigt er die Verwandtschaft des Erzeugten mit dem Erzeuger und beurteilt die verschiedenen poetischen Produktionen als verschiedene Früchte verschiedener Lebensepochen des Dichters.*
>
> *Er hat den abwechselnden Gang meiner irdischen Laufbahn und meiner Seelenzustände im tiefsten studiert und sogar die Fähigkeit gehabt, das zu sehen, was*

23 Ibid. 117

ich nicht ausgesprochen und was sozusagen nur zwischen den Zeilen zu lesen war. Wie richtig hat er bemerkt, daß ich in den ersten zehn Jahren meines weimarischen Dienst- und Hoflebens so gut wie gar nichts gemacht, daß die Verzweiflung mich nach Italien getrieben und daß ich dort mit neuer Lust zum Schaffen die Geschichte des Tasso ergriffen, um mich in Behandlung dieses angemessenen Stoffes von demjenigen freizumachen, was mir noch aus meinen weimarischen Eindrücken und Erinnerungen Schmerzliches und Lästiges anklebte. Sehr treffend nennt er daher auch den "Tasso" einen gesteigerten "Werther." ' (Emphasis mine)[24]

Although certain details of this passage are untrue (he did not find Italy conducive to writing *Tasso*, for example, and his first ten years in Weimar were not unproductive in a literary sense), it nevertheless shows the kind of reader Goethe sought for himself as one who empathized with him and engaged in the task of attempting to relate his work closely with his life. From his reader he sought a personal interest, involvement, and sympathetic understanding, in other words; his work was both a work of literature but also the fruit of the life he lived, and he did not wish the latter to be lost for the sake of the former. Friends, he knew, would bring all of the necessary qualities to bear on their reading; from critics he sought exactly the same, but here he was to be disappointed – indeed, from both quarters he was to experience a growing sense of disappointment as time went on, with the result that after his return to Weimar in 1788 he began to develop an even more esoteric, more markedly self-protective attitude than before in much of what he wrote. In the early years he had achieved the impact he sought from a much wider public than the one that truly mattered to him; from 1776–86 the 'public' he courted was in the main a group of friends and admirers, chief of whom was his beloved Frau von Stein. From early 1787, however, he began to feel himself misunderstood and unappreciated as a writer, even by some in his more intimate circle, which led him into a period of disappointed solitude such as he had never really known before. And yet his disappointment was largely inevitable, for the demands he placed on his readers could only be met by very few, if at all. In rewriting existing works to accord with his own inner development since their first composition, he

24 Eckermann 539 (3 May 1827)

expected to augment the acclaim these works had already received, but such was not always the case by any means. Weimar society responded critically to the new *Iphigenie*, for example, and with moral outrage towards *Egmont*.[25] To the rewritten *Werther* there was no response at all, however; it simply passed by its contemporary reading public as little more than a reissuing of the original. Unfortunately we have done little to take serious account of the new text ever since.

A Closer Look at Our Critical Responses to *Werther*

In his Foreword to the 'definitive English translation' of Goethe's *Werther*, first published in 1971, W.H. Auden made the following observations:

> Living in the twentieth century, not the eighteenth ... *Werther* reads not as a tragic love story, but as a masterly and devastating portrait of a complete egoist, a spoiled brat, incapable of love because he cares for nothing and nobody but himself and having his way at whatever cost to others. Had Goethe, from the bottom of his heart, really wanted his readers to admire Werther, why did he introduce the story of the servant who is in love with his widowed mistress? ... Goethe not only introduces this character but also makes Werther, the future suicide, identify the murderer's situation with his own, thereby making it impossible for the reader to think of suicide as 'noble.'[26]

What this critic does here is surprisingly characteristic of a great many others, even though his wholly negative view of Werther is not altogether representative. While Auden is not a Goethe scholar, many who are fall into error in just the same way that he does, attributing to Goethe intentions that justify their own reactions to the work. Most, however, do not reveal the shifting sands of their critical responses to

---

25 Cf., for example, Goethe's negative reaction to the critical response to his final version of *Iphigenie*, March 1787 – Gräf 2,3: no. 2529; also May 1787 (no. 2530). He was even more upset by the response of his close friends to the completed *Egmont*, in particular by their disapproval of Klärchen; cf. ibid. 2,1:no. 409, 410, 417, 423.
26 *The Sorrows of Young Werther*, trans. by Elizabeth Mayer and Louise Bogan, Foreword by W.H. Auden, 1984, xif.

the novel quite so clearly. First of all Auden emphasizes the distance in time between the era in which the book was written and the present day, formulating a negative response to the hero on the basis of values he implicitly lays claim to as those of the twentieth century to which he belongs. So far so good. But he then goes on to an equally robust assertion that concerns Goethe's intention in writing the novel, now *dispensing with* that very historical time-gap he himself has just established as the justification for his responding to the work as the tale of a contemptible egomaniac. Goethe, he implicitly claims, meant none of his readers, contemporary or otherwise, to admire Werther, or else he would not have worked the story of the farmboy into the novel in the way he did. Is this a valid comment on *Werther* or on its author? Auden's comments have a surprisingly exemplary quality for much of *Werther*-scholarship, for the process by which many critical opinions on Goethe's intentions are arrived at seems to run on an unconscious level as follows: 'I: can't stand / reject / feel embarrassed by / feel threatened by / Werther. Goethe evidently meant me to have this reaction to the work.' Thus the notion of inner distance to the central character called forth in the reader as the result of a seeming clash between his own value system and that of the work is neatly, if unconsciously, transformed into a declared distance attributed to the intention of the author.

But what of the text itself and of the reader to whom it specifically makes its opening appeal, an appeal never abandoned but, rather, heightened in Version Two by the biased editorial comments of the final section allegedly written after Werther's death? In the view of Gerhard Storz, 'die Mitteilung von Werthers Nachlaß wirbt um Teilnahme am Geschick und an der Person eines unglücklichen Menschen.'[27] Is this a sympathy which the modern reader can simply no longer feel? Is there a key here perhaps to much of what has been written about the novel over a very long period? Goethe always wrote for a particular coterie of sympathetic readers, a smaller and smaller group as time went on, but readers who shared his preoccupations and goals,[28] who were willing to subordinate their mind and heart to what they read,[29] and to engage in a creative encounter with what-

---

27 Storz, *Goethe-Vigilien* 20
28 Eckermann 253 (11 October 1828)
29 See Introduction, note 8.

ever they found there.³⁰ Wayne Booth writes: 'The author ... makes his reader as he makes his second self, and the most successful reading is one in which the created selves, author and reader, can find complete agreement.'³¹ Now while one might make certain well-founded objections to such a view, this is nevertheless the view adopted by Goethe, and the degree to which we find ourselves at odds with Werther is not necessarily to be explained by the author's desire that we should be so, hence by any assertion that he has specifically written this work in such a way as to call forth in us (or in his contemporary readers) a sense of distance. 'Teilnehmer, Freunde, Liebhaber des Verfassers' were those for whom Goethe wrote;³² and the following note from Zimmermann to Charlotte von Stein is characteristic of contemporary reactions to *Werther* when it was first published: 'Ce roman si vrai, si naturel, si ressemblant à tout ce qu'on a senti mille et mille fois en sa vie ... la naissance et la marche de l'amour le plus vif y est peint avec le pinceau de la nature même.'³³ Perhaps, as Auden declares, no twentieth-century reader can respond to either version of the work in this way, but if not, then he must be careful in attributing to the author views that may in fact simply be his own.

According to Roger Paulin, the modern reader, while having no difficulty in discussing Werther's attitude to love or religion, feels less than comfortable in any discussion of his tears.³⁴ And yet, to cite Stefan Blessin on the subject of the novel: 'Keine Interpretation des Romans ist ... möglich, die nicht auf die Selbsterfahrung des Lesers, auf der dialogischen Auseinandersetzung gegründet wäre, die dieser mit sich in den affektiv besetzten Rollen des Wertherfreundes und Wertherkritikers führt.'³⁵ Here we have a problem, do we not? For

---

30 Cf. HA *Briefe* 2:224f., 3:456, 3:382f., 4:35.
31 Wayne Booth, *The Rhetoric of Fiction*, 1983, 138
32 See *West-Östlicher Divan*, 'Noten und Abhandlungen,' HA 2:195; also letter to Schiller, 14 June 1796, HA *Briefe* 2:224f.
33 Hermann Blumenthal, *Zeitgenössische Rezensionen und Urteile über Goethes 'Götz' und 'Werther,'* 1935, 101. Another typical reaction, this time of a younger man (a friend of Ludwig Tieck), is cited by Düntzer in *Studien zu Goethes Werken*, 1849, 172: 'Ich war siebzehn Jahr alt, als Werther erschien. Vier Wochen lang habe ich mich in Thränen gebadet, ... in der Zerknirschung des Herzens, im demüthigenden Bewußtsein, daß ich nicht so dächte, nicht so sein könne, als dieser da ...'
34 Paulin 57
35 Blessin, ' "Die Leiden des jungen Werthers" im Rückblick,' in *Die Romane Goethes*, 1979, 269–301, here 271

in reading a novel that is known to end in suicide we almost inevitably establish a certain inner distance from the notion that this may be a valid end for any human being; we naturally tend to establish a distance from any line of argument or set of experiences whose only truthful and logical outcome would be the taking of one's own life. To endorse the suicide of another, after all, is to come close to acknowledging the irreproachability of the decision-making process that led up to his action, and such acknowledgment is difficult both objectively and subjectively for the normal human being whose own hold on life is secure.[36] The ready alternative that comes to mind is to find Werther unhinged, a pathological case, a man who threatens not only himself, but society around him. And so in the tale of the farmboy we take up a position on the side of society, against Werther. Although both we and he hold the young man guilty of the murder of his rival, rather than be obligated, however obliquely, to share Werther's fate, we declare him rejected by Goethe and find in the rewritten version of the novel a newly distanced narrative stance that indicts the central character.[37] However, convincing proof of our right to do so remains problematic from within the text, and so we either find 'proof' from elsewhere, such as in later utterances by Goethe, or we set about reconstructing a narrative that will serve our purpose of divesting ourselves of a sense of discomfiture, if not threat. 'Goethe war einmal Werther, aber er war es nicht mehr, als er den Roman schrieb'[38] – this is a commonplace of *Werther*-criticism, accurate enough perhaps for the original version of the novel, which was written long after Goethe had overcome his anguish concerning Lotte Buff, yet it is a view that is surely more an article of faith than any critically secured assertion of literary scholarship for Version Two, in which Werther's

---

36 Anselm Haverkamp perceives an inevitable clash between the admiring stance of the fictive narrator and that of the actual reader ('Illusion und Empathie: Die Struktur der "teilnehmenden Lektüre" in den *Leiden Werthers*,' in *Erzählforschung: Ein Symposion*, 1982). Haverkamp postulates the establishment of a fictive reader in the preface to the novel, one who will empathize with Werther but who is not then given the possibility of doing so.

37 The notion of distance is widespread throughout the critical literature on the revised *Werther* – cf., for example, Ingrid Engel, *Werther und die Wertheriaden: Ein Beitrag zur Wirkungsgeschichte*, 1986, 54; Martin Swales, *Goethe: The Sorrows of Young Werther*, 16, 20f.; Welz 52f; Reiss 20; Reuter 105f.; see also notes 45–49 below.

38 Gose 9

anguish is intensified rather than diminished. As I have tried to show, by the time Goethe came to revise his novel for republication in 1786, he was caught up in the painful awareness that he was living out Werther's story in essence all over again in Weimar. This Weimar story mattered far more to him than the Wetzlar/Frankfurt story every had, involving, as it did, the most important love relationship of his life, a relationship that had dominated his thoughts and actions for more than a decade.

For over a century now, however, the dominant theory about Goethe's authorial stance vis-à-vis the second version of his novel has been that of distance. Examining closely the new Editor's Report in the rewritten *Werther* already in 1875, for example, Erich Schmidt claimed that it was more convincing, more objective, and written in a cooler tone,[39] and yet, as we saw, this section of the novel seems in fact geared to presenting Werther in a less objective, more favourable, if more anguished, light than was the case in the corresponding section of the original version. Similar assertions in one form or another to those made by Schmidt are by now legion, however, and represent the overt or covert starting-point for most of the critical literature on *Werther* of the past hundred years and more. Even in the late 1830s Hegel looked on Werther as 'ein durchweg krankhafter Charakter, ohne Kraft sich über den Eigensinn seiner Liebe erheben zu können,'[40] so the reader's rejection of Goethe's tragic lover goes back a very long way indeed.

While it may be our task as critics to read one text and become the author of another that deals with the first, we are surely not at liberty to declare our own responses the intention and achieved goal of the author of the original. And yet many of us seem to work hard at doing precisely that, however little we may be aware of the process or mean to engage in it. Stefan Blessin has already successfully pointed out deficiencies in the work of several critics who portray Werther as a self-conscious and aggressive rebel against society, a model for modern revolutionary man,[41] and Reinhard Assling has also chal-

---

39 Erich Schmidt, *Richardson, Rousseau und Goethe: Ein Beitrag zur Geschichte des Romans im 18. Jahrhundert*, 1875, 136ff.; cf. Schmidt, *Charakteristiken* 1:297.
40 From *Vorlesungen über die Ästhetik*, cited in *Goethe im Urteil seiner Kritiker*, ed. with introduction and commentary by Karl Robert Mandelkow, 1975–84, 2:152.
41 Blessin, *Romane* 276–9.

lenged others for not reading the novel as it is but using it as a means to serve their own particular standpoints.[42] A recent critic who *has* attempted to scrutinize the text very closely and who has arrived in this way at conclusions that are both significant and convincing is Thomas Saine, who has perceived aggression rather than sacrifice in Werther's suicide even in the original 1774 version of the novel,[43] and has made us aware of a greatly altered Lotte in Version Two.[44] In general, however, we tend to see in this second version clear evidence of a different author, while ostensibly devoting our whole interest and critical acumen to the text itself. Welz, Müller, Fittbogen, and Burdach, for example, take as a fundamental 'given' that Goethe changed in his early years in Wimar from a stormy, inspirational writer to one who was a great deal more calm and controlled, and their reading of the second *Werther* evidently reflects this view.[45] Hans Heinrich Reuter – and he is not alone here by any means – writes of 'Goethe's intention to objectivize the happening of his novel in the rewriting,'[46] and seems to draw without any critical distance of his own on the author's comments in *Dichtung und Wahrheit* to substantiate the presentation of Werther as an objective portrayal of bourgeois man in the later eighteenth century.

In the examples I have just referred to, the link made by the critic between the work and its author is explicitly formulated, but others *implicitly* attribute to Goethe's writing what may in fact be nothing other than their own reading, finding a greater distance to Werther in the Editor's Report of the revised version than in that of the original.[47] The style of this part of Version Two is seen by one critic, for example, as 'ein sachlicher, wacher Dokumentarstil'[48] even though such a style prevails only very briefly in the text. From the same critic

42 Reinhard Assling, *Werthers Leiden: Die ästhetische Rebellion der Innerlichkeit*, 1981, 3–5
43 Saine, 'Passion and Aggression'
44 Saine, 'The Portrayal of Lotte'
45 Dieter Welz, passim (cf. 50); Peter Müller 205ff.; Gottfried Fittbogen 580. See also Klause Scherpe, *Werther und Werther-Wirkung*, 1970, 105f.
46 Reuter 102; 105ff.; see also notes 37, 47, and 49.
47 Cf., for example, Klaus Hübner, *Alltag im literarischen Werk*, 1982, 86: Jane K. Brown, 'The Renaissance of Goethe's Poetic Genius in Italy,' in *Goethe in Italy 1786–1796*, 1988, 90, note 26.
48 Tadamichi Doke, 'Zur literarischen Methode der "Leiden des jungen Werther,"' *Goethe Jahrbuch*, 1974, 22

we learn that the Editor takes up a position from which he can observe and present events with greater distance and quite objectively, a view evidently shared by Stefan Blessin, Hans-Rudolf Vaget, Heinz Schlaffer, and Melitta Gerhard.[49] And yet one has the uncomfortable feeling that such assertions about the text and its author may be little more than assertions about the subjective responses of individual readers, albeit responses shared by many. Benjamin Bennett, for example, who, like others, has a great deal to say that is perceptive and sound, claims that the ending of the idyllic first part of the farmboy story (where Werther says he will not attempt to catch sight of the young man's beloved mistress in case he might be disappointed) challenges us to think objectively about Lotte, of whom 'we may at least expect that she is a habitual breaker of hearts.'[50] Not so. The difficulty here, it seems to me, is one of overinformed reader-response, the response of a reader who is not coming to the text without preconceived ideas, and it is a difficulty that asserts itself time and time again.

Eric Blackall, who perceptively spotted the partisan nature of the narrative stance in the Editor's Report, rightly says the following: 'This second narrator is no more able to get outside of Werther than Werther was able to get outside of himself.' But he then goes on: 'The narrator's inability to achieve distance therefore somehow provokes distance in us.[51] Note the word 'inability' here: what is implied is that we, as readers, perceiving an inadequacy in the narrator *somehow* are led to compensate for that inadequacy and thus end up less involved with the central character. But why should we regard the Editor's partisanship as an inadequacy? Why shouldn't we become even more involved with Werther and more sympathetic towards his fate as a result of the Editor's favourable presentation of his subject? Surely this says more about us as readers than it does about the text as constituted by Goethe. And if, as Blackall declares, 'we remain [in

---

49 Ibid.; Blessin, *Johann Wolfgang Goethe: Die Leiden des jungen Werther*, 1985, 23f.; Fittbogen 580ff.; Hans Rudolf Vaget, 'Goethe the Novelist: On the Coherence of his Fiction,' in *Goethe's Narrative Fiction*, 1983, 10; Melitta Gerhard, 'Die Bauernbursche-Episode im Werther,' *Zeitschrift für Aesthetik und allgemeine Kunstwissenschaft*, 1916, 74; Heinz Schlaffer 216f.
50 Bennet 66
51 Blackall 53f.

the Editor's Report] with Werther's point of view and yet see it *as a point of view*, not as absolute,'[52] then surely this too merely says more about our refusal in reading to relinquish our own values in response to the Editor than it says about the actual text.

According to Benjamin Bennett, Goethe abandons the epistolary form of the novel 'earlier than he absolutely needs to' because the change is 'meant to draw our attention *to our situation as readers.*'[53] That it may perhaps do so is one point, but that it is *meant* to do so quite another. And such assertions are by no means rare. Erika Nolan, another splendid critic, seems to fall into a similar trap when she tells us, for example, that the canary episode and other additions to the second version of *Werther* seem to have as their chief function to help the reader to correct Werther's idealized portrayal of Lotte.[54] Again the reader may respond to the additions in this way, but can one justifiably assert that this is their 'chief function'? And Blackall, despite his achievement in partially discerning the stance of the narrator, goes on to assert arbitrarily of the author: 'Goethe is most anxious, in this second version of his novel, that we shall see the sickness of Werther and not identify him with his author, nor ourselves with him *totally*. This amount of distance Goethe desires; not, however, so much distance that we shall not identify with Werther *at all*.'[55] I find this an extraordinary claim.

No less extraordinary, and more revealing in terms of the critic's own value-system than in terms of the text of Goethe's novel, is the following comment by Heinz Schlaffer: 'Nicht anders als bei Don Quijote wirkt die Diskrepanz zwischen der fernen Idealität des Gelesenen und der nahen Trivialität des Gelebten parodistisch ... Kaffee und Homer ... Zuckererbsen und Homer.'[56] According to Schlaffer, Werther merely creates himself out of what he reads and in turn must be read ironically. Must he? In the view of Rudolf Käser, the addition in Version Two of the note in which Werther kisses Lotte's letters and asks her not to use sand to blot them, the note asking her to give him more errands to do for her (46R), shows how ironically Werther is

52 Ibid.
53 Bennet 71
54 Nolan 209
55 Blackall 53
56 Schlaffer 215f.

portrayed in the second version.⁵⁷ But again, does it? I would suggest that this reading too says more about the critic's own stance regarding a man's attitude to his beloved than about the novel or its central character. 'Not self-loss but self-recognition would bring about Werther's fulfillment. But this he never really achieves,' writes Eric Blackall.⁵⁸ However, what of the fate of the farmboy as told in the last part of the added story? Is this not the point of self-recognition for Werther? 'Du bist nicht zu retten, Unglücklicher! ich sehe wohl daß wir nicht zu retten sind,' is his summation of events (121R). While recognizing himself in the Bauernbursche does not bring about Werther's self-fulfilment in the positive way that Blackall evidently has in mind, it does lead on to his putting an end to his present existence, which may be the only self-fulfilment possible, given the circumstances.

What all of these critics, and many others as well, have in common, despite a great deal of challenging and stimulating comment in what they write on the subject of *Werther*, seems to be a rejection of the last step the hero takes in ending his life, and a belief that Goethe must have shared this view. However, the grounds for such a belief seem rather shaky, for what Goethe had to say about suicide almost forty years after Werther's appearance on the literary scene suggests that he could conceive only of a positive, sympathetic response to his hero's end. 'Der Selbstmord,' he wrote in *Dichtung und Wahrheit*, 'ist ein Ereignis der menschlichen Natur, welches, mag auch darüber schon soviel gesprochen und gehandelt sein als da will, doch einen jeden Menschen zur Teilnahme fordert' (HA 9:583). The collective critical response to Werther's fate has been almost uniformly negative, however, for a very long time indeed. While one may perhaps understandably shy away from identifying with or endorsing suicide as a solution to an impossible love situation, I think it important to attempt to engage with the novel on its own terms, and this seems to be where we tend to fall down. 'The intact nature of Lotte's relationship with Albert is reinforced by means of Lotte's inner monologue on the

---

57 Käser 175; Rolf Zimmermann, throughout a chapter entitled 'Die Leiden des jungen Werthers,' also fails to substantiate the claims he makes about Goethe's intent, but uses such claims in order to validate his own opinions (*Das Weltbild des jungen Goethe*, 1979, 2:167–212).

58 Blackall 32

prospect of Werther's departure,' writes Käser,[59] who again is not alone,[60] and yet the changes made to the original text at the very point cited seem to undermine rather than to highlight Lotte's deep and exclusive emotional commitment to her husband in the revised novel, as we saw.

Dieter Welz, who bases his reading of the second version on Goethe's newly gained composure in Weimar and on the changes in style introduced into the second version as evidence of his adherence to courtly norms prevailing there, cites Adelung, the dominant manual of style in 1786, without realizing that by doing so he weakens his own case: 'Nach Adelung ist "unedel, was in der eigenthümlichen Denkungs- und Empfindungsart der untern Classen gegründet ist, und sich eben dadurch von der erhöheten und veredelten Denkungs- und Empfindungsart der obern Classen unterscheidet."'[61] We only need to recall the glorification of the lower classes in both versions of *Werther*, augmented by the story of the farmboy in Version Two, to see that Goethe could not have been in sympathy with Adelung's views, despite all willingness to have his revised manuscript conform to the latter's rules of spelling and syntax.

In the critical stance adopted by almost all who have addressed themselves to the task of interpreting *Werther* since the second version was written there has been a degree of historical consensus that does less than justice to the work and its author. For too long we have treated the existence of the two Werther-novels in a somewhat cavalier fashion, choosing to deal with either one or the other as we see fit without subjecting them to any very close comparative scrutiny.[62] As I said in my Introduction, the distinct nature of each of the two ver-

---

59 Käser 173
60 Cf. Gräf 1,2:553ff.; Reiss 21f., for example.
61 Welz 35
62 Many scholars seem to feel free to pass critical judgments on the novel without even bothering to distinguish the second version from the first. Peter Wapnewski, for example, deals with the 1775 edition, yet discusses the farmboy story, which was not published until twelve years later ('Zweihundert Jahre Werthers Leiden oder: Dem war nicht zu helfen'). Even Thomas Saine chooses to deal only with Version One as 'in some respects [unspecified!] artistically more successful than the revised version of 1787' ('Passion and Aggression' 327), but the same claim is made for Version Two by Hans Reiss (21f.). Emil Staiger makes little or no distinction between the two versions (see Introduction, note 29), while Hans Gose deals with the second version only in the last two pages of his book.

sions was pointed out more than a century ago, but this has not yet been taken seriously enough or explored in depth as it should. It would be a pity if we were to continue to develop readings that neither do full justice to Goethe's definitive text, nor take account of the role that writing played for him during the years that lay between the two versions of his novel.

Werther: A Summary of the Need for Review

If I have gone to some considerable lengths to suggest that a different part of Goethe's life lay behind the second writing of *Werther* from that which is so widely believed, and to lend weight to my suggestions by means of a brief look at several other works from that perspective only, it is chiefly because many of our long-current critical views on the novel do not seem to have their basis in the text itself, but in certain preconceptions regarding the course that Goethe's development took both as a man and as a writer during his first eleven years in Weimar. The second version of the novel continues to be read as if the background to the revision were Goethe's experiences in Wetzlar in 1772, as if the new Lotte were Charlotte Buff and the new Albert her husband, Johann Christian Kestner.[63] This assumption is so widespread that it no longer plays any declared role in scholarly interpretations of the work, but it continues to bolster up a whole catalogue of commonplaces of *Werther*-criticism that provide a foundation for the development of new approaches and insights that, while stimulating in themselves, often seem to have a rather insecure foundation in the text of Version Two.

The belief that the poet underwent an inner development during his first five years in Weimar from turbulent defiance to serene endorsement of society's rules has given rise to the view that he rewrote

---

[63] One of the most recent examples of the assumption that the emotional background to both versions of *Werther* was Goethe's love for Charlotte Buff is Horst Flaschka's book, *Goethes 'Werther': Werkkontextuelle Deskription und Analyse* (1987); see also Rudolf Käser 133ff. Other recent critics who share the conviction that Wetzlar remained the background to the novel include Bruno Hillebrand, *Goethes Werther – ein deutsches Thema*, 1982, 6f.; Alfred Ehrentreich, 'An der Peripherie von Goethes "Werther,"' *Goethe Jahrbuch*, 1983, 266–71; Hans-Heinrich Reuter 86ff.; Blessin, *Johann Wolfgang Goethe* 17ff.

Werther from a distanced, more mature, and more critical standpoint. 'Evidence' is found in the text to support this view, 'evidence' too in an altered preface Goethe wrote for the second printing of Version One (1775), in which he added a cautionary admonition to those readers who might seek to emulate Werther's suicide: 'Sei ein Mann und folge mir nicht nach.'[64] And yet Goethe, when preparing the novel for the new Göschen edition in 1786, removed these words and returned to his original preface of 1774, where the reader had been told of the various reactions this story would elicit: admiration, love, sorrow, and a sense of consolation. There is no evidence of inner distance here, but what of the remainder of the novel? The theory gives rise to certain difficulties throughout the text, difficulties that have been overlooked, rather than disregarded, I believe, simply because even the scholarly reader has difficulty in accepting the notion that suicide is a comprehensible or acceptable response to life, however anguished or despairing, and therefore seeks his own reassurance in Version Two, using long-prevalent, if unarticulated, notions of Goethe's development in support. The poet's own account in *Dichtung und Wahrheit*, which allegedly deals with Version One, helps the reader believe what he wants to believe, and that too has an impact on his reading of the second version. In an attempt to help us focus on the need for renewed scrutiny of this text as the basis for establishing clearly whether it represents an aesthetic advance or decline in comparison with the original, let me now bring together some of the most salient textual difficulties that seem closely bound up with the theory that Version Two represents the establishment of the author's critical distance from his hero.

If Goethe distanced himself from Werther's fate in the second version, then why did he go to some lengths to show that Lotte really did love Werther, even though that love could not be expressed actively or openly? Is this an effective distancing technique? Does it not, rather, seem geared to making the unprejudiced reader more likely to empathize with Werther in his torment and even with the solution he ultimately chooses for himself? Does it really suggest Goethe's own inner distance from the hero or his conscious attempt to relativize Werther's

---

64 See HA 6:528. Benjamin Bennett, for example, sees the [temporarily] altered preface as 'the ethical message' of *Werther* (76), while claiming there is 'no formulable ethical doctrine' in the novel itself (77).

plight as that of a pathological lover who deserves to be rejected? If so, why are the former indications of Lotte's love for her husband weakened and relativized in contrast to her newly revealed feelings for Werther (134–5L/R)? Why did Goethe add this passage through which it becomes clear that she can no longer be happy with Albert alone, but needs Werther as her lifelong companion? Why does she cast Albert as the man to whom she sees herself inescapably bound, and of whose good qualities she is aware – all qualities likely to afford another woman happiness, but not herself? She characterizes her husband in Version Two, we recall, as '[der] Mann, mit dem [sie sich] auf ewig verbunden [sah], dessen Liebe und Treue sie kannte ... dessen Ruhe, dessen Zuverlässigkeit recht vom Himmel dazu bestimmt zu seyn schien, daß eine wackere Frau das Glück ihres Lebens darauf gründen sollte' (134–5R). If Goethe had wished to establish a distance from Werther when rewriting the novel by emphasizing his pathological state, would he have taken out Lotte's reflections on 'ihre Liebe zu ihrem Mann' (134L) and presented this love as mere fondness ('dem sie von Herzen zu gethan war' [134R])? Would he have had her expressly consider for the first time, then reject, the idea that Werther ought to marry one of her friends (135R)? And would he have introduced the canary episode to show the footing of intimacy she encouraged on the part of this man to whom she could never be more than a friend (97R)?

And why did Goethe write the farmboy story? Why heighten the reader's awareness of the hero's inner anguish at the course his own love was taking? Is this story proof that Goethe no longer empathized with Werther's fate when he came to rewrite his novel? Only the third part of the tale could conceivably lessen the reader's sympathy for Werther, and yet precisely this part is not included in the central figure's own account, but carefully presented in the Editor's Report between two newly written passages, the one showing how unfair he is capable of being towards Albert, the other how incapable he is of sustaining that unfairness. Werther's justification of the murder he believes the farmboy to have committed is thus short-lived, his mental balance thus carefully restored before he sends for Albert's pistols. Does this not mean that his suicide is lent an aura of even greater self-awareness and heightened self-sacrifice, of greater urgency, than it had in the original? Surely the imperative to put an end to the present situation is newly validated by Werther's fear of what his own emotions can lead him into, rather than undermined as the act of a man who has lost hold of his senses? Society will take the life of the farm-boy, Werther will take his own, hoping to find in 'escape from this world' the possibility of realizing in eternity that love whose fulfilment temporal reality denies to him. Did Goethe distance himself from Werther by means of the farmboy story? The assertion is unassailed throughout centuries of scholarly interpretation.

But what of the way in which the guilt of this man is presented? Why did Goethe not see to it that no doubt surrounds the farmboy's action in committing the murder? A single sentence would have been enough to establish that he was indeed guilty. To Werther's cry, 'Was hast du begangen, Unglücklicher!' the young man would only have had to say something like 'Ich mußte es tun' or 'Mir blieb nichts anderes übrig.' Instead of that, the text oddly reads: 'Dieser sah ihn still an, schwieg und versetzte endlich ganz gelassen: Keiner wird sie haben, sie wird keinen haben' (120R). Is this a confession of guilt? An unnoticed lacuna by the author in the writing? And why is Werther totally convinced that the farmboy is guilty of the crime immediately he learns the identity of the murder victim? Why does he not even seem to hear the reply the young man gives to his question? Is it not because he, Werther, has already felt within himself the potential for violence towards his own rival, Albert, and can therefore readily identify with the notion of murder? It was just before his discovery of the farmboy's eviction from the widow's household, we recall, that he became aware of this urge within himself:

> Manchmal will wohl ein freudiger Blick des Lebens wieder aufdämmern, ach! nur für einen Augenblick! – Wenn ich mich so in Träumen verliere, kann ich mich des Gedankens nicht erwehren: wie wenn Albert stürbe? Du würdest! ja, Sie würde – und dann laufe ich dem Hirngespinste nach, bis es mich an Abgründe führet, vor denen ich zurückbebe. (92L/R)

Death to Albert as the fruit of dreamy imaginings: so run Werther's thoughts in both versions of the novel, but only in the second is this built upon through the tale of the young farmhand. Again, do we really have evidence here of Goethe's desire to distance himself from Werther's inner state? It seems more probable on the basis of the text, and given the massive self-investment he made in most of his works, that the opposite is the case.

This also appears to be borne out by the altered and more weighty role of the Editor in Version Two, for through him Werther is presented in a more sympathetic light than in Version One. While claiming for himself a role rather like that of a meticulous biographer, the Editor constantly creates or manipulates his material in a way that seems hopelessly biased in favour of his subject. Why the change? Did Goethe truly use the Editor in either version as a means through which emotional distance to Werther might be achieved or criticism of his suicide introduced? If so, did he not then even more surely fail rather than succeed in this goal in Version Two in terms of the sympathetic reader whom he sought to address?

If Albert is 'improved' in Goethe's rewriting – and indeed various manifestations of jealousy on his part towards Werther and indifference towards Lotte are deleted in Version Two – then why is that 'improvement' diminished by the addition of information that places him more squarely than ever before among the ranks of those Philistine husbands whose chief concern is to give the neighbours no cause for gossip? 'Er liebte Lotten über alles,' his friends tell the Editor (117R), but yet it is not because he wishes to have more time alone with her that he wants her to ensure that Werther's visits are curtailed: 'Ich wünsch' es auch um unsertwillen,' he says, 'und ich bitte dich, siehe zu, seinem Betragen gegen dich eine andere Richtung zu geben, seine öftern Besuche zu vermindern. Die Leute werden aufmerksam, und ich weiß, daß man hier und da drüber gesprochen hat' (122R).

These are only some of the difficulties that need to be resolved if a great deal of what has been written about Goethe's revised novel is to be regarded as demonstrably valid. For two centuries now critical scholarship has seen in Version Two nothing more than the minor rewriting of a work in which past personal sufferings of the author, long since overcome, and hence set at a distance, have been recorded. However, as I hope to have shown, such a view conflicts both with Goethe's real-life situation and with his whole mode of writing in 1786. His approach to literary creativity was at that point even more personal than it had been in the years before his arrival in Weimar, his ability to write on different planes within one work at one and the same time more highly developed. His enormous talent enabled him to establish, rejoice in, play with, deplore, attack, defuse, or otherwise deal with his own current preoccupations in whatever way he liked, while at the same time creating a work of lasting literary substance. The rewritten *Werther* is just one example of this multiple mode of writing, and what I have tried to do here is to highlight the hidden level of confession that it contains that makes it distinct from Version One, which had its own hidden level at the time of first writing, a level that did not remain hidden for long, and one that Goethe readily admitted to, however much he may have disliked the attempts by others to discover the exact details of events that had lain behind his writing of the original. He never made such an admission with regard to the second version of 1786, but this does not mean what we have for so long believed, namely, that no new personal experiences of a similar kind lay behind it. Everything he wrote at that time was in a significant sense a reflection of all that he thought or felt, and his experiences in love from 1776 to 1786 remained so painful for him that even when he was seventy-five years old he shied away from rereading what he had written. As he said to Eckermann of *Werther* in 1824:

> Das ist auch so ein Geschöpf, das ich gleich dem Pelikan mit dem Blute meines eigenen Herzens gefüttert habe. Es ist darin so viel Innerliches aus meiner eigenen Brust, so viel von Empfindungen und Gedanken, um damit wohl einen Roman von zehn solcher Bändchen auszustatten. Übrigens habe ich das Buch, wie ich schon öfter gesagt, seit seinem Erscheinen nur ein einziges Mal wieder gelesen und mich gehütet, es abermals zu tun. Es sind lauter Brandraketen! – Es wird mir unheimlich dabei, und ich fürchte den pathologischen Zustand wieder durchzuempfinden, aus dem es hervorging.[65]

Contrary to what he had sought to assert some ten years before in *Dichtung und Wahrheit*, he claimed here that the novel was not chiefly a reflection of the spirit of the age, but of his own personal circumstances and emotions. To Eckermann, who was simply repeating Goethe's own earlier view of Werther as a representative of the time, he retorted somewhat sharply: 'Es waren vielmehr individuelle, naheliegende Verhältnisse, die mir auf die Nägel brannten und mir zu schaffen machten und die mich in jenen Gemütszustand brachten, aus dem der "Werther" hervorging. Ich hatte gelebt, geliebt, und sehr viel gelitten! – Das war es.'[66]

---

65 Eckermann 468 (2 January 1824)
66 Ibid. 469. Note, by contrast, the earlier universalizing and depersonalizing tendency in his remarks in Bk. 3, ch. 13 of *Dichtung und Wahrheit* (HA 9:589ff.).

How much more true this was of the period in which he wrote the second version of *Werther* than the first is evident, for whereas he had waited two years before committing his experiences to paper the first time, when he rewrote his novel in 1786 he was still very much caught up emotionally in another triangular love relationship, this one even more tormenting than the first. We appear to have completely overlooked or paid scant attention to a remark that Goethe made in old age: 'Was mir in Wetzlar begegnete, ist von keiner großen Bedeutung.'[67] The course that his life took after 1775 suggests that this was quite true, as do all the various changes he made to *Werther*.

While the proper task of criticism may indeed *not* be 'to untangle the connection between the work and the author, or to try to reconstruct a thought or an experience through the text,' but to 'analyze the work in its structure, in its architecture, in its intrinsic form, and in the interaction of its internal relations,'[68] this task can only be validly addressed by a mind that is truly open to the text. In the same way, there can be no sound analysis of any author's development without a respect for the integrity of each of his texts as the primary evidence of that development. What I have tried to do here has been to bring home the need for an opening up of our collective critical mind so that the final text of *Werther*, as an important building block in Goethe's development as a writer, can be more fully explored and adequately evaluated in aesthetic terms, for many important questions have yet to be answered with authority. Is this a seriously flawed work, for example? Is it so personal a statement by an author caught up in his own conflicting emotions at the time of writing that we cannot help but read it against the grain? Or have the non-aesthetic values of the writer and his readership quite simply long since ceased to coincide, leading us to a negative judgment on the hero? In that case, we must be careful about how we formulate our judgment, careful not to fill in the gap that exists between our values and those of the work with any doubtful declaration of authorial intent; to speak with Mukařovský: 'Die im Werk enthaltenen außerästhetischen Werte [dürfen] nicht

---

[67] Quoted by Ehrentreich (270), who has some difficulty in making sense of the statement, since he is convinced, like everyone else, that the well-known events in Wetzlar formed the background to both versions of *Werther*.

[68] Michel Foucault, 'What Is an Author? 1975, 605

automatisch mit den entsprechenden außerhalb des Werks geltenden Werten gleichgesetzt werden.'[69] And which version of the novel is demonstrably superior in a purely aesthetic sense? Why? These are all valid questions to which valid answers must still be found, more than two centuries after the first appearance of Version Two.

My own view is that this second version is on the whole emotionally superior, yet often artistically inferior to the first. Here and there it offers evidence of its author's growing command of his talent for the expression of emotional intensity, but in some places it lacks the sustained rigour of thought and logic necessary for the new additions and deletions to function as improvements to the existing text. When Goethe writes new passages that reveal Lotte's profound feelings for Werther, for example, or other new passages that add to Werther's wrath and lamentation at the behaviour of the aristocracy, he adds to the power of the conflict experienced by his hero in terms that lend this conflict greater credibility; when he simply adds, deletes or rewords a sentence here or there, the resulting text is often clearly improved; yet when he creates certain new seams by the addition of new notes or letters, the transitions are often flawed. To say this, however, is by no means to do justice to the final version of the novel as a work of literature. Paradoxically, what I hope to have shown here is the need for a meticulous study in its own right that would engage seriously with both versions and provide a contrastive analysis of their structure, their architecture, and the interaction of their internal relations, without reference to the genesis of the two works or to the biography of their author. Where a re-examination of the biography has been most useful has been in clearing the critical path towards this end, but it also has certain broader implications.

The final version of *Werther* is important both in itself as a discrete literary entity and also in relation to the rest of Goethe's oeuvre. The only piece of major writing/rewriting that he completed before going to Italy, it reflects a particular relationship with his own talent for literary creativity that began in his early years and underwent an intensification process in Weimar that lasted until around 1790. Already written in its original form in 1774, the novel was rewritten throughout a period of varied yet constant literary activity shared with

---

[69] Jan Mukařovský, 'Das dichterische Werk als Gesamtheit von Werten,' 1967, 43

one specific mental, emotional, and spiritual partner, Charlotte von Stein. Contrary to accepted scholarly opinion, and to the opinion that Goethe himself sought to promote as a smokescreen to protect himself from unwanted scrutiny, he was not a frustrated and unproductive writer in his first period in Weimar. He wrote a great deal in the decade prior to his journey to Italy, much of it good, much of it bad, but almost all of it bearing some mark of his relationship with Frau von Stein. It is important, I believe, to realize that despite all the emotional upheavals of this relationship, his life with her in Weimar brought him much happiness that derived in significant measure from a profound sense of shared creativity as well as of shared conspiracy, so the loss of this most important partner inevitably had its own impact on his work. After the final break with Charlotte, Goethe found himself in a state of isolation greater than he had ever before experienced, an isolation that was to last until the mid-1790s, when he began to collaborate with Schiller, an altogether different kind of literary partner.

In 1809 Goethe wrote to Reinhard, expressing confidence in the power of art to endure and to triumph over generations of critics; in his words: 'Das Gedichtete behauptet sein Recht, wie das Geschehene.'[70] The work of literature can begin to assert itself in Goethe's terms, however, only if it is allowed the room to do so. By modifying our notions of the life that the poet led up to 1789 ('das Geschehene'), and by looking closely at the multifaceted role played by writing in that phase of his life as well as the great importance he attached to it, I hope to have freed the final version of *Werther* from the stranglehold imposed on it by too great a concentration in the past on the events that lay only behind Version One. During the years up to and including the final phase of the writing of *Tasso* Goethe lived and relived his life through his literary creations, whether borrowed or not, daring to give vent there to his own innermost thoughts and feelings, but always in a way that protected his inner core from penetration by those who were not kindred spirits. 'Sagt es niemand, nur den Weisen, / Weil die Menge gleich verhöhnet, / Das Lebend'ge will ich preisen, / Das nach Flammentod sich sehnet': so run the opening lines of 'Selige Sehnsucht,' written for the *West-Östlicher Divan* in 1814 (HA

---

70 HA *Briefe* 3:117

2:18), but neither the evident esotericism nor the willingness to risk one's all for the sake of experiencing a heightened sense of life as expressed in these lines represents any new thought or any change in direction on Goethe's part, for by that time he had already been writing in accordance with these principles for a good forty years. The principle of 'Hineingeheimnissen,' believed to be characteristic only of the older Goethe, in fact had its roots in his youth but gained greatly in momentum in and through the relationship with Frau von Stein. Drawn to secrets and conspiracies by instinct and temperament from the start, in the early years in Weimar he developed certain elements of a writing style that would be of increasing importance for his work in maturity.

By relinquishing our old ideas on the second *Werther* in order to grant to the text the level of analytical scrutiny that it has so far been denied, perhaps we can take a first step on the road to reflecting clearly and freshly on the whole question of Goethe's development as a writer up to and including the first journey to Italy.

Appendix: A List of the Substantive Changes to *Werther*

Small additions/alterations:

One or more sentences:
1771: 16 June, 28L/R
      13 July, 42L/R
      26 July, 46L/R
      8 August, 48–9L/R
1772: 20 January, 77L/R
      9 May, 88–9L/R
Editor's Report, 124L/R

Complete notes or letters:
1771: 26 July, 46R
      undated, between 8 and 10 August, 50R
1772: 8 February, 78–9R
      16 June, 90R
      5 September, 96R
      12 September, 97R
      27 October, 102R
      22 November, 106R
      26 November, 107R

Large additions/alterations:

1771: Farmboy's story (i) 30 May, 16–18R
1772: Farmboy's story (ii) 4 September, 93–6R
      Farmboy's story (iii) Editor's Report, 117–23R

Appendix

Editor's Report, 116–17L/R
128–9R
134–6L/R
149–51L/R

Bibliography

PRIMARY SOURCES

Works

Goethe, Johann Wolfgang von. *Goethe: Berliner Ausgabe.* 23 vols. Berlin: Aufbau, 1972–8
- *Goethe: Sämtliche Werke.* Ed. Karl Richter in co-operation with H. Göpfert, N. Miller, and G. Sauder. Munich: Hanser, 1985ff.
- *Goethes Werke: Hamburger Ausgabe.* 14 vols. Ed. Erich Trunz. 11th rev. ed. Munich: Beck, 1978
- *Goethes Werke.* Commissioned by the Grand Duchess Sophie von Sachsen. 4 parts; 133 vols. in 143. Weimar: Böhlau and Böhlaus Nachfolger, 1887–1919
- *Der junge Goethe.* 3 vols. Ed. with an introduction by Michael Bernays. Leipzig: Salomon Hirzel, 1875
- *Werke Goethes.* Vol. 1. Prepared by Erna Merker. Berlin: Akademie Verlag, 1954

Stein, Charlotte Albertine Ernestine von. *Dido: Ein Trauerspiel in fünf Aufzügen.* Ed. Heinrich Düntzer. Commissioned by *Der Freie Deutsche Hochstift*, Frankfurt/Main. Leipzig: F.A. Brockhaus, 1867
- *Rino: Ein Schauspiel in drei Abtheilungen 1776.* In *Goethes Briefe an Frau von Stein*, vol. 1, pp. 398–400. Ed. Adolf Schöll. Frankfurt/Main: Rütten and Loening, 1883–5

Letters, Diaries, and Conversations

Briefe an Goethe: Gesamtausgabe in Regestform. Nationale Forschungs- und Gedenkstätten der klassischen deutschen Literatur in Weimar, Goethe- und Schiller-Archiv. 2 vols. Ed. Karl-Heinz Hahn. Weimar: Hermann Böhlaus Nachfolger, 1980, 1981

Eckermann, Johann Peter. *Gespräche mit Goethe in den letzten Jahren seines Lebens.* Ed. Regine Otto. Berlin and Weimar: Aufbau, 1982

Goethe, Johann Wolfgang von. *Briefe und Aufsätze von Goethe aus den Jahren 1766–86*. Ed. Adolf Schöll. Weimar: Landes-Industrie-Comptoir, 1857
- *Goethe Tagebücher der sechs ersten Weimarischen Jahre*. Ed. Heinrich Düntzer. Leipzig: Verlag der Dyk'schen Buchhandlung, 1889
- *Goethe in vertraulichen Briefen seiner Zeitgenossen*. 3 vols. Compiled by Wilhelm Bode. Rev. and ed. by Regine Otto and Paul-Gerhard Wenzlaff. Berlin and Weimar: Aufbau, 1982
- *Goethes Briefe: Hamburger Ausgabe*. 4 vols. Ed. Karl Robert Mandelkow. Hamburg: Wegner, 1962–7
- *Goethes Briefe an Charlotte von Stein*. 2 vols. in 4. Ed. Julius Petersen. Leipzig: Insel, 1923
- *Goethes Briefe an Frau von Stein*. 2 vols. Ed. Adolf Schöll. 2nd enlarged ed. Prepared by Wilhelm Fielitz. Frankfurt/Main: Rütten and Loening, 1883, 1885
- *Goethes Gespräche*. 5 vols. in 6. Ed. Flodoard Freiherr von Biedermann. Enlarged and ed. by Wolfgang Herwig. Zurich and Stuttgart: Artemis, 1965–72
- *Goethe über seine Dichtungen: Versuch einer Sammlung aller Äußerungen des Dichters über seine poetischen Werke*. Ed. Hans Gerhard Gräf. 3 vols. in 9 parts. Darmstadt: Wissenschaftliche Buchgesellschaft, 1968. Repr. of Frankfurt/Main ed., 1901
- *Tagebücher und Briefe Goethens aus Italien an Frau von Stein und Herder*. Ed. Erich Schmidt. Schriften der Goethe-Gesellschaft, vol. 2. Weimar: Verlag der Goethe-Gesellschaft, 1886

Grumach, Ernst, and Renate Grumach, eds. *Goethe: Begegnungen und Gespräche*. 5 vols. to date. Berlin: De Gruyter, 1964ff.

Herder, Johann Gottfried von. *Briefe: Gesamtausgabe 1763–1803*. 9 vols. Published under the direction of Karl-Heinz Hahn, Goethe- and Schiller-Archive. Weimar: Hermann Böhlaus Nachfolger, 1977–88

Kestner, A., ed. *Kestner, Goethe und Werther: Briefe Goethens, meistens aus seiner Jugendzeit*. Stuttgart and Augsburg: Cotta, 1855

Knebel, Karl Ludwig von. *Karl Ludwig Knebels Briefwechsel mit seiner Schwester Henriette 1774–1813*. Ed. Heinrich Düntzer. Jena: Friedrich Mauke, 1858
- *K.L. von Knebels literarischer Nachlaß und Briefwechsel*. 2 vols. Ed. K.A. Varnhagen von Ense and Th. Mundt. Leipzig: Gebrüder Reichenbach, 1840

Rothmann, Kurt, ed. *Johann Wolfgang Goethe, die Leiden des jungen Werthers: Erläuterungen und Dokumente*. Stuttgart: Reclam, 1971

Reference and Resource Materials

Deutsches Wörterbuch von Jacob und Wilhelm Grimm. Ed. Deutsche Akademie der Wissenschaften, Berlin. 16 vols. Leipzig: S. Hirzel, 1854–1960

Das Goethe-Wörterbuch. Ed. Akademie der Wissenschaften, Berlin, Göttingen,

and Heidelberg. Under the direction of Wolfgang Schadewaldt, Werner Simon, and Wilhelm Wissmann. Stuttgart, Berlin, Köln, Mainz, 1978ff.
Goethes Leben von Tag zu Tag: Eine dokumentarische Chronik. 5 vols. to date. Ed. Robert Steiger. Zurich and Munich: Artemis, 1982ff.
Wörterbuch zu Goethes Werther. Prepared by Erna Merker, in co-operation with Johanna Graefe and Fritz Merbach. Berlin: Akademie Verlag, 1958–66

SECONDARY SOURCES

Assling, Reinhard. *Werthers Leiden: Die ästhetische Rebellion der Innerlichkeit*. Frankfurt/Main, Bern: Peter Lang, 1981
Atkins, Stuart. 'Observations on Goethe's *Torquato Tasso*.' *Carleton Germanic Papers* 1 (1973):41–59
Auden, W.H. Foreword to *The Sorrows of Young Werther and Novella*, trans. by Elizabeth Mayer and Louise Bogan, pp. ix–xvi. First publ. 1971 by Random House. New York: Modern Library, 1984
Bennett, Benjamin. 'Goethe's *Werther*: Double Perspective and the Game of Life.' *German Quarterly* 53 (1980):64–81
Bielschowsky, Albert. *Goethe: Sein Leben und seine Werke*. 2 vols. Munich: Beck, 1896, 1902
Blackall, Eric. *Goethe and the Novel*. Ithaca, NY: Cornell University Press, 1976
Blessin, Stefan. *Johann Wolfgang Goethe: Die Leiden des jungen Werther*. Frankfurt/Main, Berlin, Munich: Moritz Diesterweg, 1985
– *Die Romane Goethes*. Königstein/Taunus: Athenäum Verlag, 1979
Blumenthal, Hermann, ed. *Zeitgenössische Rezensionen und Urteile über Goethes 'Götz' und 'Werther.'* Literarhistorische Bibliothek. Berlin: Junker and Dünnhaupt, 1935
Bode, Wilhelm. *Charlotte von Stein*. Berlin: Siegfried Mittler, 1919
– 'Frau von Stein als Figur im "Werther."' In *Stunden mit Goethe*, 10 vols., ed. Wilhelm Bode, vol. 6:215–19. Berlin: Siegfried Mittler, 1905–21
Booth, Wayne. *The Rhetoric of Fiction*. 2nd ed. Chicago: University of Chicago Press, 1983
Boy-Ed, Ida. *Das Martyrium der Charlotte von Stein*. Stuttgart: Cotta, 1920
Boyle, Nicholas. *Goethe: The Poet and the Age*. Oxford: Oxford University Press, 1991
Braun, Julius, ed. *Goethe im Urtheile seiner Zeitgenossen*. 3 vols. in 2. Berlin: Luckhardt, 1883, 1885
Brown, Jane K. 'The Renaissance of Goethe's Poetic Genius in Italy.' In *Goethe in Italy 1786–1796*, ed. Gerhart Hoffmeister, pp. 77–94. Amsterdam: Rodopi, 1988
Burdach, Konrad. *Die Wissenschaft von deutscher Sprache*. Berlin and Leipzig: De Gruyter, 1934
Conrady, Karl Otto. *Goethe: Leben und Werk*. 2 vols. 2nd rev. ed. Königstein/Taunus: Athenäum Verlag, 1984

Dawson, John. 'Peter Absconditus: Delving into Werther's Neuroses.' *AUMLA* [Journal of the Australasian Universities Language and Literature Association] 68 (1987):251–60

Diener, Gottfried. *Goethes 'Lila.'* Frankfurt/Main: Athenäum Verlag, 1971

Doke, Tadamichi. 'Zur literarischen Methode der "Leiden des jungen Werther."' *Goethe Jahrbuch* 91 (1974):11–23

Düntzer, Heinrich. *Charlotte von Stein: Goethes Freundin*. 2 vols. Stuttgart: Verlag der J.G. Cotta'schen Buchhandlung, 1874

– *Die drei ältesten Bearbeitungen von Goethes Iphigenie*. Ed. and with two essays on the history and critical comparison of the play by Heinrich Düntzer. Stuttgart and Tübingen: J.G. Cotta'scher Verlag, 1854

– 'Goethes Eintritt in Weimar.' *Deutsche Vierteljahrsschrift (DVjS)* CXXI (1870), 3:1–111

– 'Goethe's "Lotte" und "die Leiden des jungen Werthers." Nebst einer Übersicht der Werther-Literatur.' In *Studien zu Goethes Werken*, pp. 89–209. Elberfeld and Iserlohn: Julius Baedeker, 1849

Ehrentreich, Alfred. 'An der Peripherie von Goethes "Werther."' *Goethe Jahrbuch* 100 (1983):266–71

Eissler, Kurt Robert. *Goethe: A Psychoanalytic Study*. 2 vols. Detroit: Wayne State University Press, 1963

Engel, Ingrid. *Werther und die Wertheriaden: Ein Beitrag zur Wirkungsgeschichte*. St. Ingbert: Röhrig, 1986

Fairley, Barker. *Goethe as Revealed in His Poetry*. London: Dent, 1932

– *A Study of Goethe*. Oxford: Oxford University Press, 1947

Fischer, Kuno. *Goethes 'Tasso.'* Heidelberg: Carl Winter, 1890

Fittbogen, Gottfried. 'Die Charaktere in den beiden Fassungen von Werthers Leiden.' *Euphorion* 17 (1910):556–82

Flaschka, Horst. *Goethes 'Werther': Werkkontextuelle Deskription und Analyse*. Munich: Wilhelm Fink Verlag, 1987

Foucault, Michel. 'What Is an Author?' *Partisan Review* 42 (1975):603–14

Fricke, Gerhard. 'Goethe und Werther.' In *Studien und Interpretationen*, pp. 141–67. Frankfurt/Main: Hans F. Menck, 1956

Friedenthal, Richard. *Goethe: Sein Leben und Seine Zeit*. Munich: Piper, 1963

Gerhard, Melitta. 'Die Bauernbursche-Episode im Werther.' *Zeitschrift für Aesthetik und allgemeine Kunstwissenschaft* 11 (1916):61–74

Gose, Hans. *Goethes 'Werther.'* Bausteine der deutschen Literatur. Ed. Franz Saran. Vol. 18. Halle: Max Niemeyer, 1921

Graham, Ilse. *Goethe: Portrait of the Artist*. Berlin and New York: De Gruyter, 1977

Grimm, Hermann. *Das Leben Goethes*. Stuttgart: Kröner, 1959

Haverkamp, Anselm. 'Illusion und Empathie: Die Struktur der "teilnehmenden Lektüre" in den Leiden Werthers.' In *Erzählforschung: Ein Symposion*, ed. Eberhard Lämmert, pp. 243–68. Stuttgart: Metzler, 1982

Heitner, Robert R. 'Goethe's Ailing Women.' *Modern Language Notes* 95 (1980):497–515

Hillebrand, Bruno. *Goethes Werther – Ein deutsches Thema*. Abhandlungen der

Akademie der Wissenschaften und der Literatur, Mainz, vol. 7. Wiesbaden: Steiner, 1982

Hof, Walter. *Goethe und Charlotte von Stein*. Frankfurt/Main: Insel, 1979

Hotz, Karl, ed. *Goethes 'Werther' als Modell für kritisches Lesen: Materialien zur Rezeptionsgeschichte*. Collected and with an introduction by Karl Hotz. Stuttgart: Klett, 1974

Hübner, Klaus. *Alltag im literarischen Werk: Eine literatur-soziologische Studie zu Goethes 'Werther.'* Heidelberg: Julius Groos, 1982

Käser, Rudolf. *Die Schwierigkeit, ich zu sagen: Rhetorik der Selbstdarstellung in Texten des 'Sturm und Drang.'* Bern, Frankfurt/Main, New York, Paris: Peter Lang, 1987

Kayser, Wolfgang. 'Die Entstehung von Goethes Werther.' *Deutsche Vierteljahrsschrift (DVjS)* 19 (1941):430–57

– *Kunst und Spiel: Fünf Goethe-Studien*. 2nd ed. Göttingen: Vandenhoeck and Ruprecht, 1967

Konersmann, Ralf. 'Goethes Subjektivität.' *Germanisch-Romanische Monatsschrift* 38 (1988):106–19

Koranyi, Stefan. *Autobiographik und Wissenschaft im Denken Goethes*. Bonn: Bouvier, 1984

Kurz, Gerhard. 'Werther als Künstler.' In *Invaliden des Apoll: Motive und Mythen des Dichterleids*, ed. Herbert Anton, pp. 95–112. Munich: Fink, 1982

Lange, Victor. 'The Metaphor of Silence.' *Goethe Revisited*, ed. Elizabeth M. Wilkinson, pp. 133–52. London, New York: Calder, Riverrun, 1984

Lauterbach, Martin. *Das Verhältnis der zweiten zur ersten Ausgabe von Werthers Leiden*. Strasburg: Trübner, 1910

Lohss, Otti. 'Goethe und Charlotte von Stein.' *Goethe Jahrbuch* 103 (1986): 365–83

Lukács, Georg. *Goethe und seine Zeit*. Bern: Francke, 1947

– 'Die Leiden des jungen Werther.' In *Deutsche Literatur in zwei Jahrhunderten*, pp. 53–68. Neuwied and Berlin: Luchterhand, 1964

– 'Die Leiden des jungen Werther.' In *Faust und Faustus: Vom Drama der Menschengattung zur Tragödie der modernen Kunst*, pp. 17–30. Reinbek bei Hamburg: Rowohlt, 1968

Mandelkow, Karl Robert, ed. *Goethe im Urteil seiner Kritiker*. 4 vols. Ed. with introduction and commentary by Karl Robert Mandelkow. Munich: Beck, 1975–84

Mann, Thomas. 'Goethes Werther.' In *Goethe im XX. Jahrhundert: Spiegelungen und Deutungen*, ed. Hans Mayer, pp. 9–25. Frankfurt/Main: Insel, 1967

Marahrens, Gerwin. 'Der "Welt"-Begriff in Goethes Wahlverwandtschaften.' In *Sinn und Symbol: Festschrift für Joseph P. Strelka zum 60. Geburtstag*, ed. Karl Konrad Polheim, pp. 113–28. Bern, Frankfurt/Main, New York, Paris: Peter Lang, 1987

Maurer, Karl. 'Die verschleierten Konfessionen: Zur Entstehungsgeschichte von Goethes Werther.' *Die Wissenschaft von deutscher Sprache und Dichtung: Festschrift für Friedrich Maurer zum 65. Geburtstag*, ed. Siegfried

Gutenbrunner, Hugo Moser, Walter Rehm, Heinz Rupp, pp. 424-37. Stuttgart: Klett, 1963
Meyer, Heinrich. *Goethe: Das Leben im Werk*. Hamburg: Stromverlag, 1951
Migge, Walther. *Goethes 'Werther': Entstehung und Wirkung*. Frankfurt/Main: Insel, 1967
Mommsen, Katharina. 'Goethes Vorstellung von einer idealen Lesergemeinde.' *Seminar* 10 (1974):1-18
Morris, Max. 'Frau von Stein und die Königin der Nacht.' In *Goethe-Studien*, pp. 310-17. 2 vols. in 1. 2nd rev. ed. Berlin: Conrad Skopnik, 1902
Mukařovský, Jan. 'Das dichterische Werk als Gesamtheit von Werten.' In *Kapitel aus der Ästhetik*, pp. 34-43. Frankfurt/Main: Suhrkamp, 1967
Müller, Peter. *Zeitkritik und Utopie in Goethes 'Werther.'* 2nd rev. ed. Berlin: Rütten and Loening, 1983
Müller-Salget, Klaus. 'Zur Struktur von Goethes "Werther."' *Zeitschrift für deutsche Philologie* 100 (1981):527-44
Nobel, Alfons. *Frau von Stein: Goethes Freundin und Feindin*. Frankfurt/Main: Societätsverlag, 1939
Nolan, Erika. 'Goethes "Die Leiden des jungen Werther": Absicht und Methode.' *Jahrbuch der Deutschen Schiller-Gesellschaft* 28 (1984): 191-222
Paulin, Roger. 'Wir werden uns wieder sehn!: On a Theme in Werther.' *Publications of the English Goethe Society* (PEGS) 50 (1980):55-78
Reiss, Hans. 'Die Leiden des jungen Werthers.' In *Goethe's Novels*, pp. 10-67. London: Macmillan, 1969
Reuter, Hans-Heinrich. 'Der gekreuzigte Prometheus: Goethes Roman "Die Leiden des jungen Werthers."' *Goethe Jahrbuch* 89 (1972):86-115
Riemann, Robert. *Goethes Romantechnik*. Leipzig: Hermann Seemann Nachfolger, 1902
Riemer, Friedrich Wilhelm. *Mittheilungen über Goethe*. 2 vols. Berlin: Düncker and Humblot, 1841
Rieß, Gertrud. *Die beiden Fassungen von Goethes 'Die Leiden des jungen Werthers': Eine stilpsychologische Untersuchung*. Breslau: Trewendt and Granier, 1924
Rueff, Hans. *Zur Entstehungsgeschichte von Goethes 'Torquato Tasso.'* New York and London: Johnson Reprint, 1968. First publ. Marburg, 1910
Saine, Thomas. 'Passion and Aggression: The Meaning of Werther's Last Letter.' *Orbis Litterarum* 35 (1980):327-56
– 'The Portrayal of Lotte in the Two Versions of Goethe's *Werther*.' *Journal of English and Germanic Philology* 80 (1981):54-77
Scheidemantel, Eduard. *Zur Entstehungsgeschichte von Goethes Torquato Tasso*. Weimar: Druck der Hof-Buchdruckerei, 1896
Scherpe, Klaus. *Werther und Werther-Wirkung*. Bad Homburg, Berlin, Zurich: Gehlen, 1970
Schlaffer, Heinz. 'Exoterik und Esoterik in Goethes Romanen.' *Goethe Jahrbuch* 95 (1978):212-26

Schmidt, Erich. *Charakteristiken*. 2 vols. Berlin: Weidmannsche Buchhandlung, 1886, 1901
- *Richardson, Rousseau und Goethe: Ein Beitrag zur Geschichte des Romans im 18. Jahrhundert*. Jena: Eduard Frommann, 1875

Schöffler, Herbert. ' "Die Leiden des jungen Werthers": Ihr geistesgeschichtlicher Hintergrund.' In *Deutscher Geist im 18. Jahrhundert: Essays zur Geistes- und Religionsgeschichte*, pp. 155–81. Göttingen: Vandenhoeck and Ruprecht, 1967

Schöll, Adolf. *Goethe in Hauptzügen seines Lebens und Wirkens*. Berlin: Wilhelm Hertz, 1882

Schöne, Albrecht. *Götterzeichen, Liebeszauber, Satanskult: Neue Einblicke in alte Goethetexte*. Munich: Beck, 1982

Seuffert, Bernhard. 'Philologische Betrachtungen im Anschluß an Goethes "Werther." ' *Euphorion* 7 (1900):1–47
- 'Skizze der Textgeschichte von Goethes "Werther." ' *Goethe Jahrbuch* 21 (1900):246–51

Silz, Walter. 'Ambivalences in Goethe's *Tasso*.' *Germanic Review* 21 (1956): 243–68

Staiger, Emil. *Goethe*. 3 vols. Zurich and Freiburg/Breisgau: Atlantis, 1952–9

Stein-Kochberg, Freiherr von. 'Goethe in seinen Beziehungen zu Schloß Großkochberg und dessen Theater.' In *Das Goethe-Jahr in Weimar*, ed. Directorship of the German National Theatre in Weimar, pp. 43–5. Munich: Verlag Theaterkunst Otto Glenk, 1932

Storz, Gerhard. 'Die Leiden des jungen Werthers.' In *Goethe-Vigilien: Versuche in der Kunst, Dichtung zu verstehen*, pp. 19–41. Stuttgart: Klett, 1953

Strelka, Joseph. *Esoterik bei Goethe*. Tübingen: Niemeyer, 1980

Susman, Margarethe. *Deutung einer großen Liebe: Goethe und Charlotte von Stein*. Zurich: Artemis, 1951

Swales, Martin. *Goethe: The Sorrows of Young Werther*. Cambridge: Cambridge University Press, 1987

Vaget, Hans Rudolf. 'Goethe the Novelist: On the Coherence of His Fiction.' In *Goethe's Narrative Fiction*, ed. William Lillyman, pp. 1–20. Berlin and New York: De Gruyter, 1983

Viëtor, Karl. *Goethe*. Bern: Francke, 1949

Voss, Lena. *Goethes unsterbliche Freundin, Charlotte von Stein: Eine psychoanalytische Studie an Hand der Quellen*. Leipzig: Klinkhardt and Biermann, 1921

Wahl, Hans. 'Sebastian Simpel.' *Jahrbuch der Goethe-Gesellschaft* 11 (1949): 62–77

Wapnewski, Peter. 'Zweihundert Jahre Werthers Leiden, oder: Dem war nicht zu helfen.' In *Zumutungen: Essays zur Literatur des 20. Jahrhunderts*, pp. 44–65. Düsseldorf: Claasen, 1979

Warrick, E. Kathleen. 'Lotte's Sexuality and Her Responsibility for Werther's Death.' *Essays in Literature* 5 (1978):129–35

Welz, Dieter. *Der Weimarer Werther: Studien zur Sinnstruktur der zweiten Fassung des Werther-Romans*. Abhandlungen zur Kunst, Musik- und Literaturwissenschaft, vol. 35. Bonn: Bouvier, 1973

Zimmermann, Rolf. *Das Weltbild des jungen Goethe*. 2 vols. Munich: Fink, 1969, 1979

www.ingramcontent.com/pod-product-compliance
Lightning Source LLC
Chambersburg PA
CBHW071152070526
44584CB00019B/2762